*Scarecrow Film Score Guides*

*Series Editor: Kate Daubney*

1. *Gabriel Yared's* The English Patient: *A Film Score Guide*, by Heather Laing. 2004.

Gabriel Yared © Carole Morgane

# Gabriel Yared's
# *The English Patient*

## *A Film Score Guide*

### Heather Laing

*Scarecrow Film Score Guides, No. 1*

The Scarecrow Press, Inc.
Lanham, Maryland, and Oxford
2004

# SCARECROW PRESS, INC.

Published in the United States of America
by Scarecrow Press, Inc.
A wholly owned subsidary of
The Rowman & Littlefield Publishing Group, Inc.
4501 Forbes Boulevard, Suite 200, Lanham, Maryland 20706
www.scarecrowpress.com

Estover Road
Plymouth PL6 7PY
United Kingdom

British Library Cataloguing in Publication Information Available

The hardback edition of this book was previously cataloged by the Library of
Congress as follows:

Laing, Heather.
    Gabriel Yared's The English Patient : a film score guide / by Heather Laing.
      p. cm.—(Scarecrow film score guides ; no. 1)
    Includes bibliographical references (p.   ) and index.
Filmography: p.
    1. Yared, Gabriel. English patient. I. Title: English patient. II. Title. III.
Series.
ML410.Y35 L35 2003
781.5'42—dc22                       2003017933
   ISBN-13: 978-0-8108-4965-5 (hardcover : alk. paper)
   ISBN-10: 0-8108-4965-8 (hardcover : alk. paper)
   ISBN-13: 978-0-8108-5910-4 (pbk : alk. paper)
   ISBN-10: 0-8108-5910-6 (pbk : alk. paper)

™
⊖ The paper used in this publication meets the minimum requirements of
American National Standard for Information Sciences—Permanence of
Paper for Printed Library Materials, ANSI/NISO Z39.48-1992.
Manufactured in the United States of America.

To Tim

# CONTENTS

# FIGURES

# EDITOR'S FOREWORD

This is the first volume in the new Scarecrow series of Film Score Guides (formerly published by Greenwood), a set of books dedicated to drawing together the variety of different analytical practices and ideological approaches in film musicology for the study of individual scores. Much value has been drawn from case studies of film scoring practice in other film music texts, but these guides offer a substantial, wide-ranging and comprehensive study of a single score. Subjects are chosen for the series on the basis that they have become and are widely recognized as a benchmark for the way in which film music is composed and experienced. A guide explores the context of a score's composition through its place in the career of the composer and its relationship to the techniques of the composer. The context of the score in narrative and production terms is also considered, and readings of the film as a whole are discussed in order to situate in their filmic context the musical analyses which conclude the guide. Furthermore, although these guides focus on the score as written text, bringing forward often previously unknown details about the process of composition as they are manifested in the manuscript, analysis also includes exploration of the music as an aural text, for this is the first and, for most audiences, the only way in which they will experience the music of the film.

This volume on *The English Patient* has benefited immeasurably from the cooperation and input of the score's composer, Gabriel Yared, for which the series editor and Scarecrow Press are extremely grateful. Mr. Yared kindly agreed to a frank and wide-ranging discussion of his career; his technical, intellectual and personal views on film music; and most valuably of his experiences of composing this particular score. He also gave Dr. Laing access to the manuscript of the score and several of his other scores and concert suites, and his staff at YAD

Music gave invaluable help with access to their resources. The value of this contribution is striking in musicology where scholars must in most cases rely on texts and archival materials alone and can only hypothesize and deduce what a composer intended. In film musicology, however, the input of the composer is particularly valuable, because while filmic experience is necessarily subjective to the audience, it is also subjective to the composer. Learning how a composer translates this to the compositional process enhances and expands the ways in which we may interpret and analyze film music, an advantage which will continue to stimulate scholars and filmgoers alike. This volume is a vibrant, detailed and incisive account of the score's place in a complex text, but it is written in such a way that whatever the reader's level of musical knowledge or understanding, there is much to be learned and understood about what part the music plays in casting the spells of this enthralling film.

Dr. Kate Daubney
Series Editor

# ACKNOWLEDGMENTS

There are numerous people to thank in connection with this book. First and foremost, my thanks go to Gabriel Yared himself, for a level of help and enthusiastic involvement that stretched far beyond my expectations. This included granting me access to the scores held at the offices of YAD Music in Paris, hosting a substantial interview in his own home after which he continued to add information and answer questions by e-mail correspondence, and reading and commenting on the final draft of the text. I am eternally grateful for his indulgence. A great debt of gratitude must also go to Jean-Pierre Arquié, who managed and coordinated so much of this correspondence, hosted my visit to YAD Music and provided me with endless amounts of information.

Kate Daubney, who first approached me to write this book, has been a constant source of support, encouragement and advice, and read several drafts of the work. Miguel Mera and Valerie Orpen, along with Kate, also read and commented on the final draft of the text. Thanks also go to Miguel for providing the all-important initial introduction to Gabriel Yared and Jean-Pierre Arquié, and to Valerie for her invaluable support in researching and clearing copyright in France and Belgium. Further thanks for help of various kinds go to Rachel Moseley, Clive McClelland and Lukas Kendall.

There are many people to thank for their support and assistance in clearing copyright on the extracts of scores and interviews used in the book. Particular thanks go to Wolfgang Frank at Fantasy Records, Rachael Johnson at Music Sales, Naomi Moran at Rykomusic, Aidan Walker at Rotovision, SA., Ulrike Klinger and James Pagram at *The Daily Telegraph*, Laurent Lhermitte at SACEM, Yaël Bensoussan at EMI Virgin Music Publishing France, Sacha Walters at *The Guardian*, Matt Smith at Warner Chappell, Tegan Kossowitz at Famous Music,

Julie McDowell at Hal Leonard Corporation, Carine Leblanc at Cargo Films, Mylène Azar at La Marguerite–Cargo Films, Michel Leempoel at *Ciné Télé Revue*, Françoise D'Inca at *Studio Magazine*, as well as to Gabriel Yared for permission to use extracts from the score of *37°2 le matin* and Carole Morgane for allowing me to use the photograph that appears in the opening pages of this book. Thanks also go to Bruce Phillips, Jeff Wolf, Melissa Ray, Debra Schepp and Niki Averill at Scarecrow Press for their advice and guidance throughout the editorial process.

Finally, thanks to Tim Ayling for practical and intellectual help, as well as lots and lots of patience.

# INTRODUCTION

One of the biggest surprises attending the huge success of *The English Patient* (1996) seemed to be that audiences and critics, just perhaps, secretly yearned for a return to an old-fashioned kind of story told in a classical way. Drawing comparison with some of cinema's greatest romantic historical epics and melodramas, it seemed to take its place immediately as a classic of its genre. Its nostalgic appeal, some even suggested, was the reason behind its overwhelming success at the Academy Awards. As it left the competition behind with its nine Oscars, critics marveled only at the fact that it hadn't won more.

Most notable in this respect was its failure to win the Best Actor and Actress awards for Ralph Fiennes and Kristin Scott Thomas who, having initially been considered by some to be of doubtful box office interest, were now the talk of Tinsel Town. Indeed, in the years that followed, a fair number of cinematic couples were doomed to share the trajectory of their characters in *The English Patient*, Almásy and Katharine: fate, in all its fickle grandeur, brought them together despite apparently insurmountable barriers, only to tear them apart the moment they had finally found happiness. No successor to *The English Patient*, however, quite seemed to capture its particularly poignant sense of loss, regret and the tragic irretrievability of the past.

There are many factors that may account for its success in this respect. It is, after all, set in the past twice over. The past of World War II, the focus of intense social, cultural and personal nostalgia, gives way to a more distant past that presents us with another world altogether. The juxtaposition of the two is harsh. Whereas the war roots us firmly in time and reminds us constantly of mortality, corporality, duty and obligation, the world of the desert explorers appears timeless in its fantasy-like removal from the sights, sounds and concerns of everyday life. It is a time and place of impossible glamour, chivalry, erudite conversation, wit and, above all, exotic adventure. Until the intervention of the war, it really seems that this world could go on forever, locked into its own historical concerns and unperturbed by the processes of modernization.

Between two so very different times and places, it is the human element alone that is shared. This, it seems, doesn't change whatever the circumstances. The scope of this emotional continuity is further broadened by the key role played by the ancient text of Herodotus's *The Histories*, which imbues the film with a sense of the eternal cycle of love, betrayal, pain and loss. Almásy, Katharine, Hana (Juliette Binoche), Kip (Naveen Andrews), Caravaggio (Willem Dafoe) and all the others are, therefore, not only characters brought together for one particular story but also figures who represent the inevitable, repetitive, unchanging course of human-emotional history. Despite the very different circumstances in which the film's audience may find themselves, they are therefore likely to recognize something in *The English Patient*'s emotional concerns.

An important element of both the nostalgic and the emotional appeal of the film lies in its score. In and across the war and the desert, music reveals how people think, feel, rejoice and suffer in their common human experience. The success of the score within the film and in its own right was a testament not only to the teamwork of composer Gabriel Yared and director Anthony Minghella but also to the continued appeal of a classical, noncommercial style of scoring that avoided the use of contemporary pop music. The film does, of course, contain a great deal of popular music, but only that which is contemporaneous to its diegetic spaces. This is popular music that implies paired dancing and romance and that has itself passed into history as classic of its type.

The fact that the audience are never asked to sympathize with the characters by being wrenched back into the present, perhaps with the oft-used montage-and-song format, contributes significantly to the film's timeless feel and potentially classic status. Combining the temporal 'neutrality' that has accrued, in film music terms, to the late Romantic style of scoring, and popular music that enjoys an equally classic, timeless status avoids the risk of the film ever becoming musically 'dated.' Thus it supports the film's setting of its characters in a world of both eternal nostalgia and historical continuity; just as they are not in our present, neither will they ever seem quite fully in the past.

While Yared was already a celebrated film composer in France, the country that had long been his home and the site of most of his work in cinema, this score rocketed him, via the Academy Awards, into the international industrial and public consciousness. Most important to Yared, however, was the personal and artistic milestone that it represented in his transition to full maturity as a film composer. *The English Patient* is therefore significant on many musical counts, not only as a film, but also as a particular point in the career of its composer. This book will explore each of these aspects in the context of the other.

Both the journey toward and away from the central film is the subject of the first two chapters. Chapter 1 considers Yared's musical background, from the earliest influences of his childhood through his career in popular music to his experiences over more than two decades as both a film and ballet composer. Chapter 2 explores his film composition technique, his partnership with Minghella and the ways in which *The English Patient* may be placed at the center of his developmental process. The film itself is the subject of chapter 3. In preparation for the full analysis of the non-diegetic score presented in chapter 5, this begins with a broad consideration of the film's history and narrative themes, as well as the generic and theoretical parameters within which the score operates. The soundtrack in its entirety is the subject of chapter 4, which focuses on its essential narrative function, including the roles of sound effects, sound editing and diegetic music. Chapter 5 then places the non-diegetic score into this whole context, in a consideration of both its own narrative role and its place within Yared's creative output.

# 1

# GABRIEL YARED'S
# MUSICAL BACKGROUND

Most . . . composers . . . say: "We work for film music but, on the
side, we have a secret garden for clever people, for more intelligent
people who can understand our music." I think this is completely
fake and cynical. What you have to give to film music . . . is really
your soul, your best.[1]

Gabriel Yared does not see himself specifically as a film composer but
simply as a *composer*, who approaches all his work, whether film or
ballet scores, jingles or television theme tunes, with an equal sense of
conscience. He feels that the cinema audience should never be treated
as less worthy of hearing high quality music than the concert hall audience. This is because, as far as he is concerned, music should not be
written for more or less sophisticated audiences. Rather, music for
different media and/or different functions should be, quite simply, different music. For Yared, there is no "secret garden."[2]

He is a man of great passion and enthusiasm, who sees music as a
gift that he must not sully, betray or destroy. His musical ideas come
to him, he says, as if 'given' from somewhere outside himself. As a
result, he feels himself to be less the author of his own work than "the
worker who fertilizes the first seed," the channel through which the
musical ideas come and are expanded out into a whole texture.[3] As he
works these ideas into his film scores, he sees an opportunity to ele-
vate the audience "to the highest understanding of the universe" and to
make both the picture and the music "shine."[4] He is dedicated to an
ideal way of working that many directors and producers are unwilling
to countenance but which, throughout the 1980s and 1990s, has garnered many awards including an Academy Award for the score of *The
English Patient*.

Despite his success in this field and by his own confession, however, he is no great film enthusiast. When he approaches a film, he
prefers to work from the script and discussion with the director and
actors before the shooting has even begun. In this way he seeks to find
and encapsulate in his musical ideas the very essence of both the
drama and its characters, long before his music is molded to the picture
itself. He has also, he says, by no means given all he has to give. He
continues to crave variety and self-development in his own work, as
well as making opportunities to pass on his knowledge by supporting
the development of younger and less experienced composers.

# Childhood, Studies and Early Career

Gabriel Yared was born on 7 October 1949 in Beirut into a family with
neither musical nor artistic traditions and a strictly pragmatic attitude
to education and employment. He was sent to a Jesuit boarding school
at the tender age of four with an eventual view, in his family's eyes, to
a respectable profession in either medicine or law. Thrown into such
emotional isolation, however, the young Yared found a solace in music
that was to lead him toward quite a different future. To counter his
loneliness, music became, in his own words, "his family." He lived
and breathed it "like air," and became so dependent upon it for his
emotional sustenance that without it, he felt he would not have been
able to retain his sanity.[5] He took weekly accordion lessons and, from
the age of six, also added half-hour piano lessons to his schedule.

Even at this early stage, however, he knew that he would never be
a great performer. Instead, his keener interest in reading, analyzing and
understanding music was already pointing him toward composition.
He was determined that he should be able to read music as easily as he
could words, and every break between lessons was spent in the pursuit
of this goal. By virtue of the fact that his piano teacher, Bertrand Ro-
billiard, was the organist at the Jesuit Church in Beirut, Yared also
gained access to the church's organ loft. Here, he discovered the scores
of Bach, Buxtehude, Pachelbel and many others, and whenever possible, he hid himself away to play the organ and read his way through
this wealth of musical history. So much did he concentrate on analyzing rather than practicing his pieces, that after a year of music lessons,
his teacher advised his father that he would never make a musician.

Although the majority of Yared's spare time and energy was spent
on music, it was also during these early years that he had his first ex-

perience of cinema and established a relationship to the filmic image that survives almost unchanged to this day. The boarding school allowed pupils to go into the town every Thursday in order to visit either the dentist or the optician. Thus Yared, in his own words, "became myopic."[6] While in town he was able, although only three or four times a year, to go to the cinema. What he found there, however, was that he was unable to separate the fiction being played out on the screen from his own sense of reality. Whatever happened to characters in the film felt, to Yared, as if it was actually happening to him. Although he enjoyed adventure films and particularly Roman epics, he therefore found that he could not stand to witness violence in films, a proscription that remains with him to the present.[7]

Furthermore, whether to do with this confusion of images and reality, his increasingly poor eyesight or what he felt to be his abandonment at such an early age, he found himself naturally prone to introspection. Perhaps as a result of all these things, the cinematic experience has never held any particular draw for Yared, and it remains his contention that this presents no hurdle to being a successful film composer. For him, the single most important quality that a film composer must possess is the ability to understand the essential drama of a narrative and to realize exactly what it *needs* from its score. In order to do this successfully, there is no necessity to be a *"cinéphile."*[8]

When Yared left school at sixteen years old, his father refused outright to allow him to become a composer. After failing to gain admittance to study medicine—his second choice of profession—he enrolled in Beirut University to study law. The only consolation for the unbearable boredom that he suffered as a student was that the School of Law was next to the same Jesuit Church where he had played the organ and learned about music throughout his school years. He was therefore able to continue with his musical studies on a private basis and, during his second year at University, gave a public organ recital. When he subsequently announced that he wanted to quit law for music, however, his father remained intransigent. Yared was forced to take his future into his own hands.

In 1969, he left Beirut for Paris, where he embarked on his first formal musical study. He entered the École Normale de Musique for a one-year course, studying composition with Henri Dutilleux and orchestration with Maurice Ohana. During these studies, finding himself surrounded by already highly trained and talented students, he realized his ignorance of the musical theories and rules that, Dutilleux warned him at the end of the year, he would have to learn if he ever wanted to have the freedom to move beyond them in his own compositions. Instead of going further with his formal studies at this point, however, Yared was to return to the world of popular music.

Back once again in Beirut, he was offered the opportunity by a Brazilian music promoter to work with a lyricist and singer as the representative of Lebanon in a song contest in Rio de Janeiro. Yared grabbed his chance and, at the end of the summer of 1970, he left Beirut for a stay of two weeks in Brazil. With lyricist and singer Gwen Owens, he composed the song *Song without Love* which took third prize in the contest. Finding that he liked Brazil, his intended short stay then gave rise to a residency of eighteen months and the beginning of his professional musical career. Working as a pianist and conductor in a band and meeting musicians such as Jorge Bem, Ellis Regina, Edu Lobo and Ivan Lins, he composed during the day and played in the evenings at the Number One Club in Ipanema. He had been entirely self-taught in composition and now his first experiments in orchestration, still working solely by ear, led to his orchestrating an album for Ivan Lins.

In 1972, however, he was to make a second unexpected move, following a visit to Paris in the hope of securing a grant from the Lebanese government. Intending to stay for two weeks, his subsequent residency in France became permanent. He began working with the Costa Brothers and recorded an album of twelve songs with them called *Costa-Yared-Costa* as cocomposer, orchestrator and singer. News of his talent soon spread, and so began a prolific period of work in Paris as composer of countless advertising jingles and theme tunes for television and radio and as composer and orchestrator for major popular music artists such as Johnny Halliday, Sylvie Vartan, Michel Jonasz, Françoise Hardy, Mireille Mathieu, Henri Salvador, Gilbert Bécaud, Enrico Macias and Charles Aznavour. This proved an important area for his development as an orchestrator, giving him the opportunity to learn in greater detail about writing for string, brass, vocal and rhythm sections.

In 1976, he released an album of his own music, composed to lyrics written especially for him by Michel Jonasz, called *Yared Words and Music*. As a result of this, he decided to develop into producing as well as orchestrating albums. He felt ideally placed for this new role, knowing, as an orchestrator, how every element of the music should work within the overall sound mix, as well as already having been involved with the technical aspects of music recording. He focused his career as a producer on artists Michel Jonasz and Françoise Hardy, undertaking composition, orchestration, conducting, sound direction and even choice of album covers. This work continued until 1979, when Yared found himself facing something of a watershed year and a period that would consolidate several aspects of his career so far.

# Film Music Composition

Throughout the 1970s, while working in popular music, Yared had maintained his childhood love affair with score reading, and all the money he earned was put toward building a private library of music for this purpose. While continuing to produce albums for Jonasz and Hardy, he decided in 1979 to resume his formal music studies. He visited Julian Falk, a retired teacher from the Conservatoire National de Musique de Paris, and showed him some of his compositions. Falk recommended that he learn counterpoint and fugue, and Yared studied with him every Saturday for the next two years. When, in the same year, Françoise Hardy's husband, Jacques Dutronc, suggested Yared to Jean-Luc Godard for his film *Sauve qui peut la vie* (1980), Yared was determined to use his newly developed compositional skills to the full. In an interview in 2000, he described his working method with Godard, which involved:

> read[ing] a script—there was nothing visual. . . . I told him I didn't know anything about making music for a movie. He said, "don't worry, just use your imagination."[9]

In response to Godard's 'carte blanche' brief, Yared composed forty minutes of music from a basic thematic cell of four bars taken from the Overture of the second act of Ponchielli's *La Gioconda*.[10] While he worked independently of the film, Godard visited him periodically to take away recordings of his work. The film was then edited to these pieces of music.[11]

*Sauve qui peut la vie* proved a turning point in Yared's professional life, marking the beginning of a decade devoted primarily to composing film music, mainly for French films, an area in which he was to become increasingly famous and revered. His film music was eclectic in style and he was interested in anything that stretched or broke the rules of scoring. His compositional technique tended toward tightly constructed counterpoint and he began to view himself as a highly skilled worker, "a real goldsmith" in Juliette Michaud's words,[12] working out the musical possibilities of those ideas that seemed to come from outside himself. He saw in world music an opportunity to examine the original meaning and spirituality of music and, in 1982, spent a month in Bali studying gamelan music. Then through his work on *Malevil* (1980), he was introduced to the Fairlight Synthesizer and developed his understanding of sampling and composing with sound. He created a score using his own voice and various environmental sounds as source material, as well as instruments such as the quanoun and the oud. Looking back in 2001, he confessed that he considered himself extremely lucky to have had the chance to experience so many diverse areas of music so early in his career.[13]

In an interview in 1994, he also claimed that this first experience with Godard was "decisive" in determining his preferred approach to film music composition.[14] He espoused an ideal working method based on this experience, a method that, he continues to claim, should be standard to the industry. Yared's plea to directors was to involve composers from the very earliest point of the film's inception and not, according to the prevalent practice of Hollywood and the international industry, to request a score after the shooting and editing was already finished. He felt that by being one of the first, rather than one of the last people involved in the film, a composer could have sufficient time to absorb the drama of the story and, in his own words, to "dig" for musical ideas and their development, and have sufficient "time to be wrong."[15] Essentially, he was pleading for the right of music to be integral to the actual creation of the narrative—to be part of its very sense rather than just underlining particular scenes—and for the composer to play a much more prominent role in the creative process than merely arriving 'after the event' to fill whatever gaps were left in the final edited film. The director-composer relationship should, he stated in 1992, be as "equal to equal; novice to novice; discoverer to discoverer."[16]

This ideal working method was borne of an avowed belief in a need to serve music and to give back what he refers to as its "gift" to him.[17] More important than fitting music to a scene, he feels, is to "dive into the ocean of possibilities" offered by the essential drama of a script and to work through all the ideas that arise from it, to explore until he feels he has gone as far as he possibly can. If in the completed film, "only half a page is left" or "the most beautiful of those possibilities are not used," he therefore considers that he has, nevertheless, fulfilled his proper role as a *composer* rather than specifically as a film composer.[18] Accordingly, in interviews in 1985 and 1990, he called for film composers in France to be salaried for the entire time spent working on a score rather than being forced to work solely on commission, suggesting in turn that the composers themselves should try to restrict their commissioned work.[19] True to his own counsel, he strove for selectivity in his own work, explaining in the same 1985 interview:

> Writing thirty or forty minutes [of music] twice a year is enormous on its own. I have saved myself because, to begin with, I want to choose the films, I don't want to take on anything that's offered to me without seeing the script. And then before anything else there are the personal relationships with the directors to consider. Finally, I want my music to be real music, which can be listened to without the film.[20]

One of his most famous and productive collaborations was with Jean-Jacques Beineix who, according to Yared in a 1994 interview, approached him to work on *La Lune dans le caniveau* (*The Moon in the Gutter*, 1983) after hearing his music for *Sauve qui peut la vie* and *Malevil* on television in 1982.[21] This film, developing upon the discoveries he had already made through working with Godard, "allowed [him] to see exactly how much impact music could have on the shooting of a film."[22] In all three of their collaborations, Yared was prepared for work by Beineix through reading and discussing the scripts and also, in the case of *37°2 le matin* (*Betty Blue*, 1986), the original novel, as well as by meeting the actors and discussing their characters.[23] He wrote the music before shooting began and, as Beineix first took to the set, his completed music was played to the cast and crew.

Although *La Lune dans le caniveau* was the film for which he won his first award, the Grand Prix de la SACEM in 1984, Yared considered his greatest collaborative success with Beineix to be *37°2 le matin*.[24] For this film, they agreed the score should be "very intimate,"[25] a feeling that was achieved to a great extent by the drawing of non-diegetic themes from the diegetic world of the characters and, in particular, the integral role of a piano duet in the relationship of the central protagonists. This duet was composed by Yared in accordance with the musical abilities of the actors themselves and is played by their characters Betty (Béatrice Dalle) and Zorg (Jean-Hugues Anglade) in the piano shop that they manage during the final stage of their passionate and tempestuous relationship.[26] The melody of this duet, however, permeates the non-diegetic score in a variety of instrumental arrangements, recalling their emotional interaction, closeness and dependency throughout the film. Since the scene in which they play the duet did not exist in the novel on which the film was based, Yared considered this to be solid evidence of music's potentially active influence on a film, even at the scripting stage.[27] Following the success of this film, Yared worked with Beineix on one further film, *IP5*, in 1991.

His working practices with Robert Altman and Jean-Jacques Annaud were similar in many ways to his experiences with Beineix. His first film with Altman had been *Beyond Therapy* in 1987, for which he was required to write a score using only the George Gershwin song *Someone to Watch Over Me* as thematic material. This gave him "an opportunity to renew [his] acquaintance with jazz,"[28] while also allowing him to compose in his preferred way, fertilizing that first 'seed' of music. He worked entirely away from the film and by the time he saw it for the first time, he had written many variations and fugues on the first eight notes of Gershwin's melody. His compositional techniques were borrowed from J. S. Bach's *The Art of Fugue* and included mirror and retrograde fugue forms. As a result of this method, he told an interviewer in 2000 that "all this work was creative to [him], although [he] didn't do the main theme."[29] He continued to compose away from the film with their next collaboration, *Vincent and Theo* (1990). In this case, as well as looking at the script, he turned to Van Gogh himself for inspiration, particularly his 1887 painting *Sunflowers*. He described his process in 2000:

> "The Sunflowers" became a leitmotif for me and I drew on it for inspiration for the Vincent theme. . . . I had a book of the paintings and I used different ones to inspire the music for different scenes.[30]

Although, in another interview in 2000, Yared considered the result of this work to be "maybe the most creative music [he had] done,"[31] the production itself proved problematic. According to Yared, Altman left France, leaving the production in the hands of a French company and Yared had never, at least up until this interview, seen the finished film.[32]

His first experience with Annaud followed immediately afterwards. In an interview in 1994, Yared described him as being "like Beineix" in that he "actually listen[ed], and . . . ha[d] a taste for risk."[33] He told how, for their first collaboration on *L'Amant* (*The Lover*, 1991), Annaud approached him a year before shooting was due to begin with "a wealth of information on music in 1930s Vietnam."[34] As he worked, however, it was Annaud's description of the love story that lay at the heart of the film that provided Yared with the vital inspiration for the central theme.[35] Once again, his music was written in response to the essential drama of the narrative and away from the image itself. This director-composer relationship was so satisfying that the pair worked together again in 1993 on the 3D IMAX™ film *Wings of Courage* (1994).

In the meantime, with other directors such as Maroun Bagdadi and Bruno Nuytten, and through his first forays into writing for ballet, Yared had the opportunity to develop different aspects of his compositional style. In 1988 he produced his first ballet music for *Shamrock* by Carolyn Carlson, which was performed by the Het National Ballet at the Het Theater in Amsterdam. This was followed by music for Roland Petit's *Le Diable amoureux* in 1989, performed at the Théâtre des Champs-Elysées in Paris. Throughout the 1980s and into the early 1990s, his films with Bagdadi offered him an opportunity to return to his cultural roots and to "marry [his] eastern culture with western music,"[36] a possibility that would arise again most strikingly with *L'Amant* in 1991 and *The English Patient* in 1996. With Nuytten's *Camille Claudel* (1988), on the other hand, he was able to explore his longing for the "almost morbid romanticism" of Mahler's Tenth Symphony—a work with which he was preoccupied at the time.[37] Although he found both the working process and the final editing of this score far from ideal, this personal musical development meant that he was still able to enjoy "a great experience"[38] writing a score that *Première* lauded as having, itself, "the magnitude of a symphony."[39]

By the end of the 1980s he had already won several awards, including the Grand Prix de la SACEM for *Hanna K* in 1984, the Victoires de la Musique in 1986 and 1989 for *37°2 le matin* and *Camille Claudel* respectively, and César nominations for the latter two as well as *Agent trouble* (1987). According to *Studio Magazine*, his work on *37°2 le matin* had made him "one of the most sought after musicians in cinema"[40] and in 1990, just as he approached a second watershed point in his film music career, he was acclaimed by *Le Film Français* as "'the' film music composer."[41]

# Disillusionment and the Académie Pléiade

Throughout the 1980s, Yared had gained a reputation for perfectionism evidenced by his refusal to compromise, even at the cost of a "potentially meteoric rise" to fame,[42] and by the sheer length of time that he devoted to each of his film scores.[43] His popularity, enviable reputation and numerous awards, however, could not counter his growing frustration with both the industry and his own work.

In 1990, the year of the first public concert of his film music, he declared film composition to be "a grocer's profession," which he was about to quit forever.[44] He had always been a proponent of breaking away from the conventions of film music scoring that he felt had remained largely dominant since the 1930s.[45] Now, he found that he no longer felt creative as a film composer and that he was, in his own words, "just walking in [his] own footsteps" with every score that he wrote.[46] He considered that economic and commercial constraints in film and television disallowed composers, except in very rare circumstances, from experimenting and thus from developing.[47] Added to this was the concern that directors often did not recognize the full narrative potential of music. Yared considered this problem as being rooted in the failure of most film schools to offer courses in the basics of the styles, instrumental sounds and affective potential of music.[48] Perhaps as an extension of this, he also saw the continued use of temp tracks as a serious hindrance to composers. It was quite understandable, he suggested in 2001, that directors who had grown accustomed to the sound of a particular temp track were less likely to give their composers the chance to make their own voice heard or to revolt against convention.[49]

At this point in his career, he therefore decided to finish his existing film projects and to return to writing music for commercials and pop songs. As if to signify his break from the past, he left Paris and settled in the quiet community of L'Ile aux Moines in Brittany. In these new surroundings, he hoped to find a much-desired opportunity to return to composing for its own sake. He entered into a period of intense improvisatory work, much of which would later be used in the ballet score for *Clavigo* (1999).[50]

His disillusionment had also focused his attention on the question of the general education and opportunities offered to composers wishing to work in film. From around the mid-1980s he had in fact been nurturing the idea of creating his own academy to address these very concerns. He felt that his own early background as a self-taught composer rendered him particularly well equipped to teach young composers about the kind of direct experience of working in the music and film industries that they could not learn in a formal educational setting. Involvement in such a venture would also, he hoped, be beneficial to his own development as a composer. By 'giving away' what he already knew, he would in turn compel himself to explore his own new avenues of discovery. The students, in the meantime, would learn more than they could from conventional film music composition courses— more than what he saw as a film music "vocabulary."[51] Rather than teaching them how to compose for film through examination of the 1930s Hollywood precedent, he wanted to open their eyes to the work of classical composers such as Bach, Janáček, Mahler and Bartók. Furthermore, he aimed to offer them actual support and help in becoming established as professional composers. Thus the idea of Académie Pléiade was conceived—its name meaning, in Yared's words, "many stars who shine together in constellation and yet remain independent of one another."[52]

In 1994, in association with Jean-Pierre Arquié, who he had first met in 1991 when Arquié worked as Music Supervisor on *L'Arche et les déluges*, he began his attempt to bring the idea to fruition. In 1996, he was commissioned by the music rights agency SACEM and the French Minister for Culture to provide a one-year course of study, including a series of meetings with film directors, orchestrators and sound engineers, as well as a visit to his own recording studio, for six young composers. It was the hope of both Yared and Arquié that a center could eventually be established in which to base this work as an ongoing project, with financial support from the original commissioning bodies. When this proved impossible, however, they decided to continue the project themselves under the banner of YAD Music, an organization that they founded in 1998 to promote the music of both Yared and the Académie Pléiade composers.[53]

He had begun with sixteen composers under his wing, but at this point the number was reduced to three who, at the time of writing, remain with Pléiade. These composers, Jérôme Charles, Nathaniel Méchaly and Stéphane Moucha, study with Yared and work both in association with him and by his recommendation. Most importantly, when they work on a project for which he is the primary composer, they receive full credit alongside him. By encouraging producers who approach him for work to give one of his students an opportunity, Yared hopes to encourage a more open-minded attitude to new composers. Thus he aims to provide a bridge between inexperienced, unknown composers and the film industry.

# Anthony Minghella and After

Even as Yared was preparing to take his leave of the world of film music, however, he was already being lured back by the beginnings of his partnership with Anthony Minghella. In the early 1990s, Minghella, who had been impressed by the scores for both *37°2 le matin* and *L'Amant*, approached Yared to compose the music for his first Hollywood film, *Mr. Wonderful* (1993). While Yared was happy to accept the offer, Warner Brothers, the film's producers, were unfamiliar with his work. As a result, their proposed collaborative debut ended before it had even begun. Minghella persisted, and approached him again some time later with what was to become their first joint venture: a series of six commercials for the telecommunications company Mercury. Most importantly, as Minghella suggested, this gave them "a way to be engaged before being married."[54] When he subsequently enticed Yared from retirement with the script of *The English Patient*, their long-awaited 'marriage' was immediately evident as one of true soul mates. In Yared's view, Minghella was a writer who wrote as "a musician"—a musician who was eclectic and knowledgeable and who was, most importantly of all, "an explorer."[55]

It was undoubtedly the particularity of this relationship and his first experience of working with sound editor Walter Murch that enabled him to exorcise a further problematic issue of his past film music career. Alongside his public declaration of the problems of working in the film industry, it is also possible that Yared had felt a different kind of frustration with his own work. He has said that in working on *The English Patient*, he "became a film composer"—his earlier work being "only the very arrogant look of a composer at a picture."[56] In the past, he felt, he had composed his music in an "overall" sense with no real idea of how to fit it to the film.[57] The only model he could find was that of the classical Hollywood style, which repelled him because of what he saw as scores becoming "musically nothing" as soon as they were pitted against the more important forces of dialogue.[58] As he said in 1990, he did not want to be "a slave-composer who adjusts his melodies to the images."[59] For him, it was the music itself that was the most important thing, and without being willing to subject it to such compromise, he could find no effective alternative way of working.

Despite his immense enjoyment of working on *The English Patient* (a detailed account of his working practices with Minghella and Murch can be found in chapters 4 and 5) and his development into what he considered a fully-fledged film composer, Yared was nevertheless completely stunned by the success of this score. Just three years after *Studio Magazine* had proudly witnessed that "[his] objective [was] not to end up in Hollywood with an Oscar,"[60] that was exactly the position in which he found himself. His Academy Award for *The English Patient* hit him, in his own words, "like a nuclear bomb."[61] He soon found, however, that his newfound fame was something of a mixed blessing. The next two projects that he undertook ended in disappointment and failure; his scores for both Iain Softley's *The Wings of the Dove* (1997) and Bille August's *Les Misérables* (1998) were rejected. The award, he felt, had changed nothing in his life as a film composer, except that he was now branded as the *"English Patient* composer."[62] As he saw it, this identification with a particular style and quality of music garnered only more and more offers to write the same kind of score. Indeed, *Film Score Monthly* suggested that since scoring *The English Patient* and *City of Angels* (1998) he had become "the chosen voice of tragic romance."[63]

Unsurprising though it was, given the overwhelming success of *The English Patient*, he found himself once again frustrated at the limitations being imposed on him by the film industry. He yearned to work across the variety of film genres and musical styles that he had explored and enjoyed during the 1980s and early 1990s and felt that his work on films such as *37°2 le matin* and *L'Amant* had been largely forgotten.[64] In the course of time, it was Minghella, once again, who he sees as having led him out of this second impasse, this time with his adaptation of Patricia Highsmith's dark thriller *The Talented Mr. Ripley* (1999). Both this film and their subsequent project, *Cold Mountain*, demonstrate in Yared's view that Minghella is "the only person who really understands who [he is], and who always expects [him] to go where [he has] never been before."[65]

Yared's continued development nevertheless maintained the consolidation of past and present that has proved a constant feature of his career. One aspect of scoring that he was more than happy to revisit with *The Talented Mr. Ripley*, according to a 1999 interview, was composing his own title song. He had composed his own songs for French films such as *Tatie Danielle* (1990) and *Les Marmottes* (1993), and for this new film he composed *Lullaby for Cain* to lyrics written by the director.[66] In general, Yared was uncomfortable with the rise of the use of pre-composed pop songs in film, seeing the phenomenon, in the same interview, as chiefly a manifestation of the commercial stronghold exercised by producers and record companies over films and their composers. Rather than thinking about their films' scores in

purely musical terms, he felt producers were now either forced, or
welcomed the opportunity, to take into account the commercial potential of the soundtrack. In particular, he bemoaned the growing phenomenon of including songs on soundtrack CDs that did not even appear in the film.[67] Although he confessed that his own experiences of
working on Hollywood scores that incorporated pop songs had been
various and not altogether unsatisfactory, his preference for writing his
own songs, in a variety of styles, remained. After *The Talented Mr.
Ripley*, he took on this role again within his scores for films including
Neil LaBute's *Possession* (2001) and Jean-Paul Rappeneau's *Bon voyage* (2003).[68]

In 1999, he also made a return to the world of ballet, working once
again with Roland Petit on *Clavigo*. Interestingly, he now applied his
preferred method of composing for film to this very different genre.
The first thing he did after being approached by Petit was to read the
Goethe novel on which the ballet was to be based, in order, he
claimed, to imbue himself with "the spirit of the work."[69] Having finished the composition of the main themes, just as he had done with
directors such as Beineix and Minghella, he made a demonstration
recording that formed the basis for his further discussions with Petit, as
well as allowing the ballet dancers to have an idea of how the final
music would sound. He sought, as he stated in 1999, to challenge the
boundaries of his own compositional experience in order that the music should be as much a pleasure to write as to dance to.[70] *Clavigo*
premiered at the Paris Opera House in November 1999 and was re-
vived in January 2002.[71]

In the meantime, his film music suites were receiving increasing
attention from concert audiences. In October 2000 he was invited to
conduct a concert of his own music in Valencia, and a year later he
shared the concert platform at the 28th Flanders International Film
Festival with Elmer Bernstein. He continues to compose for films and
feels that his work on *The English Patient* has cured him of the self-
perceived inability to fit his scores to their films. His work on *Possession* involved writing 72 minutes of music, of which 65 minutes were
what he terms "underscore."[72] His eight months of work produced a
score which he believes is both complementary to the scenes with
which it plays and successful in independent terms as music. This, he
has said, is the ideal of what he would like to achieve in writing film
scores.[73]

# 2

# YARED'S TECHNIQUE OF
# FILM SCORING

Yared's philosophy of film scoring and his ideal working method stem from the belief that the film music composer should seek to capture the very essence of the narrative within the music. In his view, the composer's involvement should begin at the scripting stage, the point from which the drama is first conceptualized, in order that the music may grow alongside its characters, themes and overall narrative design. This gives the composer time to think and explore, to know the drama intimately and to develop the music as a meaningful and integral element. As long as the composer has had sufficient time to take this process as far as possible, then the work of composition has been properly completed even if only a small proportion of the resultant music is actually used in the film. In these terms, therefore, the film itself forces the composer to shift his or her thoughts from the emotional subtext of the narrative to its everyday, scene-by-scene, diegetic detail.

This working method means that Yared has often completed a significant amount of the music for a film before he has seen any of it. Clearly, at least in the initial stages of composition, this renders impossible a shot-by-shot approach to scoring. The music fits the spirit of the film first, the detail of its presentation second. The question of how his theory of film music composition is translated into the actual practice of scoring therefore becomes paramount in an investigation of Yared's style. Added to this must be his own pinpointing of moments of creative frustration and development throughout his film-scoring career. This chapter will prepare for the case study analysis of *The English Patient* by contextualizing it within the overall picture of Yared's musical and musical-narrative language and the stylistic developments that resulted from his work with Minghella and Murch.

# Mode of Scoring

Given that the encapsulation of the essence of the narrative is Yared's single most important aim, it is perhaps inevitable that his approach to scoring tends to adhere to a broadly melodramatic model. In this context, the presence of non-diegetic music in a film attests to the emotional, moral or ethical 'truth' that underlies the surface of everyday events.[1] Peter Brooks suggests that the melodramatic mode suspects the potential superficiality or inadequacy of spoken communication. It finds that "truth," rather than residing in such concrete meaning, is more likely to be found in the desemanticized "gesture" of nondenotative signs.[2] While such signs encompass elements such as mise-en-scène, acting style, tone of voice and physical gesture, music, of course, enjoys an obviously definitive role.[3] Its very particular constitution as a system of sounds that nevertheless eschews the concrete meaning of language, seems to allow it to provide the starkest contrast to the rational, 'real' world of the diegesis. Robert Lang even goes so far as to suggest that "[i]n melodrama's use of music, . . . we identify an impulse to fly free of the codifications of the symbolic."[4]

The non-diegetic score is privileged in this respect above diegetic music because of its physical distance from the 'realities' of the diegetic world. Removed from both the control and knowledge of the characters, the non-diegetic score is free to reveal secret thoughts and restrained emotions, to create associations between apparently disparate situations and characters and even to contradict emotional falsehood and deception. It is therefore particularly well suited to proving the existence of Brooks' moral universe—the level of human existence defined solely by an emotional and moral veracity that transcends social constructions, codes and definitions. Such a guarantee of emotional truth, which supersedes any ruses of behavior, language or diegetic music that a film or its characters might throw up, is vital to Yared's method.

Yared does not seek to score actions as much as the emotional undercurrents that inform those actions. As a result, his music is often so deeply 'intimate' with the narrative that it negates, to some extent, the importance of his occasional lack of control over its actual placing within the film. He almost never apes physical action in the manner generally referred to as *mickey-mousing*,[5] and only imitates movement in his music when it implies a similar emotional contour. In *The English Patient*, therefore, in his accompaniment of Hana swinging up into the ceiling of the church at Arezzo and then from one side of the ceiling to another, the ascending string arpeggio and harp glissandi express more of Hana's sudden bursts of exultation than her actual physical movements.

By working away from the film, using novels, screenplays and discussion with directors and actors, he aims to find the real human significance of the everyday situations of which his music will be a part, and it is this dramatic core that he seeks to bring alive in the film. A score may therefore be primarily concerned with the emotional state of one individual and may suffuse all events with a sense of their very singular outlook or experience. Such extreme intimacy can lend the films that he scores a peculiar and even uncomfortable emotional depth. He has the ability to render characters completely open and their narratives, as a result, can become particularly involving, moving and memorable; audiences are certainly left in no doubt that they have been into the inner world of the central protagonist. Where characters suffering from extreme emotional anguish or illness are concerned, such as the eponymous Camille Claudel (Isabelle Adjani), Vincent van Gogh (Tim Roth) and Tom Ripley (Matt Damon), this can be an experience of almost painful proximity. The same level of involvement with a wily old devil like Tatie Danielle (Tsilla Chelton), on the other hand, has a completely different result. It deepens the awful wickedness of her actions in the face of her mock innocence while still, amazingly, making them seem the funniest you have ever seen.

Part of the intimacy between score and narrative arises from the way in which Yared creates both direct and indirect links between music within the diegesis and the purely emotionally motivated non-diegetic music. The emotions represented at the non-diegetic level thus appear so much more a product of the characters with whom they are associated and an extension of their actual world. Perhaps *37°2 le matin* offers one of the most obvious examples of a direct link, with both of the main non-diegetic themes being anchored to the world of the characters through their own diegetic renditions (a more detailed account of this can be found later in this chapter). Similarly, perhaps, while the sourcing of themes from J. S. Bach and Mozart reflects the period in which *La Putain du roi* (1990) takes place, it is also momentarily linked to the diegetic musical practice, and by extension the private emotional life, of Jeanne (Valeria Golino) and her husband.

More indirect links, which unite the non-diegetic score in spirit rather than through actual themes with the diegetic world, are also common. Even though the Bach played by Hana in *The English Patient* does not transfer directly into her non-diegetic musical representation, the retention of its style suggests that the film is adopting her own chosen mode of musical expression to reflect her deeper interiority. Tatie Danielle sings an aria from *The Merry Widow* as she 'accidentally' tramples on Odile's (Neige Dolsky) flowerbeds. While she never sings the actual title song that introduces her story, its wry operetta style nevertheless reflects perfectly this rather theatrical brand of naughtiness. In *City of Angels*, by the same virtue, although the pop and blues music that Maggie (Meg Ryan) listens to never transfers directly into the non-diegetic scoring, her initial appearance is highlighted by the use of a pop idiom. This suggests the rather brisk way in which she currently relates to the world and thus prepares for the depth of her shock at subsequent events in the operating theater.

Conversely, Yared often uses the distinction between the diegetic environment and its music and the non-diegetic score to emphasize the concealment of a character's interiority—the difference between their real emotions and the image that they choose to convey. In any melodrama, the void between what a character claims to feel and what the non-diegetic music tells us that they actually feel can be extremely poignant. Not only do we feel their frustration at being unable to reveal their real emotions but we also feel, on a more universal scale, the pain of being verbally disempowered, of being unable to express freely what we think and feel. When a character willfully or unwittingly compounds the repression or misrepresentation of their real emotions through the use of diegetic music, however, the contrast seems all the more painful. Although characters may believe that music can be trusted and relied upon to tell the truth about themselves or others, the film audience knows that diegetic music can deceive; only non-diegetic music can really be relied upon to reflect the truth of a character's interiority.

Poor Jojo/Jockey (Sekkou Sall) in *IP5*, for example, represents himself through his own performance of streetwise rap, creating all the instrumental sounds vocally (except for a non-diegetic drum track) and chanting lyrics that sum up his bleak view of his own existence with a sense of bravado that is characteristic of that musical style. He is only a little boy, but already appears gruffly independent, tough, humorous, resilient and completely confident in his interaction with adults. Through Leon (Yves Montand), however, he is offered the paternal wisdom and guidance that he so sorely misses from his own alcoholic and entirely dependent father.

Walking through the forest in search of the Ile aux Pachydermes, Leon teaches Jojo and his friend Tony (Olivier Martinez) to feel and understand their place in the universe and its history and the magnitude of their decisions, actions and surroundings. The non-diegetic music representing the emotion that he brings into their lives is in complete contrast to Jojo's rap music, connoting by turns a sense of steadfast strength, deep compassion and gentle affection. This is epitomized in the scene where Leon encourages the boys to rest their heads against huge, ancient trees in a forest glade in order to feel their age and the history that they carry within them. Tony is skeptical and resistant, but Jojo seems gradually comforted by the feeling of the tree and relaxes against its trunk. All is still and focused, until Leon flings him arms into the air with a guttural cry, cueing the sudden appearance of the main theme. Its even pacing and stepwise descending intervals imply strength and constancy, while the interplay of ascent and descent in the sequential repetition of the melody suggests a calming, benevolent influence (see figure 2.8). Only after Jojo has found someone strong enough to support and love him can he reveal the desolate, lonely child that hides behind his constant wisecracking carelessness.

A similar divide exists in tragic romances such as *La Lune dans le caniveau* and *L'Amant*, both of which place their characters in an environment of decadent dance music, only to reveal their innermost emotions through extremely lyrical and romantic non-diegetic themes. In *City of Angels*, Yared himself has suggested that the mixture of pop songs and classical scoring worked extremely well in positively supporting the division between the terrestrial life of Maggie, the main female character, and the otherworldly existence of Seth (Nicholas Cage), her self-appointed guardian angel.[6] As will be examined later in this chapter, however, this division also allows for a dramatic contrast between Maggie's apparent self-confidence as a surgeon, Seth's presumed transcendence as an angel and the deep anxiety and pain, as well as the love and compassion, that unites them at a deeper level.

In both *The English Patient* and *The Talented Mr. Ripley*, the non-diegetic scores reveal subjectivities that are entirely at odds with outward appearances. Rather than being the cold-hearted, austere character that Almásy would have others believe, he is, in fact, a deeply emotional, intensely passionate man, not only where Katharine is concerned, but also in terms of his beloved archaeology and ancient history. Tom Ripley's interiority, similarly, is not worn on his sleeve. The very nature and self-consciousness of his disguise, however, means that the contrast of diegetic music to non-diegetic music is actively foregrounded.

# Partnership with Anthony Minghella

It is easy to see how Yared felt that he had found an ideal working partner in Anthony Minghella. Interviews and reviews of Minghella's work throughout the 1980s and 1990s reveal him to have an approach to narrative that is very similar in essence to Yared's approach to scoring. Both, firstly, are interested in representing and exploring what lies at the heart of a drama and with the emotions, rather than the superficial actions and events, of situations. Minghella's work delves beneath the surface of the everyday to explore the emotional makeup, motivations, strengths, confusions, misunderstandings and weaknesses of people as they negotiate their relationships and the social and moral frameworks within which they see themselves.

He is interested, he has said, in "what it means to be human"[7] and perhaps unsurprisingly, therefore, his original writing as well as his screen adaptations often deal with extreme and irreconcilable emotional complexity. In a review of his Channel 4 drama *What If It's Raining?* (1986), Minghella explained:

> Too often drama nominates good guys and bad guys. I prefer to inhabit more than one perspective: groups of people operating within their own moral or ideological framework who crash into other people navigating by their own lights. . . . I think life is messy: it doesn't yield to easy analysis.[8]

Complex though the human journeys that he represents may be, however, his aim is not to observe and judge, but to inhabit the same journey and encourage his audience to recognize elements of themselves in the characters. "If the character is so distant from anybody that we know or understand," he says, "it's very hard to learn anything. You adjudicate rather than recognise."[9]

Perhaps the most important aspect of this shared philosophy is a belief in music as a key to such humanity, interiority and recognition. Undoubtedly as a result of his own background as a musician and his previous experience of writing for radio, Minghella believes that "sound in film is as important as image."[10] In Yared's view, Minghella has "a vision of how the music could be with the scenes" as he writes.[11] This view is perhaps borne out by Minghella's own admission that he "always listen[s] to music while [he] write[s]."[12] Of particular note in this respect is the fact that both Yared and Minghella, before working together, had explored the role of diegetic music in revealing the interiority of characters and/or the emotional truth of their relation-ships: Yared in *37°2 le matin*, for example, and Minghella in *Cigarettes and Chocolate* (1988) and *Truly, Madly, Deeply* (1991), for which a musical duet was the starting point of the story.[13] In both *37°2 le matin* and *Truly, Madly, Deeply*, the diegetic duets that the protagonists play clearly express the synergy of their togetherness and, consequently, the bleak loneliness of their separation. (The construction of the piano duet as an expression of this relationship in *37°2 le matin* is considered later in this chapter.)

For both Zorg in *37°2 le matin* and Nina (Juliet Stevenson) in *Truly, Madly, Deeply*, the association of their relationship with this music is such that the musical instruments played by their late lovers become iconic, to varying degrees, of their absence. When Zorg has murdered Betty, he closes all the pianos in the shop in a gesture of finality after playing a fragment of her melody line from their duet. Before the reappearance of Jamie (Alan Rickman), Nina continues to play their duets alone, filling in Jamie's line with her own voice. Then, when asked to lend his cello to her nephew, she equates the request to being asked to hand over her late lover's body.[14] The moment when we understand that she has accepted his death, therefore, is when she carefully and reverently places the instrument into its case and locks the lid shut. In both of these films, the interdependence of the two parts of the musical duet becomes paradigmatic of the relationship of the characters playing them. Adopting the usual meaning of non-diegetic music, Zorg and Nina's adherence to their respective duets attests to the continuation of their emotions, whatever has befallen their partners. The duet cannot lie; it protects the genuine nature of their emotions against any accusations of falsehood and testifies to the unfathomable depth of their grief. The poignancy of the void left by the missing line of a duet played solo speaks far louder than words.

Working together on *The English Patient* and *The Talented Mr. Ripley*, however, Minghella and Yared have evolved ever-more complex relationships of personal identity to diegetic music. Entire schemes of signification then arise centered on diegetic music and its distinction from non-diegetic scoring. The full effect of the contrast of diegetic to non-diegetic music in *The English Patient*, and the relationship of each to Almásy's own personality and his engagement with other characters, is fully examined in chapters 3, 4 and 5. For the purposes of mapping this particular development, however, it is necessary to note at this point that the film maximizes on the potential for the concealment of self through the use of diegetic music. In particular,

Almásy uses music, consciously or unconsciously, to disguise or to close off his identity and real personality by precluding active engagement with those around him, an ironic move given Caravaggio's eventual identification of him partly through his encyclopedic musical knowledge. The idea of actively seeking to conceal one's personal identity through a particular choice of diegetic music is exploited to the full in *The Talented Mr. Ripley*. Minghella has said how he "tried to construct an argument in the film between classicism and jazz," stemming from Tom's natural alignment to the former and Dickie's (Jude Law) to the latter.[15] In order to ingratiate himself with Dickie, Tom relies on the general belief that the kind of music that a person likes will reflect the truth of their personality. He fakes a love of jazz and in so doing, easily fools Dickie into believing that they must be kindred spirits despite all appearances to the contrary. Ripley's use of diegetic music thus becomes more insidious than the mode of personal concealment and emotional control employed by Almásy in *The English Patient*. In Ripley's hands, it becomes a means of purposefully projecting a completely false persona.

The destructive fluidity of this false persona is then, perhaps appropriately, epitomized through diegetic music. As Tom acquaints himself with jazz before setting off for Italy, he listens to a recording of Chet Baker singing *My Funny Valentine*. Much later, as he sits with Marge (Gwyneth Paltrow) and Dickie on their yacht, the introduction to the song starts, continuing over an edit to Tom walking with Marge through the streets of Mongibello as she tells him how she first met Dickie when he used to play that very song in a Paris club. As soon as she mentions the song, the words begin on the soundtrack and because of the similarity of the voice, we may be forgiven for thinking that this is the version to which Tom had been listening in New York. It continues to accompany what we, Silvana (Stefania Rocca) and Tom know to be an emotionally loaded scene between Dickie's legitimate fiancée and illicit lover, before following Tom and Marge to Dickie playing a game in the street with some local men. Marge jokes with Dickie that she may run away with Tom; Dickie pretends not to mind then jokily mimes throttling his friend. A cut then takes us to Tom and Dickie horsing around, with Tom giving Dickie a piggyback ride down the street and Marge laughing at them. They run into Silvana and Dickie sings to her, momentarily chancing upon a fragment of the diegetically unheard song. We then see Tom hanging on rather too tightly to Dickie on the back of his moped, with Dickie admonishing him for "breaking [his] ribs."[16]

This happy summer montage, however, effectively catalogs the emotional disjunctures between all of its characters. Marge loves Dickie and, as Peter Smith-Kingsley (Jack Davenport) will later recite, "Dickie loves Marge." But Dickie also loves Silvana, after a fashion at least, and both Silvana and Tom also love Dickie. Whereas for Marge the love song signifies the beginning of their relationship in Paris, Dickie sings it just as happily to Silvana and both she and Tom would gladly adopt it to express their own relationship with him. Finally, however, when we locate the source of the music, the meaning of everything we have seen is altered once again. It is Tom, rather than Chet Baker who sings the song, glancing up to smile at Dickie who is accompanying him on the saxophone. As Minghella has said: "Tom can speak to Dickie through that song."[17] In retrospect, therefore, the song re-frames the montage in the light of Tom's gradual attempts to usurp Marge and Silvana as Dickie's lover. Just as he imitates everything else about him, he now attempts to adopt his role as seducer through the very song that has been so successful in that capacity for Dickie.

Once again, however, the impossibility of a false relationship to music proves the undoing of poor Tom. After a while, the superficiality of Dickie's interest in both his beloved saxophone and his new best friend becomes apparent as he prepares to move on to the pastures new of drumming, San Remo, his old friend Freddie (Philip Seymour Hoffman) and his marriage to Marge. Having murdered Dickie and assumed his identity, however, the one pretence that Tom cannot support is the all-important allegiance to jazz. Instead, he clearly feels safe in returning to his true loves of classical music and opera. Freddie's instinctive knowledge that Dickie would never take an interest in classical music then plays a significant role in arousing his suspicions about the apartment in Rome that ostensibly belongs to Dickie. As a result, he too is duly dispatched by the desperate interloper.

Tom finally meets classical musician Peter on the mutual home ground of the opera house. The pair seem almost to recognize each other at first sight, and are immediately and instinctively 'at home' with one another on a level far deeper than Tom's relationship of musical and sexual falsehood with Dickie. In a relationship where his own natural mode of musical-emotional expression is understood and reciprocated, however, he begins to lose his vital capacity for self-concealment. He sits at the piano and plays Vivaldi's beautifully mournful *Stabat Mater*, the piece that Peter is currently engaged in rehearsing, and talks of a locked room full of secrets to which he yearns to throw Peter the key. Peter cannot realize just how right he is when he says that this is "the music talking," but this is a musical-emotional convention of which Tom can now never be a part. His web of lies is already such that he is soon denied the chance of happiness with his true soul mate. The sudden reappearance of Meredith (Cate Blanchett) as he and Peter leave Venice means that he is forced to kill his new lover who, as the only character who is completely true to his own diegetic music, is marked as the only really genuine man in the narrative. Perhaps the final irony of this discursive musical relation-ship, as Minghella himself points out, is that at heart, it is Tom who has the improvisational soul of a jazz musician, rather than Dickie, who is actually formulaic and conventional in spirit.[18] It is in the face of such complex schema of diegetic music that the melodramatic role of Yared's non-diegetic score takes on such a particular importance.

# Compositional Style

One of the most notable qualities in Yared's writing is his stylistic eclecticism and versatility, not only across different types of film, but also within individual scores. First and foremost, having such a broad musical palette at his disposal allows him to approach films entirely on their own terms and to identify a musical style that matches the life and emotionality of the characters and their drama with tremendous flexibility. It also, however, allows him the potential for greater control over the scoring of the whole film, particularly in terms of continuing to compose original music where other composers may turn to pre-composed sources.

A broad overview of Yared's output immediately reveals the tre-mendous variety of his musical expertise: *La Lune dans le caniveau* encompasses blues saxophone, percussive dance music, a tango and a grandiose late-Romantic symphonic style; *37°2 le matin* ranges from fairground barrel organ music, blues saxophone and the simple, child-like style of the piano duet, to overdriven electric guitar riffs, pulsating synthesizers and Latin American dance music; *Camille Claudel* re-mains faithful throughout to a full string orchestra and a late-nineteenth century, specifically Mahlerian, idiom; *Tatie Danielle* opens with a brashly comic cabaret song sung in overblown operatic style that is transformed into quirky waltz and blues settings; *L'Amant* contrasts the ethereal mix of Eastern and Western instruments and styles of its main theme with diegetic dances including a tango, a fox-trot and a waltz; *City of Angels* contrasts aching symphonic appoggia-turas with washes of synthesizer sound, ballad-style guitar and a light, contemporary pop idiom; *The Talented Mr. Ripley* begins with its theme song, set in turn as a berceuse and then a classical concert piece, before alternating jagged Herrmann-esque dissonance and ostinati with light jazz. [19]

In the cases where he does employ pre-composed music, however, his originality remains uncompromised thanks to his compositional invention. *La Putain du roi* takes music by J. S. Bach and Mozart as original source material for its non-diegetic score. *Beyond Therapy* subjects George Gershwin's *Someone to Watch Over Me* to the rigor-ous variation described in chapter 1, and Ponchielli's *La Gioconda* is similarly treated in *Sauve qui peut la vie*. Finally, the score for *Sarah* (1983) uses cells from the second movement of Schumann's Piano Quintet.

There is, therefore, no doubt that his eclectic expertise enables Yared to tackle a wide diversity of genres and subject matter with equal success. What is perhaps surprising, however, given the broad range of styles that he routinely encompasses, is that this does not mean that his scores are loosely constructed, inconsistent or indistin-guishable as his own work. In fact, it is the very nature of their diver-sity that provides one of the hallmarks of his distinctive idiom. Perhaps inevitably, given his training with Julian Falk and the resultant compo-sitional method through which he seeks to explore musical ideas to their limits, Yared tends to base his scores in all their variety on rela-tively economical thematic material. Some, as a result, become object lessons in musical invention and imagination. In any one score, a theme or thematic cell may be subject to variation through instrumen-tation; fugal, contrapuntal or ostinato settings; melodic, rhythmic and harmonic development; and arrangement into musical styles such as jazz, swing and pop and set types such as classical aria, waltz and samba. Yared's overall approach and variety of techniques therefore mean that he is able, simultaneously, to make his music intrinsic to the spirit of the narrative, adaptable within and across its diegetic and non-diegetic levels and musically satisfying in itself.

## Orchestration

Along with stylistic eclecticism, and perhaps inevitably for a com-poser with such a strong background in orchestration, a broad range of instrumental color is also a characteristic of many of Yared's scores. He is clear that he sees orchestration as an intrinsic part of composition and that this is a role that he cannot conceive of delegating. Although he has worked with orchestrator John Bell since *The English Patient*, he maintains a strict control on this aspect of his work. With the help of his sound engineer Georges Rodi, he creates an exact synthesizer version of each cue, which is then translated by Bell into actual instrumentation. "But," says Yared, there is "not one note to add, not one harmony to change, not one counterpoint to add—it's all there and it's divided into many tracks. . . . [E]verything is set and I don't want anything to be added, and anything to be subtracted, from that."[20] The synthesizer demo for *The Talented Mr. Ripley* is therefore, according to Yared, indistinguishable from the final instrumental tracks that appear in the film. When composing a theme for a film, he contends that the composer must "think of the color,"[21] and this directive is clearly followed in his own work.

Qualities of sound and timbre are a vital means by which he inflects his themes with very particular nuances of meaning, feeling and atmosphere. His palette, accordingly, frequently encompasses orchestral instruments and choral or solo voices, as well as traditional instruments of, for example, Latin America, the Middle East and Asia. Perhaps most interesting, however, is his use of the synthesizer as a very particular sound source. While his score for *Malevil* indicated early on in his career that he viewed the synthesizer as more than just a substitute for acoustic instruments, it was used in that capacity in some of his later films.[22] Nevertheless, Yared has continued to make use of the synthesizer as an instrument in its own right, exploiting in particular its capacity for lending a peculiarly ethereal or unearthly sound to scores either as a solo instrument or in combination with other instruments. The precision with which he creates his ensembles in order to achieve specific timbres and moods is then centered on his aim of encapsulating the essence of characters and drama in the music. Contrasting and combining instrumental sounds and styles can speak volumes, in Yared's scores, about the emotional undercurrents and influences of humans and their relationships.

In *37°2 le matin*, for example, Yared uses a whole scheme of instrumental color, performance style and musical placement to map the relationship between the central characters, Betty and Zorg. He introduces one of the two themes with which they are most closely associated through Zorg cheerfully humming its first two phrases as he waltzes a pan of his beloved chili around the private diegetic space of his beach hut. As Betty subsequently arrives, the theme expands to a fuller length and appears in purely non-diegetic instrumental ensembles. As it transfers to the melodramatic site of emotional 'truth,' it also takes on something of a tender and melancholy air that transforms it significantly from Zorg's solo version and suggests Betty as a lonelier and more complex figure. Its arrangement is very gentle as she first appears in an aerial long shot, with the melody sounding tentatively in the guitar with only a light accompaniment. As Zorg later indicates that she may move in, the solitary voice of the accordion maintains the air of sadness while intensifying the tenderness of Zorg's kind action and Betty's grateful response. It then reappears in the diegetic space of the beach in the more disjointed, improvisational style of Georges's (André Julien) diegetic saxophone playing.

Transferring the theme so freely across the diegetic and non-diegetic spaces and between so many voices this early in the film gives the sense that the whole world of the central couple is imbued with the emotions of their relationship; from the moment that they meet, everything they do and feel is immediately centered on each other. After this point, the theme appears only non-diegetically until the very end of the film. It inflects the quieter moments of their often tempestuous life together with its continuing air of melancholy tenderness by foregrounding the delicate and lonely voices of the saxophone, guitar and accordion. Only after Zorg has murdered Betty in her hospital bed does the cheerfulness of his initial rendition reappear, cruelly, as their theme emerges from what might be assumed to be the diegetic source of a radio within the bright sound and carefree rhythm of a Latin American dance ensemble. It is as if Zorg is now doomed, rather than delighted, to be reminded of his love for Betty in every piece of music or every sound, just as he tells her in the hospital that he still hears her voice in their apartment.

## Characterization

The most crucial element of Yared's hallmark intimacy of character, drama and music is, of course, the way in which he constructs his themes. Music that bears no apparent relationship to the characters it represents, no matter how cleverly it is integrated into the narrative, will reveal nothing of great importance. Yared's real achievement in this respect is the incredible depth of connotation with which he is able to invest his themes and their development, and the resultant sense that

narrative and music are integrated at a level far beyond that of match-
ing on a shot-by-shot basis.

Tatie Danielle's very particular kind of robustness and self-
centeredness, for example, is conveyed through a song, *La complainte
de la vieille salope*, sung in an operatic style that alternates the breath-
less, coquettish wavering of the verse (figure 2.1) with the wide, de-
clamatory intervallic leaps and strident melody of the chorus (figure
2.2).

Figure 2.1: *Tatie Danielle* (Gabriel Yared) sc 1220562 (1990).
*La complainte de la vieille salope*. Extract of verse melody line.
Music by Gabriel Yared. Lyrics by Florence Cibiel and Catherine
Ringer.
© EMI Virgin Music Publishing France. All rights reserved.
Reproduced by kind permission of EMI Virgin Music Publishing
France – 20, rue Molitor, 75016 Paris.

Figure 2.2: *Tatie Danielle* (Gabriel Yared) sc 1220562.
*La complainte de la vieille salope*. Extract of chorus melody line.
Music by Gabriel Yared. Lyrics by Florence Cibiel and Catherine
Ringer.
© EMI Virgin Music Publishing France. All rights reserved.
Reproduced by kind permission of EMI Virgin Music Publishing
France – 20, rue Molitor, 75016 Paris.

The use of the 6/4 and 3/4 time suggests the old-fashioned sound of a waltz, which in combination with the overblown singing style evokes a figure of fading grandeur, a *grande dame* who has not lost her sense of self with advancing age. The music also suggests, however, that her character is not without a certain sense of irony and self-awareness; the melodrama of the opening song and its instrumental versions in sleazy but comic jazz and blues settings cast a wry tone over even the worst of her antics.

Perhaps one of the most interesting and intricate examples of this, however, can be found in the main theme of *The Talented Mr. Ripley*. This begins life as a berceuse before its various motifs are adopted and transformed in the non-diegetic score. As the film opens and before any image has appeared on the screen, the very first bars of the music, which interlock repeated notes an octave apart in the piano, indicate that we are dealing with disjuncture and doubling. The initial minor tonality and relentless downward contour of the melody sets a melancholy tone, but this is almost immediately inflected with constantly shifting chromaticism that suggests a degree of eerie instability. A faint wash of tinkling chimes behind the piano notes adds a sense of chaos and disarray, no matter how gentle, and the later introduction of acciaccatura notes in the bass line of the piano suggests the splitting of wholeness in a very literal way.

The breathy timbre of a woman's voice enters and weaves its way down the chromatic twists and turns of the opening line of the song, at the end of which Tom Ripley begins to appear in fragmented, tinted shards across the screen. The sung melody, which begins as part of the interlocking texture, slowly breaks away and begins to subvert the sense of meter and barline, both sustaining notes over accented beats and accenting weak beats. The sense of fluidity and instability that this creates is compounded by occasional changes of meter, alternating between 4/4, 3/4 and 2/4. This melody becomes the source of most of the thematic material that accompanies Tom through his narrative, even seeming to underlie the jazz themes that are introduced into the score as soon as Dickie enters his life. Such a connection to the original song, at whatever level, underpins Tom's actions from the outset as motivated not by evil but by irrationality caused by the intense sadness and feeling of disjuncture contained in the music, a disjuncture that we soon learn to be personal, social, cultural and sexual.

Tom is an incomplete character, as fragile as the intricate structure of the lullaby. He is perhaps still something of a child, for whom the boundaries of morality, behavior and identity remain fluid. He has a highly developed musical sensibility and ability, but instead of being a musician or a member of the elite audience, he is an ex-piano tuner working as a concert hall cloakroom attendant. As a person who does not fit comfortably into any walk of life, Tom becomes defined by a tragic fluidity; his impressionist party tricks become a way of life in which he becomes unable to separate himself from those he loves, admires or wants to be.

The hint of chromaticism contained in this introductory music thus becomes increasingly exaggerated as Tom loses his emotional grip on his situation, culminating in the moment of complete madness in which he murders Dickie. Yared is, in general, relatively sparing in his use of real dissonance and this sets his representation of Tom's sad but slightly creepy insanity completely apart from that of a character such as Camille Claudel. Camille's innocently soulful passion, and the tortured madness that results from the end of her love affair with Rodin (Gérard Depardieu), are captured instead in searing Mahlerian chromaticism and major-minor tension. Her pain and illness are thus granted a gravity and veracity of terrifying proportions.

## Thematic Style, Unity and Development

While scores such as *37°2 le matin* and *The Talented Mr. Ripley* demonstrate the thematic complexity and development that is characteristic of many of Yared's scores, the sheer variety of his work makes generalization about points of compositional style more difficult. A certain number of techniques, however, are identifiable across a wide range of scores and may therefore be considered as typical of his approach to the composition and development of his themes and the overall musical unity of his scores.

### *Melodic Style and Motivic Coherence*

Yared's scores are typically very lyrical. He employs long melodic themes that are often drawn out from their accompaniment by their setting for solo instrumental voices. Together with their often relatively slow tempo, this isolation can lend a characteristically wistful, even elegiac tone to his themes. Like the scores as a whole, the themes are tightly constructed, with a great deal of reliance on motifs and sequential repetition. The original non-diegetic version of the theme discussed above from *37°2 le matin*, for example, consists of four short phrases. Each begins with the same pattern of a four-note ascending scale leading to a dotted figure that resolves onto a sustained note (figure 2.3). For the first two phrases, the ascending pattern remains the same, although the dotted figure is inverted. The third phrase transposes the whole first phrase down a tone before the fourth returns to the original pitch and ends with an octave displacement of the final note.

Figure 2.3: Gabriel Yared, *37°2 le matin* (*Betty Blue*, 1986).
Betty and Zorg's theme.[23]
© 1986 by Gabriel Yared.

A similar combination of motivic structuring and sequential repetition can be found in the melody of the piano duet theme (figure 2.11) and in Betty's 'madness' theme (figure 2.4),[24] as well as across other scores as diverse as *La Lune dans le caniveau*, *IP5* (figures 2.7, 2.8, 2.9 and 2.10), *Tatie Danielle* (figures 2.1 and 2.2), *The English Patient* (see chapter 5), *City of Angels* and *The Talented Mr. Ripley* (figures 2.5 and 2.6). It is from the elements of this strong melodic coherence that Yared builds a sense of unity across the score as a whole, without compromising the need for significant musical variation and flexibility to the narrative. In some cases, even when the instrumental range that he employs is relatively restricted, he may still alter the sound of themes to such an extent that audiences for films such as *IP5*, *City of Angels* or *The Talented Mr. Ripley* are perhaps unlikely to recognize, on a conscious level at least, how coherent the scores actually are and the effect that this has on their comprehension of the narrative.

Figure 2.4: Gabriel Yared, *37°2 le matin.* Betty's 'madness' theme.
© 1986 by Gabriel Yared.

Figure 2.5: *Ripley* theme from Paramount Pictures' and Miramax
Films' *The Talented Mr. Ripley* (1999). [25]
Music by Gabriel Yared.
Copyright © 1999 by Famous Music Corporation.
International Copyright Secured. All Rights Reserved.

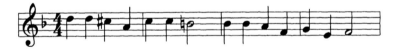

Figure 2.6: *Lullaby for Cain* (opening bars of melody) from Paramount
Pictures' and Miramax Films' *The Talented Mr. Ripley.*
Lyrics by Anthony Minghella. Music by Gabriel Yared.
Copyright © 1999 by Famous Music Corporation.
International Copyright Secured. All Rights Reserved.

Many of his scores connect a range of apparently very different themes through common motivic traits, making it difficult to identify exactly which theme constitutes what might usually be called the 'original' version. In *IP5*, for example, the whole non-diegetic score arises from variations on the same basic melodic and rhythmic pattern, which crystallizes into notably different melodies in association with particular characters, emotions or relationships.

The first version of the theme (figure 2.7) helps to create an emotional bond between Tony and Gloria (Géraldine Pailhas) during their first meeting, a bond that Tony deftly manages to break through his subsequent misconceived gestures of affection. It then becomes more prevalent in suggesting the importance of Leon as an influence on Tony, not only as a representative of Tony's potentially loveless future if he fails to find and make up with Gloria, but also as an older, more experienced man who understands what Tony is feeling. Thus it accompanies the pair as they walk without Jojo through the forest and, crucially, the moment when Tony encourages Leon not to give up his own search for love. Finally, after Leon learns of his long lost love, Clarence's, tragic fate, his lonely figure trudging along the railway tracks offers a salutary warning of the penalties of failing both to listen to your heart and to understand what is most important to your own happiness.

The next version (figure 2.8) is used as Leon, Jojo and Tony enter the forest together for the first time, immediately after Leon has rescued the boys from the site of their car crash and the wreck has exploded into flames behind them. Its arrangement for synthesizer and piano gives it a combined sense of simple clarity and the ethereal. Perhaps appropriately, therefore, its significance seems to lie in the mysterious and benevolent territory and influence that both the forest and Leon offer the boys, and perhaps Jojo in particular. It returns as Leon throws his face and arms skyward after he has encouraged the pair to feel their place in history with the help of the forest trees, and again as Jojo cries over Leon's dying body in the car at the end of the film.

The third version is used in both an even (as in figure. 2.8) and uneven rhythm (as in figure 2.9) and signifies the importance of the Ile aux Pachydermes, and everything that it symbolizes, to Leon. It first appears after he has led the boys into the forest and is suddenly gripped by the conviction that he has finally found the place for which he has been searching. The rhythm is smoothed out into even notes as he walks on the water of the pond where he believes he first met Clarence. The theme reappears later when he thinks that Jojo has found the right place, and again as he finally reveals his story and the reason for his quest. Despite Tony's protestations, the spiritual and romantic connotations that Leon's story has lent the theme then inflect the younger man's midnight swim and call to Gloria with more than just a lustful urge. Finally, as we see the scenery and lake that surround Leon's death in the car, the theme appears for one last time.

The final and least frequent version (figure 2.10) is used to create tension at two vital points. Firstly, it appears as Tony is overtaken by his creative urge and undertakes to paint a massive roadside billboard that the trio come across as they drive through the open countryside. Its repetitive rhythmic and melodic patterns repeat and build until the moment when Jojo accidentally fires Leon's revolver, thereby beginning the sequence of events that will finally end in Leon's death. Tony's passion is then translated into pride as Gloria, having overheard Jojo's testimony to his friend's love at Leon's hospital bedside, rushes out to find him sitting in a café opposite the hospital. As she stands looking at him through the window, the theme accompanies Tony's apparently angry and confused prevarication. When he sees that Gloria has given up, however, he runs out into the street to catch her.

Figure 2.7: Gabriel Yared, *IP5* (1991).
Cue title: *The Landing—Tony and Gloria.*[26]
© Editions La Marguerite–Cargo Films 1992.

Figure 2.8: Gabriel Yared, *IP5*. Cue title: *The day breaks.*
© Editions La Marguerite–Cargo Films 1992.

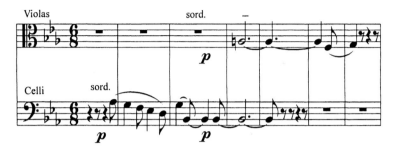

Figure 2.9: Gabriel Yared, *IP5*. Cue title: *The Island of Elephants.*
© Editions La Marguerite–Cargo Films 1992.

Figure 2.10: Gabriel Yared, *IP5*. Cue title: *Juke Box—Hospital.*
© Editions La Marguerite–Cargo Films 1992.

Apart from the obvious musical coherence that this creates, such thematic unity is also employed as a means of reflecting overarching narrative themes and structures. As has already been mentioned, the sourcing of many of the themes and motifs of *The Talented Mr. Ripley* from the material of the opening song links the score in an unusually close way to Tom's unique subjectivity. In a similar way to *The English Patient*'s focus on Almásy's emotional view of events (see chapters 4 and 5), this suggests that much of the course of the narrative is a result of his overinvestment, rightly or wrongly, in his own desires. The unity of musical themes in *IP5*, however, suggests the uniting of the three otherwise very different male protagonists in their search for love.

Much of the score of *City of Angels*, similarly, is based on material arising from a 3-note ascending scale pattern. This appears in variations including a pop synthesizer version for a view of angels overlooking the city; a piano variation that intersperses the ascent with lower notes to create a rocking pattern for the death of the little girl at the beginning of the film; and a string theme that extends the basic pattern into a cadence with an agonizing appoggiatura to underpin Seth's sympathy for Maggie's grief. The unity of these themes allows the compassion and serenity of the angels to embrace the painfully raw mortality of the hospital. While the diegetic music maintains the clear ethereal-terrestrial division, referred to in both chapter 1 and earlier in this chapter, between heavenly voices and pop and blues music, this non-diegetic theme is therefore able to connect the underlying, unspoken emotions and desires of Seth and Maggie.

*Ostinato and Counterpoint*

Within such versions of his themes and their own separate variations, Yared employs a range of structural devices and settings that, although consistent across his scores, are often used to very different musical, emotional and narrative effect. Arpeggiated accompaniments, for example, often in the form of ostinato basses, are a frequent means by which he adds to his characteristic foregrounding of melodies at the same time as using their firm regularity to enable fluid, sometimes almost improvisatory melodic writing. The first melody of *IP5*, for example, is introduced as Tony speaks with Gloria for the first time (figure 2.7). The languorous melodic line is foregrounded in the guitar, with an extremely delicate arpeggiated piano accompaniment, allowing it to reflect the tentative nature of the developing emotions between the couple while still remaining prominent. *Message in a Bottle* begins, similarly, with a harp ostinato that supports and highlights the oneiric, oceanic quality of its main theme in the strings.

The creation of interlocking relationships between accompaniment and melody, often extending into whole contrapuntal textures, is also a characteristic of Yared's scores that spans countless narrative functions. Sometimes it is used to give an added sense of lightness or delicacy to the relationship between ostinato and melody. For example, *37°2 le matin* emphasizes the fragility of the emotional interdependency of its two main protagonists through the hesitant rhythm and interlocking pattern of their piano duet (figure 2.11). In different contexts, however, the devices of both ostinato and counterpoint are used to very different ends. Such melodic freedom as is demonstrated in *37°2 le matin* can also be used to imply a potentially sadder kind of isolation, an effect that is further exacerbated in scores such as *Clean and Sober* (1988) and *The English Patient* by the actual separation of the melody from its ostinato support. In these cases, throughout the score of *Clean and Sober* and on one occasion in *The English Patient* as Hana plays hopscotch, the bass and melody appear alternately rather than simultaneously, but clearly belong together.

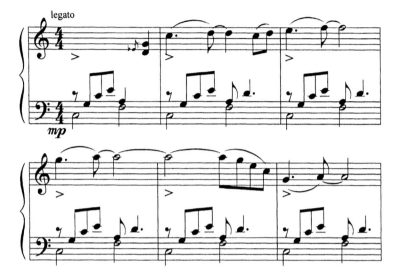

Figure 2.11: Gabriel Yared, *37°2 le matin.* Piano Duet.
© 1986 by Gabriel Yared.

A completely different affect is achieved through the almost violent rhythmic counterpoint that accompanies Gérard's (Gérard Depardieu) work as a stevedore in *La Lune dans le caniveau.* The blunt, repetitive industrial sounds of this cue express the harshness, noise, intensity and exertion of his very worldly life, providing a stark contrast to the symphonic excesses that accompany his emotional reaction to the rather otherworldly Loretta (Nastassja Kinski). In *37°2 le matin,* an insistently repeated contrapuntal pattern under a slightly dissonant melody is used to convey Betty's slide into insanity, just as the move from delicate, music box-like counterpoint to an interlocking texture of more insistent rhythms and dissonant harmonies charts Vincent's mental descent in *Vincent and Theo.*

The menacing potential of ostinati and the inherent disjuncture of contrapuntal lines are then exploited to the full in *The Talented Mr. Ripley.* Here, as was examined earlier in this chapter, the veritable schizophrenia of the score perfectly encapsulates Tom's murderous psychosis, becoming central to the mise-en-scène's representation of his fragmented personality and imaginary doubling with Dickie. A melody that in one setting seems to encapsulate the quintessence of an Italian coastal village in the full heat of summer, for example, is transformed by a thundering ostinato bass and dissonant harmonies into the most violent representation of Tom's insanity (figure 2.5).

*Drones and Pedal Notes*

Drones and pedal notes often play a similar role to the ostinato bass in terms of foregrounding and freeing melody lines and contrapuntal textures, although their effect can be slightly more doleful or portentous. They are also used, however, for some very particular effects that are difficult to imagine being fulfilled by any other kind of writing. In films such as *Wings of Courage*, *Map of the Human Heart* (1992) and *The English Patient*, for example, the use of drones helps to integrate the non-diegetic score into the narrative through imperceptible overlaps with the diegetic sound of airplane engines.

Perhaps most notably, however, sustained tones on their own or as part of more complex sound washes, particularly in the synthesizer, are often used to suggest moments of particular emotional extremity as wide-ranging as intense tension, fear and terror, speechless wonder and even the deeply ethereal or spiritual. While lower pitches are sometimes used to emphasize emotional gravity of a positive kind, such as the reconciliation of Garret (Kevin Costner) and his estranged brother-in-law in *Message in a Bottle* (1999) they often tend, perhaps naturally, to suggest situations of a more ominous nature. Each time that Wolfgang (Julian Sands) in *Tennessee Nights* (1989) encounters the mystery car with its apparently murderous inhabitants, his abject terror is underlined by low synthesizer rumbles and high-pitched tones, sometimes with the addition of repetitive interlocking patterns or rock drumming. As the young Avik (Robert Joamie) collapses in *Map of the Human Heart*, a low drone accompanies his dazed confusion and emphasizes the tension of the moment until his nose begins to bleed. Later, when he is an adult (Jason Scott Lee), a drone and pulsing beat suggest the inherent threat of war, as well as its personal impact, as Walter (Patrick Bergin) explains what is happening in Europe. Ominous synthesizer drones are used to signify the constant threat of violence in *Romero* (1989) and even in *La Putain du roi*, otherwise scored with music based on J. S. Bach and Mozart, a synthesizer tone accompanies Jeanne's view of her husband being captured and dragged away by the king's soldiers.

The piercing spiritual insight contained in the glare that Leon turns on Jojo in *IP5*, on the other hand, is conveyed through the gradual appearance of a sustained high synthesizer pitch. In *City of Angels*, by extension, the overall spiritual and corporeal tension between life and death that suffuses the narrative is expressed through a series of sustained high tones in both synthesizer and strings. These underline moments such as the tension of the operating theater, the bond of faith between patient and surgeon, the spirituality of the angels watching over the city, Seth's contact with Maggie through a glass window, the peace of the babies' ward and the final seconds before Maggie's fatal accident.

*Fugues and Fugal Textures*

More sparing, perhaps because of its relative lack of immediate flexibility to narrative events, is the use of fugue. This has already been mentioned in chapter 1 in connection with *Beyond Therapy*, but also appears in films such as *Hanna K* (1984), *La Lune dans le caniveau* and *IP5*. Given room for such cues to breathe, Yared uses complete fugal textures or fugal-style entries to very particular narrative effect. The sense of spaciousness, expansion of time and gravity that can be created by this form, for example, gives a very peculiar sense of portent to key moments in both *La Lune dans le caniveau* and *IP5*.

In the former, a fugue is built from the main theme to accompany Gérard and Loretta's drive along and away from the docks after they have narrowly missed knocking over Gérard's drunken father. As the fugue begins in the ominous, accented sound of the lower strings, it seems to reflect Gérard's horror at the sudden proximity of Loretta to his father and his realization, as a result, of the drastic dichotomy that their relationship is making of his life. As the fugue builds, it emphasizes both the epic magnificence of their industrial surroundings and the serious purpose of their journey, which reaches its climax as the fairytale church on the cliff edge finally comes into view. The breadth of the fugue carries them, therefore, out of reality and into fantasy. In *IP5*, the fugal entries of the opening bars of figure 2.8 herald the turning point in Tony and Jojo's lives as they team up with Leon and enter the forest for the first time. In a similar way to Gérard, perhaps, this symbolizes their temporary abstraction from their everyday reality and their entrance into a metaphorical space of fantasy and self-discovery.

# Placement of Music

Yared's claim that he "became a film composer" with *The English Patient* [27] suggests that working with Minghella and Murch allowed him to develop crucial areas of his technique in which he had previously felt himself to be lacking. Perhaps the most noticeable aspect of this development involves the way in which he fits his music to the detail of the image.

In Yared's earlier films, it is often noticeable that he does not write what he refers to in chapter 1 as "underscore." [28] Although his music always captures the emotion of the moment, he tends neither to mold it too closely to the intricate detail of the images, nor to score too many scenes that contain a great deal of dialogue. This means that his music is given an opportunity to breathe and to speak, to the effect that it can lend particular images, actions or episodes a profound emotional depth. Two such episodes stand out in *L'Amant*: as the Chinese man (Tony Leung) first takes the young girl's (Jane March) hand and later as she performs her languorous, erotic kiss through the window of his car. The sense of their passionate ecstasy obliterating their awareness of the world around them is perfectly encapsulated in the combination of diegetic silence and non-diegetic music. This gives the score space to play through its whole main theme uninhibited, while at the same time privileging the overwhelming emotion of their actions over their physical circumstances.

In a completely different film such as *Tatie Danielle*, however, the same combination results in quite a different effect. Here, the various versions of the title song that accompany Tatie's activities also come at moments of either little or no speech, or even complete diegetic silence. In either case, the foregrounding of music has the effect of emphasizing her personality and attitude above everything else, thus giving the audience the opportunity to relish her behavior in full. As her erstwhile family takes her on a car tour of Paris, for example, her purposefully abject boredom is expressed through a combination of diegetic silence and a non-diegetic waltz variation that slows down as she finally dozes off.

Such placement of music certainly does not, therefore, prevent it from being integrated into the narrative on an emotional level and at moments such as those described above, it is used to best effect by standing alone. In other circumstances, however, the fact that the music often seems to stop in order to make way for dialogue can prevent it from feeling quite as fully involved in the story as it might. Furthermore, even though most of his film scores do encompass at least some degree of non-diegetic music in combination with dialogue, he tends not to score around the speech. In *37°2 le matin*, he does reduce the texture of one cue, as Betty types up Zorg's manuscript, to make way for their dialogue. In *IP5*, similarly, he ends a cue mid-phrase as Leon, Tony and Jojo walk away from the burning car into the forest and holds a high synthesizer note under their dialogue before the melody returns after they have finished speaking. In many cases, however, his cues are simply reduced in volume under the dialogue.

This is most noticeable when the texture of the music is unusually dense, such as the moment when Gérard first sets eyes on Loretta in *La Lune dans le caniveau*. The increasingly grandiose symphonic style of the cue very clearly expresses the gradual but dramatic awakening of Gérard's emotions. It begins just before Loretta appears for the first time and as she enters the bar in search of her brother, the main theme is foregrounded in the solo violin. This fades out for her speech and then returns as she falls silent and Gérard gazes at her in wonder. It fades down once again for Loretta and Newton's (Vittorio Mezzogiorno) dialogue and up as they finish speaking. It then stops completely in time for Gérard himself to speak, although this sudden non-diegetic silence does lend a particular dramatic emphasis to his words. As he leaves the bar and looks at Loretta's expensive car, the music returns, only to stop on the following cut to his house. As this example also suggests, the music is often faded out during scenes or over edits rather than coming to a designed end.

As a result, undoubtedly, of his unusually interactive working method on *The English Patient* (see chapters 4 and 5), Yared has now developed techniques for designing his cues to the detail of the action without losing anything of the quality of his music. This has enabled him, in his later films, to achieve a perfect combination of the emotional and physical integrity of his score to the film. As he suggested in chapter 1, this does seem to have freed up his style and technique to a tremendous extent and his scores appear to exude a much greater confidence with the specific language of film scoring.

One important change concerns the flexibility with which he treats statements of his thematic material. Rather than necessarily stating themes or their variations in full, he allows for a greater degree of extraction and variation of shorter thematic cells, which will remain clearly recognizable even when used to score extremely brief moments. He continues to use entire themes in order to linger over long scenes or several linked scenes, but now tends in these cases to involve more complex development and combination of themes within the same cue. The way in which he begins and, particularly, ends his cues appears to be more precisely designed to the shape, diegetic music, sound effects and dialogue of the film as well as any pre-composed music that is used within the non-diegetic score.

As a result of all these things, his cues in his later films tend not only to feel more minutely integrated into the drama of which they are a part, but are also often able to imbue them with a greater sense of emotional fluidity, subtlety and immediacy. The minutest instances of integration are therefore often reserved for moments of particular emotional intensity or significance. As a conclusion to this chapter, and to prepare for the examination of the placement and development of the score in *The English Patient*, examples from *City of Angels* and *The Talented Mr. Ripley* will be used to demonstrate some of the forms that this can take.

## *City of Angels*

One of the most striking moments of visual and musical integration in *City of Angels* comes as Maggie flees the family room where she has just imparted news of the death of her patient to his wife and children. She hides in a stairwell and cries bitterly, questioning whether she could have done more to save her patient's life. Unbeknown to her, however, her grief is witnessed by invisible angel Seth. The soundtrack at this point has three layers: the diegetic sound of Maggie crying, the non-diegetic music and the interior monologue of Maggie's thoughts. The flexibility of the music to the cue allows it to create a tangible sense of emotional interaction between Maggie and Seth in a way that almost makes the action, in retrospect, seem choreographed to the music.

Before Maggie's voice-over starts, a non-diegetic cue is introduced that begins with a variation on the main theme and gradually develops into the theme itself (figure 2.12). Phrases and answering phrases are alternated, led by the violins and celli. The first segment of Maggie's voice-over coincides with the second violin phrase of this cue, in-between two answering phrases in the celli. The second of these answering phrases (bracketed in figure 2.12) repeats the first in sequence but inverts the final two notes; it thus transforms it into the first phrase of the main theme. As it begins, Seth emerges from the darkness to face Maggie, the most intense moment of his gaze at her coming on the phrase's penultimate, appoggiatura note.

The violins take up the remainder of the theme as Maggie lifts her face, unseeing, to Seth and continues her voice-over. The interplay between the celli and violins, and the progression from the first to second phrases of the theme, correspond exactly with the alternation of visual focus on Seth and Maggie. This draws the characters together and reconfigures their separate words and actions as an emotional exchange, or conversation, despite the fact that Maggie is not even aware of Seth's presence. Although the main theme is being stated in full, meanwhile, its rhythm is so fluid that it does not draw attention to itself and maintains a sense of flexibility to Maggie's much faster, almost percussive speech pattern.

As Seth then crosses his hand in front of her face to question whether she is at all aware of his presence, the violins make a sudden augmented 7th leap and begin the sequential descent of the theme's third phrase (figure 2.13). Maggie becomes more frantic about losing her confidence and repeats short phrases in her speech. The musical descent of the theme's third phrase followed by the repeated descending figures of the following phrase seems to compound her panic. The final note of the melody, however, which is suddenly expanded into a full, if unresolved chord, comes at exactly the moment that Seth places his hands over hers. The framing of these actions within one coherent musical line draws them together so that, in emotional terms, Seth seems almost to make one continuous movement from lifting one hand before Maggie's eyes to bringing both to rest in his gesture of comfort.

Certainly, as he attempts to calm Maggie he seems at least to calm the music, which cadences briefly before moving through a short bridge passage to the first fully chordal statement of the opening phrase of the main theme.

(Seth waves his
hand across
Maggie's eyes)

(Seth places
his hands over
Maggie's)

Figure 2.13: Gabriel Yared, *City of Angels*.
Seth watches Maggie grieving in the stairwell: Extract 2.
© 1998 New Regency Music, USA.
Warner/Chappell Music Ltd, London W6 8BS.
Reproduced by permission of International Music Publications Ltd.
All Rights Reserved.

This short phrase seems once again to give a conversational shape to the image, this time that of a question and answer. As we see Seth's face suddenly light up in fascination with something about Maggie's face, the first three notes of the theme rise very slowly, arousing a sense of anticipation about what he could possibly have seen. During the third note and into the fourth, we find the answer to this question in a cut to an extreme close-up of a tear running down Maggie's cheek. The appoggiatura chord on the fourth note is purposefully sustained—rather than progressing to its resolution—for the next reverse shot of an extreme close-up of Seth's eyes. The unresolved musical tension and the iconic signifier of pain offered by Maggie's tear make for a powerful combination. The tear attests to a depth of human pain that Seth can barely comprehend. In his love for Maggie he connects to this particular moment as representative of both the living emotions that he wishes to feel for himself, and the despair from which he wishes to rescue Maggie by teaching her to love being alive once again.

Whatever he may do to achieve this, however, this moment seems to foresee the ultimate futility of his efforts. Following Maggie some days later as she hides from an encounter with the wife of her patient Nathan Messenger (Dennis Franz), Seth 'touches' her hand through the window of a children's playroom. The same appoggiatura chord now resolves, suggesting the emotional inevitability and healing potential of their union. No matter what Seth sacrifices to be with her, however, their first encounter over that dissonant tear suggests that he can save neither her nor himself from the inevitability of grief.

## *The Talented Mr. Ripley*

In this film, a very short thematic cell is used to give an instant sense of Tom's encroaching madness, regardless of any other music with which it is combined. This motif is extracted from the song that opens the film and consists of a short, 5-note descending figure interspersed with a pedal note (figure 2.14). Removed from the lullaby, the figure is reorchestrated to feature celesta and glockenspiel and is often enhanced by a wordless, dissonant glissando sung by a female voice. This undermines to some extent the privileging of the upper line provided by the voice in the song and throws the interlocking texture into slightly greater relief.

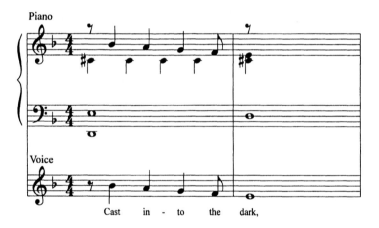

Figure 2.14: *Lullaby for Cain* from Paramount Pictures' and Miramax Films' *The Talented Mr. Ripley*.
Lyrics by Anthony Minghella. Music by Gabriel Yared.
Copyright © 1999 by Famous Music Corporation.
International Copyright Secured. All Rights Reserved.

Together with the gothic nursery rhyme quality of the instrumentation, this signifies Tom's split personality, dangerous instability and emotional over-dependency on Dickie, as well as exacerbating the sense that Tom's mentality is unnaturally childlike and eerily fragile.

Whether or not we sympathize with him as he is buffeted by a cruel and isolating fate, his actions are, as Dickie so rightly points out, "spooky." The brevity of the motif makes it infinitely flexible to any narrative situation so that, in a second, Yared can tell us that Tom is becoming more than just strange. In the buildup to the culminating moment when Tom murders Dickie, therefore, this motif is used relatively sparingly, being reserved for those moments in which Tom really is at his most dangerous.

The first real hint of this danger comes quite some way into the film, once Tom has safely insinuated himself into Dickie's house. He overhears Marge and Dickie discussing him on the terrace below the window of his room and, looking intently at himself in the mirror, he begins to impersonate them. Until this point, it could be argued that we are not fully aware of the habitual manner in which Tom appropriates other peoples' identities. He took the place of the pianist in the opening concert sequence because his friend had injured his wrist. He then impersonated Mr. Greenleaf (James Rebhorn) in order to reveal the purpose of his mission to Dickie. Creepy in effect though that was, the real potential for nastiness in his talent is saved for this latest moment. The dissonant glissando of the female voice hovers over the motif, curving incessantly downwards, before the motif gives way to a fuller instrumental rendition of the song's melody, still emphasizing the same instrumentation and interlocking texture. The next appearance of the motif then comes as Tom is startled by the sudden arrival of Dickie as he dances and sings dressed in Dickie's clothes. At the mention of rival friend Freddie, the motif cues us to the irrational depth of Tom's hatred for someone that he barely knows but instinctively recognizes as a threat to his relationship with Dickie. Once its malevolent potential has been established, the motif undergoes alteration and combination with other music in order to underline the inherent sadness of Tom's condition. His tragedy and his strangeness are therefore alternated as the story progresses toward Dickie's murder so that, by the time it happens, we are unable to condemn Tom completely for his extreme behavior.

With Freddie now firmly, if temporarily ensconced in Mongibello, Tom is feeling the "cold" that Marge describes as inflicting all of Dickie's forgotten friends. Dickie and Freddie play together in the sea and Marge approaches Tom on the yacht to offer comfort. As she begins to speak about Dickie's changeability, a solo clarinet appears above a string accompaniment, playing a short series of notes based on the melody of *Lullaby for Cain*. The effect is one of a sad but wistful isolation that creates a point of connection between Tom and Marge. When she mentions that this situation is "always the same" irrespective of the particular friend involved, a cut to Tom reveals his painful sense of rejection.

The simultaneous appearance of the motif, however, inflects his sadness with a hint of malevolence and only Marge's assurance that Tom was an especial favorite of her fiancé can temporarily retrieve the brightness of both Tom's expression and the cue. Her accidental confirmation of Tom's rejection through his exclusion from their planned skiing trip, however, is accompanied by a fuller variation on the theme song in the cor anglais. This instrument's long, doleful tones, in combination with Marge's increasing distress in attempting to explain the rather transparent reasons for this decision, hammer home the tragic consequences of Dickie's childish faddishness. We see Tom alone again on a cut to the yacht later that day, followed by Marge's sad and concerned gaze at him, both accompanied by the heightened volume of Dickie and Freddie's chummy banter. A longer shot of all four characters, however, is inflected once again with Tom's potentially dangerous reaction to their carelessness, as his motif returns to cast a final sinister air over this sequence of events. Immediately afterwards, as he watches Dickie making up to Marge through the cabin window, the motif returns to inflect the whole melody of the theme song with its creepy instrumentation and constant disjuncture. Evidence of Dickie's intimacy with anyone else clearly brings out the very worst imbalance in Tom's character.

This proximity of tragedy and danger is played out once again as Dickie finally confronts Tom and calls a halt to their time together. As he cheerfully blasts Tom's dreams apart, the cor anglais returns with the same long variation on the theme song that accompanied Marge's efforts to excuse his callousness on the yacht. Here, however, the dominance of the strings in the instrumentation of the motif places the deepest emphasis yet on the genuine pain and loneliness that underpin Tom's desperate dependence. The following events, by the same token, show Tom at possibly his most bizarre throughout the whole film. As he and Dickie travel by train to San Remo, Tom sees a rare opportunity for intimacy. As Dickie sleeps, Tom removes his glasses and tentatively rests his head against Dickie's lapel. Then, after they are momentarily disturbed by the guard, he twists his neck in order to align their faces and lips in the reflection of the corridor window. Both actions are accompanied by the otherworldliness of the glockenspiel and celesta version of the motif. The danger is clear, but Dickie is too thick-skinned to consider the consequences of his actions. Eventually, as he gives Tom the final brush-off on the boat at San Remo, the motif tells us that beneath Tom's initial stunned silence and then his hurt protestations, are feelings that Dickie could never have anticipated.

With this short motif, therefore, in its various settings and manifestations, Yared conveys the very core of his subject's tragic, murderous, almost schizophrenic disturbance, his childlike loneliness and his talent for deception. While still preferring to be considered a *composer* in his own terms, such intricacy demonstrates that he is, since *The English Patient*, most certainly *also* a film composer.

# 3

# THEMES AND ISSUES IN
# *THE ENGLISH PATIENT*

## Production History

The often difficult process of *The English Patient*'s production and the fact that it became known as the film "that was almost not made,"[1] made its eventual success a victory of independent risk-taking over Hollywood studio conservatism. In 1992, Minghella had been sent a copy of the novel and read it "in a single gulp" the day after completing work on *Mr. Wonderful*.[2] He was, as a result, "intoxicated, so stirred by the story that he wanted to see it."[3] He contacted Saul Zaentz, a producer famous for his successful film adaptations of 'difficult' literary works as well as his "maverick streak of individuality and . . . renowned penchant for calculated gambles."[4] Zaentz supported the project and in the autumn of that year he and Minghella embarked upon an unusually collaborative screenwriting partnership with the novel's author, Michael Ondaatje.[5]

From the outset, Minghella made no secret of his attitude to the adaptation:

> What excited me about Michael's book was that it was rather like reading . . . a magazine with 50 fantastic articles. . . . It was filled with great pictures, but these were only loosely connected by narrative. I felt that, unless I let go of the book, I would become ensnared by its rhythms and poetry.[6]

Thus he wrote the screenplay as a "response" to the novel, without the source material itself to hand,[7] seeking to "write [his] way back to the concerns of the novel, telling [himself] its story."[8] According to

49

Zaentz, all three men agreed that the only way the adaptation could work was by "capturing [the novel's] essence, its spirit," rather than by slavishly reproducing its every detail. Such an approach would, in any case, have been impossible in the case of so complex a story.[9] Ondaatje was therefore content to distinguish between the two works. In the foreword to the screenplay he described how he saw the relationship between his novel and Minghella's film:

> What we have now are two stories, one with the intimate pace and detail of a three-hundred-page novel, and one that is the length of a vivid and subtle film. Each has its own organic structure. There are obvious differences and values but somehow each version deepens the other.[10]

After an arduous screenwriting process that involved numerous drafts over a period of eighteen months, the funding and production of the film itself became rife with difficulties. Apparently as a result of a dispute over casting, producers 20th Century Fox pulled out of the project immediately before shooting was due to begin. According to one report, "Minghella wanted people 'not thought of as insurance policies'. Specifically, Fox said that Fiennes, if Fiennes it had to be, must be cast opposite a big American—Uma [Thurman] or Demi [Moore]."[11] Minghella and Zaentz sought new backing, which subsequently came from the independent Miramax Films. Shooting was finally able to begin but, according to *The Daily Telegraph*, this was only after "the cast agreed to take as little as a quarter of their salaries up-front."[12] "I despaired," Minghella said afterward, "thinking that the movie would never get made. Saul was the optimist to my pessimist throughout the whole process."[13]

Financial matters, however, were not Minghella's only concern. He broke his ankle during the first few months of shooting in Italy and, once in the Sahara desert, found yet more unforeseen problems.[14] As he told an interviewer in 1997:

> There's no practice in the desert. Someone walks across a virgin dune and that landscape has a flaw on it for two days, five days, a week. Then, . . . the only way to get there is by trekking in on mules with a huge convoy of film crew. We built a road and it was promptly rained off.[15]

In the end, it was the very length and depth of the screenwriting process, he claimed in the same interview, along with the caliber of his creative team, that had become his salvation in such unfamiliar and challenging circumstances: "I knew every nuance of it [the screenplay] before I began. In fact, I left it behind when I was working because it was so much in my body."[16]

With the difficulties of shooting behind him, however, Minghella remained proud of the virtue that had almost cost the film its very existence: the absence of film stars. As he stated categorically in a 1997 interview: "There are only actors in this film."[17] Despite the victory of his determination to retain his apparently noncommercial casting choices, however, he refused to condemn 20th Century Fox for abandoning the project. Instead, in the same interview, he extolled their courage in having demonstrated even an initial interest in a film "which is set in Europe, in the past, with reference to Herodotus and the politics of Kipling; with a central character who is burned beyond recognition and marooned in a bed."[18]

# Critical Responses

Despite its early setbacks, the film enjoyed a surprising and dramatic success at the American box office. In its opening weekend, in just ten cinemas, it grossed $278,439.[19] According to one report, this constituted more than double the amount grossed by any other major film.[20] The excitement soon spread and by the time of its British release it had been hailed as "one of the most eagerly anticipated films of the year."[21] It had by now taken in over $57 million at the American box-office[22] and had won two Golden Globe Awards including Best Picture—its seven nominations having exceeded every other film that year. It was nominated for twelve Academy Awards (also more than any other film that year) and thirteen BAFTA Awards (of which it went on to win six).

When it famously swept the board with nine Academy Awards, including Best Picture, it was celebrated as the most successful British film in Oscar history. Overall, it took joint place with *Gigi* (1958) and *The Last Emperor* (1988) as the third most successful film in Academy Award history. So great was its success, in fact, that many British newspaper reports highlighted those awards that it did not win, rather than those that it did. "Well," Andrew Lloyd Webber was reported as saying in his acceptance speech for Best Original Song, "thank heavens there wasn't a song in *The English Patient.*"[23]

The film also attracted the attention of the tourism, fashion and publishing industries. According to *The Times*, the Tunisian Tourist Office spent £20,000 as the main sponsor of the British première and "mounted a 17-city roadshow" in the hope of boosting Tunisia's flagging British tourist trade.[24] This same article reported that tour operators were also being encouraged by the Tunisian Tourist Office to make the most of the film and that one company was planning an *English Patient* tour for later that year. *The Times* also reported on plans to "convert the monastery of Sant' Anna in Camprena, in which Juliette Binoche tend[ed] to her dying patient, into a country hotel."[25]

The Isle of Wight council leader hoped that the director's fame would also boost interest in his own homeland. Minghella's origins in Ryde were well publicized and he had even managed to make references to the Isle of Wight in the film, saying that he "wanted to give something back to the island which ha[d] given [him] so much."[26] Furthermore, as he received his Academy Award for Best Director, he had claimed it to be "a great day for the Isle of Wight."[27] Island council leader Morris Barton, in return, said, "We now expect thousands of Americans to visit Minghella country. He has put the Isle of Wight on the map."[28] In recognition of his achievement and his community's pride in their famous son, Minghella was in fact honored by being the first person to be made an Honorary Freeman of the Isle of Wight in November 1997.[29]

Aside from tourism, fashion house Jaeger, according to *The Sunday Times*, chose to support the film's première "because its current collection . . . recreated much of the 1940s style seen in the film."[30] Perhaps the most unlikely tie-in success story, however, was Herodotus's *The Histories*, with Nigel Reynolds suggesting that "[i]f the Academy of Motion Pictures had had a category for Best Fogey-ish Film Prop, there is little doubt that the film would have won 13 nominations."[31] As early as 20 March 1997, a week after the film opened in Britain, *The Guardian* reported that "[b]ooksellers' expectations of a sales boom based on the film [were] high" and that Penguin Classics were considering releasing a special edition.[32] Only eight days later, while taking credit for having alerted them to the film's marketing potential, *The Daily Telegraph* was able to report that Penguin had indeed printed 35,000 copies of such a special edition within days of the crucial Academy Awards ceremony.[33] Penguin claimed, ordinarily, to sell approximately 15,000 copies of the classic every year,[34] but in May 1997, *Time Out* reported that the book had sold "a massive 100,000 copies" since the release of the film.[35]

Despite its undoubted commercial success, however, the film provoked a dramatic division of opinion and raised a number of critical issues amongst journalists, academics and film reviewers. Most seemed to find the passion of its central narrative overwhelmingly pleasurable and many suggested it as being at least close to a classic, particularly in terms of its welcome recollection of the style and scale of earlier Hollywood filmmaking. Many praised the contrast of the epic and the intimate that had attracted Minghella to the story.[36] Thus it was hailed as: "[T]he first film in a long time to work the Casablanca trick of making audiences care more about the problems of a few little people than about a whole collapsing world"[37] and as a film in which: "[W]ithin the momentous scale of world war, we treasure the intimacy of tiny stories."[38] Indeed, in terms, variously, of its emotional qualities, historical context, location and the perceived 'Englishness' of its moral sensibility, it attracted comparison with filmmakers such as David Lean and Powell and Pressburger and films such as *Gone with the Wind* (1939), *Casablanca* (1942), *Brief Encounter* (1945), *From Here to Eternity* (1953), *Lawrence of Arabia* (1962), *Dr. Zhivago* (1965), *Once upon a Time in America* (1984) and *Out of Africa* (1985).

For others, however, the passion at the core of the film was overly melodramatic. The contrast of intimate emotionality and world politics was therefore found to be abhorrent, particularly when it was perceived that personal passion was being privileged over national responsibility, indicating the director's vindication of the central character's own romantic self-justification. Jacqui Sadashige, for example, asserted that the film suggested that "love possesses the ability to justify almost anything" and that "loss of love provides ample recompense for betrayal."[39]

Ironically, contention over the film reflected its own internal interrogation of questions of national identity and historical veracity. Politicians and journalists who hailed the film as either an English or a British triumph on the grounds of the nationality of its director, main stars and genesis as a project, were vilified by those raising the issue of its American funding and the British government's continued lack of support for their domestic film industry. Particularly galling in this respect, suggested *Screen Finance*, was the Department of National Heritage's apparent redrawing of national definitions in order, retrospectively, to render the film European, if not actually British.[40]

At the same time, historians questioned the film's representation and possible romanticization of an actual and somewhat problematic historical figure. The real Count Laszlo de Almásy's prowess as an explorer was less in contention than the question of his actual allegiance to the German forces during World War II and his apparent homosexuality. These issues were examined, although only sometimes as a means of undermining the film, in a series of often conflicting accounts of Almásy's real feelings about nationhood and his rightful wartime role. According to one article, Elizabeth Pathy Salett claimed him to have been a Nazi agent. This was refuted by ex-Bletchley Park translator Jean Howard, who had tracked Almásy during his mission to convey two German spies across the Sahara and researched his life after her release from the Official Secrets Act in 1976.[41] According to the author of the article, Sebastian O'Kelly:

> Those who know something of the life of Almásy find the accusation that he was a Nazi spy more upsetting than the almost total fiction of the film, which at least is flattering. Hungarians, who celebrated the centenary of the explorer's birth . . . and issued a commemorative postage stamp, are mortified.[42]

The coincidental discovery of Rudi Mayer's footage of a 1929 expedition, however, which was made into the documentary film *Durch Afrika mit Automobil*, revealed that: "He [Almásy] obviously adored killing animals and regarded East Africa as a paradise for Europeans. He was extremely tall and thin, far removed from Fiennes's classic good looks, and rarely without a cigarette."[43]

Whatever the truth of the real Count Almásy, Minghella was clear that he had not seen this documentary footage before making his own film. Neither had he realized "that Almásy might have been homosexual."[44] When questioned about this aspect of the film's historical veracity, Miramax was at pains to point out that it was, in fact, "a work of fiction based on fiction." Michael Ondaatje described his version of events as "not a history lesson, 'but an interpretation of human emotions—love, desire, betrayals in war and betrayals in peace—in a historical time.'"[45] The film, of course, carried a disclaimer that acknowledged its historical touchstones but also made clear its complete independence as a story.

The main thrust of the critical response to the film, however, concerned issues arising specifically from its adaptation of Ondaatje's famously complex Booker Prize-winning novel of the same name. Many critics and academics voiced appreciation of the adaptation. Gerald E. Forshey hailed Minghella's screenplay as "almost a guidebook to the process of adapting a novel,"[46] and Stephen Amidon applauded him for having "quite simply, defied the whole current notion of screen adaptation."[47] Anne Billson felt that the film "reache[d] those parts that all those other recent literary adaptations failed to reach,"[48] Janet Maslin proclaimed it as "a stunning feat of literary adaptation"[49] and Quentin Curtis extolled its "ravell[ing of] Ondaatje's beguiling threads into a brilliant web."[50] Other critics, such as Philip French, Sharyn Emery and Douglas Stenberg, delighted in detecting poetic transmutations of narrative elements between the two formats.[51] Both Emery and Stenberg examined the theme of characterization in relation to water and aridity, while Stenberg also considered the significance of death and "eternal sleep"[52] in both the characterizations and trajectories of the patient and Hana and the parallel spaces of the Cave of Swimmers and the church at Arezzo.

Others, however, questioned the particular choices that had evidently been made in restructuring and reducing the novel's myriad narrative threads and subjectivities. While Jamal Mahjoub agreed that the strength of the adaptation was that it "create[d] something different out of the building blocks presented to the filmmaker," his question of why the "significant brick" of colonial critique had been omitted echoed the primary concern of many of those who were, at least in part, less impressed with the film.[53] Most significantly, critics in this respect focused on the reduction of the interracial relationship at the monastery and the exclusion of the culminating event concerning Kip's reaction to the news of the atom bombs being dropped on Hiroshima and Nagasaki. Nick James suggested:

> The screenplay's downgrading of the affair between Hana and Kip
> . . . from the novel's parallel main subject to a meagre subplot, leaves
> *The English Patient* open to accusations of cynicism—it's obviously
> that much harder to imagine a miscegenous relationship powering the
> film towards Oscar nominations.[54]

Sadashige accused the film of:

> [E]ffect[ing] discomforting changes in meaning: private matters
> overshadow public events; individuals appear able to transcend or
> move beyond their racialization and that of others; 'history' becomes
> most poignant when it is most personal; and personal is all but
> equivalent to romantic.[55]

And Lisa Rundle suggested:

> Through erasure of and writing over the one character in the novel
> who provided a 'post-colonial' critique, the makers of the film have
> been faithful to the larger project of imperialism which as a whole
> serves to silence colonized people and their experiences.[56]

Despite Ondaatje's avowed acceptance that all losses between novel
and film were "understandable choices . . . [which] made the film better,"[57] such accusations of manipulation of the novel's themes in order
to soften or avoid confrontation of difficult and less audience-friendly
issues, were also echoed by others such as Nigel Andrews, Quentin
Curtis and Raymond Aaron Younis.

Certain criticism of the adaptation, however, perhaps lacked full
acknowledgment of differences in literary and cinematic modes of representation and signification or the complex subtlety of the film.
Younis' consideration of Hana's motivations, for example, did not focus on the events that drive her into retreat, the patient's explanation of
her trauma to Caravaggio, her own allusions to being "cursed" and "in
love with ghosts,"[58] her place in the mise-en-scène of the film, her music or Binoche's nuanced performance of self-repressive dialogue.
Rather, it seemed to accept her assertion that she is determined to keep
the patient alive "because [she is] a nurse"[59] at more-or-less face
value.[60] Similarly, while Sadashige was correct in pointing out that
Kip's racial awakening, which constitutes such a vital culmination
point in the novel, is missing, she nevertheless missed a crucial point in
her suggestion that this is replaced merely by the image of Almásy and
Katharine's posthumous desert flight. Equally plausible in this respect—especially since the film actually ends with Hana's view from
the truck as she leaves the monastery—seems to be Mahjoub's suggestion that the demise of the patient and Hana's positive move out of the
monastery indicate that the story's conclusion lies in the death of the
prewar order of the putative 'International' Sand Club and the begin-

ning of a new era which belongs to "the Hanas and Kips of this world."[61]

Such differences of opinion and understanding may normally indicate no more than the contentious nature of the film's themes or, as Jonathan Margolis suggests, the apparent or assumed divisions in gender appeal of different kinds of story.[62] In this case, however, they also point to the characteristic narrative and moral ambiguity in Minghella's construction of his text. For, contrary to Sadashige's assertion that "for Minghella, . . . meanings are obvious and often singular,"[63] *The English Patient* is indeed much more typical of the characteristically open-ended approach to human emotional and moral conundrums detailed in chapter 2. In order to understand the whole story, however, it is necessary to consider the whole film.

*The English Patient* in fact presents its audience with an extremely complex mise-en-scène that offers many, often contradictory angles on its central story and several different interpretations of the actions and reactions of its characters. Rather than vindicating or condemning either Almásy or Katharine, therefore, Minghella does indeed achieve his avowed ideal of remaining strangely nonjudgmental in presenting his complex, multilayered story. He leaves the viewer to decide which route to take through the story.

In order to understand how he constructs such a narrative system and therefore to establish the framework within which the score operates, the remainder of this chapter will be divided into two parts. The first considers the transformation of certain key themes and motifs from the novel into the film. The second focuses on the film in its own right, specifically in terms of its relationship to its generic precedents, its construction and the narrational and emotional parameters that it sets for its characters.

# From Novel to Film

## Mode of Storytelling

> The book's defining characteristic is its fracturing, its dismantling of narrative. That was the one profound alteration I made: to construct some architecture to hold its beauty.[64]

While the film is clearly more focused and less expansive than the novel, it is far from being a mere simplification or selective literal translation. It is perhaps a reflection of the kind of interdependency that Ondaatje himself feels between the two works, that certain aspects of each version of the story seem to become illuminated and enriched by the other. A consideration of the two works in tandem may therefore offer a fruitful avenue to understanding the structure, themes and characterizations of the film in all their complexity.

The most obvious overall change that Minghella's screenplay makes to Ondaatje's novel is the placing of the eponymous character and his relationship with Katharine Clifton as the central focus of the story and the main element against which all other stories resonate. In the novel, the patient/Almásy is only one of a group of principal characters given subjective viewpoints and narrating voices in both their present context and through flashbacks.[65] Their stories in the present and the past intermingle in a contrapuntal texture; each character's subjectivity and story becomes dominant by turns and their memories, experiences and relationships resonate with and inflect each other in numerous ways. A strong teleological drive seems less the point than the overall interaction of the multiple viewpoints and experiences and the constant recontextualizing of the characters that results.

Ultimately, therefore, all enjoy an equal sense of importance and the resolution of the patient's story is no more significant to the whole than the personal discoveries made by any other character. Each person's background is offered, through their own or the novel's voice, a little at a time, and the content of flashbacks does not always have a simple or direct function in relation to present events. Crucial information on characters, events, and their relation to each other often unfolds gradually through half-formed hints and enigmatic references that serve to withhold the whole truth until the overall texture of the novel has been much more fully woven.

While the structure of the film is more easily comprehensible, its apparently smooth flow nevertheless incorporates a multitude of temporal and spatial transitions that maintain a surprisingly close affinity to the fragmented narrative style of the novel. At the same time, although many episodes in the novel have of necessity been omitted from the film, the aim of the screenwriting team to capture the spirit of the novel means that its modes of description, themes and motifs are often translated and reabsorbed into modes of representation, incidents and characters in the film.

The opening title sequence of the film illustrates some of the ways in which it absorbs aspects of the narrational style and storytelling structure of the novel. The first fragment of narrative comes through the soundtrack, with a sound of tinkling glass, the Islamic call to prayer, the breathing and grunting of camels and, as the first image appears, sporadic male voices speaking in Arabic. The accompanying image offers no clue, however, as to what this aural mosaic may signify. We are faced with a textured surface in such extreme close-up that it is difficult to determine whether it is, perhaps, ancient paper, a parched landscape or even dried skin. As the film's title appears over this mysterious background, a woman's voice enters singing some kind of Eastern folk song. The end of a paintbrush then appears and tentatively sets down a short, gently curving line on the mysterious surface. Further lines are slowly added and the camera moves along the page with the painting as it develops. All sounds have vanished except for the woman's voice. The identity of the image remains unclear, particularly since its close framing now excludes its initial lines. As the painter adds two pincer-like curves, the woman's voice is replaced by a solo cor anglais. Now the final detail is added to the painting and the head of the figure clarifies its human identity.

Several narrative themes emerge from this densely packed introduction. The soundtrack suggests the traditional cultures of the Middle East and Eastern Europe and the association of these worlds with male and female voices respectively. The image suggests the complex nature of comprehension and identity, both of which come gradually through the assemblage of otherwise enigmatic fragments. Only with the final piece of the puzzle, the site of human thought, memory and communication, are the other lines bound together in meaning. In the novel, Hana finds order in the events of the day only as it ends and she is about to fall asleep. The story of the film, for the patient at least, will begin similarly near the endpoint of final slumber and involve a return

to its beginning in order to achieve a full understanding of what events
have meant in their overall context. Completion of the full picture will
be necessary before full understanding can be reached and the 'day-
time' of the story can be satisfactorily brought to an end.

Not only, therefore, does this sequence alert us to the fact that the
story will turn on questions of representation and identification, but it
also alerts us immediately to our own methods of interpretation. The
sum of the whole story will be larger than its enigmatic constituent
parts and we should be wary of prediction, prejudgment and assumption.

## "We Are the Real Countries": [66] Personal, National and Other Identities

### Naming and Personal Identity

Questions of identity lie at the heart of both the novel and the film.
Each considers the construction and meaning of personal and national
identity and goes beyond these to examine alternative, equally meaningful modes of identification. Each shows how characters see each
other through the filter of their own needs and desires and how different ways of identifying oneself and others may preclude a clear view of
what lies beneath various accepted conventions and codes of behavior.
Stripped of the protection offered by assumption, we are left with the
sometimes shocking truth of a person's real self, values and alle-
giances.

Both novel and film examine the results of either accepting or attempting to reject such arbitrary points of identification as name, social
status and nationality, as well as the implications of more conscious
choices of self-identification made through marriage, profession, personal philosophy and self-expression. Naming—that is, the names by
which people are known—becomes emblematic in this context of varying degrees of personal, social, national and, particularly in wartime,
political, alignment, belonging and ownership. One of the key concerns
of the novel, therefore, which becomes perhaps the principal question
of the film, is the relevance of a person's name to what they or others
may consider their real identity.

In the novel, the clue to this theme offered by the anonymity of the
title is developed through the way in which each of the principal characters is introduced. The first fragment of narrative takes the form of a
short prologue, preceding even the list of contents, detailing an extract

from the minutes of a meeting of the Royal Geographical Society sometime in the 1940s. It begins:

> Most of you, I am sure, remember the tragic circumstances of the death of Geoffrey Clifton at Gilf Kebir, followed later by the disappearance of his wife, Katharine Clifton, which took place during the 1939 desert expedition in search of Zerzura.[67]

The subsequent opening section of the novel then moves straight to "The Villa," a location inhabited by two characters referred to solely as "she," "he" and other purely gender-based identifications.[68] Their relationship to the named characters in the prologue is uncertain and their situation is only revealed through the gradual accumulation of details that are often initially enigmatic. Even as their stories, thoughts and memories begin to unfold, however, their names remain a mystery.

As his eponymous status might suggest, it is the patient himself whose characterization explores this theme in the most tangible way. Early in the novel's opening section we learn that "he," following a plane crash in the desert, is unable to remember his own name and thus to reveal it. Furthermore, this accident has robbed him of any distinguishing physical features and even an identifiable accent in his English speech. Stripped of all conventional forms of identification, he has only the contents of his mind through which to re-form himself and to retrace his steps to the present. While we may assume that he has a relatively coherent picture of his nurse, including her name, nationality and how she has come to her present situation, she has only his memories and his physical state as a clue to his origins and his fate, and little information on events in between.

When we are introduced to the patient, it is through the filter of this limited knowledge and the alternative ways in which his nurse has come to know him. Significantly, therefore, she does not ask his name but rather *who he is*, thereby seeking to reach beyond superficiality to the unique qualities and experiences that really identify him. When the nurse herself is finally named, after the unexpected arrival of an avuncular figure from her past, David Caravaggio, it is only through the novel's own voice that we begin to identify her as Hana. Caravaggio himself enters the narrative only as "[t]he man with bandaged hands"[69] and his initial identification of Hana, in an effort to reach beyond her shell-shocked exterior, involves reference to their shared memories of life before the war rather than the mere detail of her name.

The full naming of Katharine Clifton, which will connect her to both the prologue and the patient/Almásy is similarly withheld through fragmentary and momentary clues that span the first half of the novel. The opening section first suggests the anonymous past significance to the patient of "*a woman* who kissed parts of his body that are now burned into the colour of aubergine." [my italics][70] Then Hana, reading from the personal notes kept in his copy of Herodotus, finds an account of "Clifton's wife" reading a poem to the assembled desert explorers.[71] Immediately following this, although its significance cannot yet be clear, are Almásy's own thoughts on the dramatic effects of new lovers. References to the mysterious "woman," Clifton's wife, and Almásy falling in love continue in turn, apparently unconnected, and only when they are finally united does he name Katharine in full.

For the patient/Almásy, Katharine's name therefore signals a tri-partite identity, wherein her social status as a married woman and her specific marital connection to Geoffrey Clifton (Colin Firth) are contrasted with her first name. Since in both novel and film Almásy refers to himself and others in the desert entirely through surnames, his use of Katharine's first name is particularly significant and suggests a highly uncharacteristic level of personal engagement. In the film, when he wishes to distance himself from her or hurt her, he reverts to the emphatic and sometimes sarcastic use of her marital title and name. Calling her "Katharine" or "K" signals not only an intimacy that is largely alien and therefore highly dangerous to Almásy, but also a crucial transgression of the social boundaries on which their group is predicated.[72]

As the film seeks to subjugate the other principal characters to the patient and his story, it therefore seems inevitable that the significance of their names and the related complexities of their identities will become diminished. Information on the patient/Almásy and Hana, which is scattered throughout the novel in numerous flashbacks, is incorporated instead into a tight introductory series of events that occur in the present and lead straight to their shared destination. The result of this reorganization is to redefine the central mysteries on which the narrative will turn.

The first scene of the sequence appears to recall the novel's prologue. Now, however, we see how a couple come to die when their plane is shot down over the desert, but we do not know who they are or why they are there. As this strand of the narrative continues, we see that the man has survived the crash but is terribly burnt, suggesting that he may be the eponymous patient. We see enigmatic clues to his identity beyond this, as the Arabs who save him examine first a thimble and then a leather-bound book full of paintings and handwritten notes. As he is subsequently interrogated at a military hospital in Italy, it is clear that despite his partial memory loss, his mental faculties are intact. The fact that he is both learned and witty is signaled through his knowledge of German and his joke about a national tendency, shared with the British, toward marriage. The parallel he draws between himself and Tutankhamun, no matter how flippant it may seem, also suggests the history of ancient Egypt as a particular frame of reference. Nevertheless, the information on the patient in both past and present is inadequate to determine either his personal or national identity.

The introduction of Hana, on the other hand, provides a stark contrast in its absolute clarity and coherence. From her first appearance, it is clear that she is a military nurse in a transient world of carnage and mud based in trains, tents and trucks. While her name is not used immediately, its withholding seems to have no real narrative purpose and it is learned casually and early as an officer shouts at her to take cover during a bombing raid. With cruelly efficient rapidity, we witness her loss of sweetheart and best friend and her resultant emotional exhaustion. She becomes the patient's nurse and through their conversation we learn that her burden of grief has developed into a belief that she is a curse to anyone who loves her. We are then briefly introduced to Kip as an unnamed bomb disposal officer, before Hana's trauma culminates in her sanctioned desertion and her establishment with the patient in the monastery.

The remaining characters, who are introduced relatively quickly in relation to this basic situation, share Hana's focus on the patient/Almásy. Katharine's identity is explained in a flashback motivated by the book, now revealed as a copy of Herodotus' *The Histories*, that we saw being retrieved from the wreckage of the plane crash. The book contains the patient's past in its scrapbook-style collection of papers, pictures and photographs. As he opens its pages, he thus opens up his past in the most literal way. Rather than fragmenting his story as in the novel, and delaying the appearance of Katharine, his memories in the film begin at a very specific point and progress as a coherent narrative in themselves. He is returned to the desert as a young, sophisticated explorer, speaking Arabic with an old man through whom he is researching desert geography. Immediately into this scene comes a woman who is identified almost before we can even see her, as

Katharine. Thanks to one of the major differences between literature and film lying in actually being bound to see characters as they make their first appearances, we are able to identify her as the woman from the opening scene.

While we realize immediately that she must come to have some connection to the patient/Almásy, we are therefore compelled to question his references to her during his earlier interrogation and immediately after this flashback as his *wife*. For Katharine is named in no uncertain terms from her first appearance in his memory as *Mrs. Katharine Clifton*, reflecting the most negative aspects of her identity from the patient/Almásy's point of view. The mystery of the film therefore centers itself on how Mrs. Geoffrey/Katharine Clifton comes to be Almásy's wife and how they subsequently end up on their fatal flight.

The arrival of Caravaggio, in a dramatic alteration to his role in the novel, introduces a secondary mystery. Caravaggio and Hana are now complete strangers with none of the shared history that is so important to the novel. His name and profession are offered immediately and this, particularly with the assurance that they come from the same neighborhood in Montreal, is sufficient to gain Hana's trust. Caravaggio is not all that he seems, however, and thus immediately highlights the fault in assuming that a name and a nationality guarantee a genuine or even coherent identity.

In fact, he conceals an alternative name and identity that motivate his search for the patient. While he was working as an Allied spy codenamed Moose, the actions of German agent Count Laszlo de Almásy led to his torture and mutilation. Now he seeks Almásy for revenge. Although we know from the very outset of his flashbacks that the patient is indeed Almásy, he continues to deny any knowledge of this in the present. Caravaggio's interrogation assures us, however, that there are now two crucial elements to the patient's story, which on the face of it seem to have no possible connection. It is left to the patient and Caravaggio to determine how the puzzle fits together and thereby to reveal the disjuncture between name and identity on which the story turns.

Caravaggio is able to identify the patient as Almásy through his placing in the desert, knowledge of music and possession of his unique book. He makes the mistake, however, of believing that he understands Almásy's whole identity through his apparent activity as a German spy. As he attempts to force him to admit his guilt in this capacity he realizes the crucial, if naïve difference in the patient/Almásy's view of his own self-identification and therefore his motivations. His accusation compels the patient to explain his actions in his own terms, which leads to an admission of his culpability in Katharine's death. In the film he attributes his inability to save her simply to having "the wrong name."[73] In the novel, however, this realization is enriched by his fuller explanation of his own, ultimately fatal naïveté:

> I said she was my *wife*. I said *Katharine*. . . . Whereas the only name I should have yelled, dropped like a calling card into their hands, was Clifton's.[74] [Ondaatje's italics]

At last the patient realizes that contrary to his own ideals, it is not the intimate significance of Katharine's first name that matters in the context of war, but the social, political and national significance of her married name. Nor does the fantasy that they have agreed upon of sharing "a different life" wherein she is "a different wife"[75] have any meaning outside of their own private concept of what is morally and emotionally, although not socially 'right.'

In any other historical context, of course, Almásy's naïvely romantic misunderstanding of the real significance of names may not have proved quite so catastrophic. Both the novel and the film, however, place his relationship with Katharine pointedly between the international space of the Royal Geographical Society and the contested space of the North African desert in wartime. The significance of names in terms of national identification thus becomes a potential matter of life and death. It is this specific association of personal and national identification that drives the second, fatal nail into the coffin of Almásy and Katharine's romance. Not only does he fail to acknowledge the value of Geoffrey's name, but he also disregards the very un-English sound of his own. Attaching Katharine to the name of Almásy is useless in terms of its social significance, but absolutely fatal in terms of its national ambiguity.

### National Identity

In tackling the relationship of personal and national identity, the film is placed at significant disadvantage in its reduction of the role of Sikh bomb disposal officer Kip. In the novel, Kip's story presents a harsh and rigorous confrontation of the insoluble and painful contradictions of personal, national, racial and colonial identity with no possibility of escape into romantic fantasy or tragedy.

Kip believes in the integrity of the English and feels proud to become part of the eccentric 'family' of his training officer in Devon. He believes he can transcend the racial protests that have landed his brother in an Indian jail and puts his life at risk on a daily basis as a member of the British army. While he is saving the Allies from mines and bombs, however, and becoming increasingly involved with his Canadian lover Hana, he suddenly finds himself faced with the news of Hiroshima and Nagasaki. Feeling that the attitude of the West to "the brown races"[76] has been put into its true perspective by this event, he tries to kill the patient, rejects Hana as his lover and leaves the villa.

The reduction of Kip's complexity in the film therefore seems to have a greater impact on this particular issue than the reduction of the reflections and memories of the other characters. Caravaggio/Moose retains the idea of national demands being able to divide a person through dual naming. Kip, however, all but loses his real name, Kirpal Singh, leaving his identity comparatively fixed rather than symbolically malleable. References in the novel to his original name and his English nicknaming after kipper grease, as well as the contrast of his name to the similar names of Kipling and his novel *Kim*, are largely lost in the film. Here, he is known primarily as Kip. Only one reference each to Kipling and Kip's surname are ever made and his nickname is never explained. His lengthy reflections on his colonial identity in the novel are concentrated accordingly in the film into a cutting response to the content of the now unnamed *Kim*, and his speech in appreciation of Sergeant Hardy (Kevin Whately) and the patient as "everything that's good about England."[77] The issue of nationality in his relationship with Hana therefore seems to become more significant as an antidote to Almásy and Katharine's downfall, rather than something on which both he and Hana reflect on their own behalves.

It is left to the characterization of Almásy and his doomed romance with Katharine to absorb as much as possible of the rigor with which the novel questions the meaning of national identity. Furthermore, Katharine's characterization is changed significantly in the film so that she becomes more a reflection of Almásy and his desires in this capacity, rather than the comparatively adversarial figure that she presents in the novel.

In both novel and film, Almásy sees the desert as the very antithesis of the idea of national boundaries and identities that he hates so much. To him, the desert constitutes a pure space immune to contamination by petty matters of politics, nationhood and social regulations.

In the novel he expresses an unguarded admiration for its ancient history, autonomy and perpetual self-regeneration:

> The desert could not be claimed or owned—it was a piece of cloth carried by winds, never held down by stones, and given a hundred shifting names long before Canterbury existed, long before battles and treaties quilted Europe and the East. . . . All of us, . . . wished to remove the clothing of our countries. It was a place of faith. We disappeared into landscape. . . . Erase the family name! Erase nations! I was taught such things by the desert.[78]

In the film, when Madox (Julian Wadham) is forced to point to the reality that eludes his friend, Almásy is scornful of what he perceives, in his own terms, to be a naïve view:

> Madox: What do we find in the desert? Arrowheads, spears. In a war,
> if you own the desert, you own North Africa.
> Almásy (contemptuous): Own the desert.[79]

Although the film's Katharine retains her literary counterpart's greater self-identification through her social and marital status, she also now shares Almásy's frustration with the perceived importance of nationhood. In this way she is contrasted rather favorably with the novel's Katharine, whose passion for the desert, significantly, is conceptualized by Almásy as temporary. She is young, barely out of university and, although she soon becomes eager to learn, initially shares comparatively little of Almásy's engagement with culture. She is sexually predatory, violent and cruel in the face of Almásy's suffering both during their affair and after their separation.

Katharine in the film, however, is a slightly different matter. Not only has their age difference been collapsed, but she also matches Almásy in learning, sophistication and temperament. In Madox's words she has "read everything"[80] and is familiar in particular with Almásy's own monograph on the desert and his beloved Herodotus. She certainly understands the importance of national allegiance in war in an intellectual sense and thus appreciates the crucial nature of Geoffrey's work and the reasons why they cannot return to England. Spiritually, however, she is a divided soul. The 'English' love of water, hedgehogs and all things green that she shares with her literary counterpart, as well as her protestation that she does not want to die in the desert, does not stop her from adopting crucial thoughts against nationality attributed to

Almásy in the novel. Her dying words in the film, and the last words that the patient chooses to hear as he himself dies, contain the essence of their shared philosophy and the tragedy of their romance: "We are the real countries, not the boundaries drawn on maps with the names of powerful men . . ."[81]

*Other Identities*

In seeking to overcome all the boundaries that come with names and nationalities, Katharine and Almásy's relationship in the film is therefore predicated on a different level of identification based on deeper, more meaningful and personal commonalities. In this way, they resonate with both the novel and film's preoccupation with the possibility of collapsing superficial identities through a concentration on shared underlying qualities. The desert was once, and in many ways remains, a sea.[82] A book's page may be like skin and "*the hollow of the roof of a dog's mouth*" [Ondaatje's italics] or "a woman's back" may be recalled in the shape of a sand dune.[83]

In the film, such depth of mutual identification imbues Almásy and Katharine's love with an irresistible authenticity, even perhaps in poor Geoffrey's eyes, which explains Katharine's inescapable drive toward infidelity and the transgression of her chosen social and marital identity. Katharine and Almásy in the film therefore offer a much more tragic picture of true soul mates than their literary counterparts. Despite the film's more detailed and sympathetic drawing of Geoffrey, including much evidence of his genuine love for Katharine and his grief on learning of her adultery, he could never be such a spiritual partner to her.

In perhaps the same way, however, the many different kinds of love that Katharine defines on her first meeting with Almásy in the film also have at least one thing in common. Although Almásy and Katharine may wish to believe that such issues can be overcome, perhaps even the purest love cannot avoid the need for possession and ownership. Almásy, in both novel and film, cannot help but coincide his most hated and loved ideals of identity in his desire to map, name and claim his lover's body. Katharine is for him at one and the same time a pure geography and a mapped territory. His beloved hollow at the base of her throat has the beauty of a desert dune, a point which the film emphasizes through its mirroring of a close shot in which her neck and throat fill the screen with the opening shot of the undulations of the desert. His love of the autonomy of the desert, however, has disappeared in his romantic love.

He wishes, in a way that parallels some of Katharine's final words in the film, for her body to bear the signs of their love. In the film, he buys her a thimble to wear around her neck, full of saffron with which he will paint her dead face in the Cave of Swimmers. After they separate, he cannot bear the fact that she does not reveal physical and emotional signs of grief in the same way as he does. He displays a loss so obvious that any cover they have managed to maintain is completely blown. Her self-control, however, convinces him that she does not care, and it is only after Geoffrey's death that he notices that she still wears the thimble as a sign of her continuing love. Ultimately, following this revelation, the flames of their burning plane engulf Almásy's body in a metaphor of his emotional suffering. He is, as it were, burned up with passion and destroyed by loss.

In the opening pages of the novel we meet him through "his black body, . . . destroyed feet. . . . the penis sleeping like a sea horse, the thin tight hips. . . . [and Hana's beloved] hollow below the lowest rib, its cliff of skin."[84] The key to his identity resides in the combination of this physicality and details of his past which emerge through his constant reminiscence. His body thus becomes, as both he and Katharine had wished in the film, a landscape of his life, a geography of mysterious features and hidden secrets which must be excavated in order to illuminate his true history. Thus as the film moves from its title sequence into the first scene, the painted figure merges with the dunes of the desert as if, like the image of Katharine's throat, we are to understand that not only is the body a landscape of a person's life, but that it will be reclaimed to the land by both death and history.

## Character, Landscape and Narrative Structure

Both the novel and the film extend the metaphorical association of body, life and landscape to parallel relationships between the main characters and the narrative itself. As each character's view of the world becomes known through their reflections and circumstances in the novel, so the mise-en-scène, temporality and story structure become reflective of their states of mind. Perhaps the most important of these relationships, particularly in transition to the film, center on the emotions and perceptions of Hana, the patient and Kip.

*Hana and the Monastery*

In both novel and film, Hana's trauma arises from the cruel disjuncture between her continual exposure to the moment of death and her powerlessness in its prevention. In the novel, the deaths of her father and lover and the termination of her pregnancy have left her able to deal with death only by emotional removal. In a symbolic gesture, she cuts her hair to prevent it catching in the blood of the wounds she tends. She knows the signs of death intimately and expertly administers the moment of passing for countless soldiers. She is tortured, however, by the geographical distance that prevented her from fulfilling this role for her own father and her trauma suspends her within the moment of his death. She wonders how and where he died and is unable to move forward from the event by returning home or, even in the form of a letter, by communicating with her stepmother.

Although the film replaces her losses in the novel with the deaths of her sweetheart and best friend, the idea of her impotence in the face of death, and the related role of the patient, remain the same. The building in which she chooses to care for the patient, to suspend his moment of death in compensation for those she could not save, symbolizes the emotional limbo state between life and death in which she herself hovers. In both novel and film, it is similarly caught between life and death in a way that is symbolized in turn by the *trompe l'oeil* vines painted on the walls of the patient's room. Bomb damage has left the whole building prey to the reclamation processes of nature so that, without human intervention, its missing or damaged walls admit weather and climbing plants that will gradually destroy it.

As Kip, in the film, enters the monastery through one such destroyed wall, he therefore acts as a force of nature that will reclaim Hana's life by remedying the past and allowing her to move into the future. Unaware of the mirror that their relationship holds up to Almásy and Katharine's, Hana's new strength comes not only from Kip's love but also from his ability to cheat death, to outwit the very weaponry and potential devastation of war. The most symbolic moment in this respect, although Hana cannot realize it, is the moment when he defuses the bomb that literally has his name on it.[85]

Her delay of the patient's death is also reflected in the film's overall structure. Whereas the novel stretches far beyond this event and in fact does not even describe it, the film is framed by the first and last moments of his death. He is, as it were, already dead, in emotional terms from the moment of Katharine's death and in physical terms from the moment of the plane crash. First the Bedouin and then Hana, however, dictate that he stay alive long enough to understand his own past. The sole purpose of the film's many movements into the past is then to allow this to happen, so that within the moment of death that Hana sustains, the patient follows his own separate trajectory.

## Almásy and the Desert

It may be that Almásy's apparent failure to recognize the harsh reality of his historical and social context stems from a similarly metaphorical relationship to the desert in which that separate trajectory is played out. Rather than being innocent of the symbolism of the space around him, however, as Hana is of the monastery, Almásy creates his own symbolism by conceptualizing the desert according to his own ideals. He sees himself as a reflection of the desert and the desert as a reflection of himself. In his view, the desert removes national and personal identity, reducing everything to a purer state of existence. It is this ideal of conceptual absolutism that he feels unites him with his surroundings.

The film compounds the idea of this inherent similarity by purifying Almásy of some of his more compromising features in the novel. The film's Almásy does not frequent brothels, neither is he *really* a spy. He lives in the old part of the city rather than a modern hotel and comes out of the desert positively infused with sand. Perhaps more so than any of his International Sand Club companions, he is truly a creature of the desert. He is even rendered at one with its landscape, his costume of blue shirt and beige shorts creating a continuous line with the horizon. His new, more autonomous nature is also defined through his use of language, as pointed out by Katharine in his desert monograph. His view that "[a] thing is still a thing no matter what you place in front of it,"[86] symbolizes not only his affectedly stark exterior, but also his ideal of pure existence.

Since he is, at least in his own estimation, so much at one with the desert, it is perhaps fitting that the activity of the desert should become complicit with his sexual and emotional desire for Katharine. As if he himself had willed it so, a timely and somewhat symbolic sandstorm strands the future couple in the private space of a truck cabin for a whole night. Their rescue is then delayed by the very processes of timeless renewal that Almásy so admires in the desert. The sandstorm has covered their all-important tyre tracks with a blank page of sand. Their consequent proximity, forced upon them by the desert, allows

Katharine to learn of Almásy's feelings through the notes that she finds concealed within his copy of Herodotus. The love that he feels for Katharine, however, once again betrays his hopelessly romantic view of the world. For him, real love must be absolute, removed from everyday surroundings and unaffected by normal circumstances. Katharine and the desert are, in these terms, almost one and the same thing.

## Kip and the Time Bomb

Stand ABSOLUTELY STILL! You're walking in a minefield![87]

Although the patient's relationship to time and space dictates the film's fluidity of temporality and the relationship of past to present, it is Kip's view of the world that structures the story he tells in the past. In the novel, Kip is more than just a bomb disposal expert; he is a man who visualizes the interiors of mines and bombs as if they themselves were narratives. He travels through the wiring of the bomb in his mind's eye, knowing that if he can understand the nature of the person who constructed it, he can beat whatever new device or trick it contains.

He also knows, however, how full of mines the wartime world is. He tells in the novel of tiny items brushed accidentally from tables detonating concealed booby trap bombs, of defusing unstable unexploded bombs and of the elaborate trickery of delayed action bombs. He spends his life within the novel treading carefully across Italy and through the villa and its gardens, looking for tripwires and seeing the potential for death everywhere. In the end, he faces the ultimate time bombs of Hiroshima and Nagasaki.

The extensive narrations that contain this information in the novel are not retained in the film, so that we have only the brief clue of the episode concerning the monastery's mined piano to understand how his mind has come to work as a result of his profession. His psychology, however, resonates through the real and metaphorical time bombs lying everywhere in the lives of the other characters.

The literalization of the emotional 'bombshell' is presented quite clearly at the very outset of the film, when Hana's knowledge of her sweetheart's death comes as a bombing raid on her temporary hospital base begins. Her best friend Jan (Liisa Repo-Martell) is then killed by a landmine. At this emotional turning point, when she can stand no more death and loss, she literally walks into a minefield oblivious to her possible fate. It is there, of course, that Kip first sees her, as he looks up from the unexploded mine over which he lies poised. His profession, and this particular introductory positioning, are the clues to his potential ability to free Hana from her ghosts.

It is too late, of course, to help the patient. In the novel, we understand through Caravaggio's reporting that Geoffrey's knowledge of his wife's affair came through his social and diplomatic network. This information, however, comes very late in the patient's story. The film reconstructs the affair as a bomb waiting to go off from a much earlier point, setting the metaphorical fuse with Geoffrey's challenge to Almásy as he leaves his wife in the desert: "Why are you people so threatened by a woman?!"[88] In the film, we also witness Geoffrey's awkward discomfort as he watches his wife and Almásy dancing, his unwitting humiliation on Christmas Day, the terrible moment when he discovers their affair and his anger as Almásy drunkenly insults Katharine after the end of their relationship. It is clear by the time of this final event that everyone in their social circle shares Geoffrey's knowledge and it is unthinkable that their actions will go unpunished.

As usual, however, Almásy is as oblivious to this as he is to anything else that takes the feelings of others or the outside world into account. He is so absorbed in his own emotions that he never stops, as Katharine does, to consider her husband's feelings in the light of his very public outbursts. When the time bomb of Geoffrey's revenge finally explodes, Almásy is therefore not only completely unprepared, but still fails to acknowledge the incredible pain he must have caused.

It is for similar reasons that Caravaggio's news of Madox's death comes as such a shock to him. In the novel, it is the patient who tells how Madox committed suicide in an English church, distressed beyond reason by the jingoistic sermonizing of the vicar. In the film, however, he is shocked to be told by Caravaggio that Madox killed himself after learning that his best friend Almásy was a spy. His romantic ideal of an absolute love has prevented him from seeing the world's view of his actions. As he says so easily and succinctly to Caravaggio: "The rest meant nothing to me."[89]

Since it is Kip who lends the metaphor of the time bomb to Almásy's narrative in the film's past, it seems only right that he should be the one to defuse it in the present and for the future. Firstly, the rhyming of his and Hana's current relationship with the patient's affair offers, as Mahjoub suggested earlier in this chapter, a way forward for the international relationship. It also, however, recontextualizes some of the important symbolic spaces and promises of the past. Unlike in the novel, it is not race in the film that ultimately separates Kip and Hana, but simply the ongoing movement of the war. He is forced to leave when the army posts him further north, and they take their leave of each other with the promise of eventual reunion in either body or spirit. If such a reunion is to take place, they suggest it may be in their contemporary recontextualization of the desert's Cave of Swimmers: the painted church at Arezzo. Like Almásy's promise to return to Katharine in the cave, they pledge always to return to their church. For them, however, the story may be just beginning rather than ending.

# Theoretical Issues in the Film

## Critical Framing and Other Stories: Narrative Structure, Subjectivity and Mise-en-Scène

The general classification of *The English Patient* as a love story in the historical epic mold conceals a greater complexity of structure that sets it somewhat apart from such classics of the type as *Gone with the Wind*, *Casablanca* and *Dr. Zhivago*. On the face of it, it certainly shares with these films the contrast of the intimate and the epic and the setting of small, personal stories against the massive backdrop of history that many critics note. An important difference with *The English Patient*, however, is the particular way in which this contrast becomes a major cause of both narrative and critical contention. The positioning of the patient as the primary narrator of his own story lies at the heart of this tension.

In the novel, all the principal characters exist in a constant state of interaction between past and present. The past is constantly alive in present events and thoughts, and memory is part of the filter through which the present is contextualized and comprehended. Flashbacks are therefore constructed as an integral part of the ongoing narrative. Reminiscence is not always spoken and almost never returns to the same point in the present at which it began, so any results of the flashbacks are rarely immediate. For all except the patient, however, the past is still clearly the past. Unlike the others, when he remembers the past, he is so fixed within his "well of memory" that if Hana moves out of the line of his gaze, "his stare will travel alongside her into the wall."[90] Sometimes he tells her stories; sometimes he merely disappears into them, his eyes open to the darkness of the night as a clear signal of his oblivion to his immediate context.[91]

In the film, the patient is alone in being allowed such extensive forays into the past. The only other character offered a narrative voice is Caravaggio, and his less extensive narratives are primarily concerned with the recontextualization of the patient's story, rather than the consideration of his own memories for his own sake. It is the patient's subjectivity, therefore, that has the most powerful influence over the temporality of the narrative as a whole. As in the novel, however, the patient does not just narrate past events—he exists equally in another place; just as for him the desert has no boundaries of time or space, so there is no distinction in this respect between the past, the present, Italy or Egypt.

As he himself says, he "died years ago,"[92] so that his life, effectively all in the past, is being viewed from the vantage point of what might be considered to be a symbolic extension of his last breath—the point at which its events flash before his eyes. This rather tenuous relationship to the present is reflected in a general state of consciousness that constantly conflates the present with the past, either by actual movement back and forth, or by a more confused merging of events in the two temporal spaces. He sings to himself when he is alone, is confused over events and sensations between the past and present and, at least on the two occasions when she reads to him, hears and sees Katharine in the desert in place of Hana in the monastery.

This parallel of two, effectively concurrent spaces dictates an almost imperceptible fluidity of movement through time in the present. The patient moves into the past through a whole series of stimuli including Herodotus, the similarity of sounds or voices and the questions or comments of other characters. Most of his narrations exist only in his own thoughts and as soon as he moves into a flashback, all sense of time in the present is lost. His memories move the present between day and night. He begins to narrate while awake and then wakes from sleep at the end of his reminiscence. During the time in which we see his memories, other characters enter or leave his room and begin or end a variety of activities.

For the majority of the film, we experience the story according to this fluid temporality, the relative physical stasis and temporal flexibility of the present giving way to the strong sense of direction in the past. As the film represents this movement through techniques not available to the novel, we also witness the merging of the two narrative strands, not only through sharing the patient's memories of sounds, but also through visual links. The dunes of the desert, for example, melt into the folds of his bedsheets, and Katharine's hand reaches poignantly across history during the fateful sandstorm to touch his face on the pillow in the monastery. Once the story in the past has begun, it becomes the principal narrative of the film and the one that gives the film its strongest sense of conventional direction. The telling of past events thus comes to dictate when the present situation will end.

This peculiarly subjective view of events and, of course, the almost unique access to narration enjoyed by the patient, allows the film to pit its historical epic framework in an unusually active way against what Mary Ann Doane terms the "ordinary" love story. This type of love story, "rather than activating history as mise-en-scène, as space, inscribes it as individual subjectivity closed in on itself."[93] Following Doane's formulation, for the patient, "[h]istory is an accumulation of memories of the loved one, and the diachronic axis of representation generates a relation governed by only one set of terms—separation and reunion."[94] It is this exclusively personal point of view, and the self-justification that arises from it, that causes so much offense to Almásy's diegetic and extra-filmic critics.

His is not, however, the film's only voice. On the contrary, the singularity of his subjectivity is constantly underlined. The very frequency of movement between present and past that facilitates his story itself draws attention to his implicit narrating voice. The questioning of his reliability as a narrator then comes most obviously from Hana's mention of the effects of morphine on his perception and from Caravaggio's interrogation. Even the film's wider contextualization of his memories throws his self-justified actions into often extremely critical relief.

George Custen, Maureen Turim and Sarah Kozloff all point out that the subjectivity stressed by a film's flashback format can never operate independently, first of all, of its present-day context. Indeed, one of the primary functions of the flashback is to "retell history *from the vantage point of a particular narrator*. This privilege allows the narrator to frame the life not just in terms of the order and content of events, but to frame its significance." [my italics][95] This also means, however, that as what Sarah Kozloff would term an embedded first-person narrator, the patient can never be the sole narrating voice of the text.[96] He will always be framed by the wider voice of the film and therefore be subject to interpretation by other levels of the narrative.[97]

He chooses to frame his story in one way, as an account of a passionate but tragically fated romance that led to the deaths of his lover, her husband and, ultimately, himself. Within and around this presentation, however, Caravaggio and the wider voice of the film both suggest alternative interpretations.

This interrogatory and critical context enables the simultaneous representation of the patient's view and alternative views of the past and must throw into question whether, as some critics have suggested, the film is completely sympathetic to the idea that Almásy's passion places him beyond all social or political blame. The one-sidedness of the patient's story is constantly offset through critical devices of framing, editing, mise-en-scène, sound design and dialogue. While the film shows us how Almásy sees things, therefore, it also emphasizes those crucial things that he does not see. The greatest tragedy of the film thus becomes his awful self-absorption and the cost that it exacts of others.

In this sense, the film is both sympathetic to and critical of its central character. Almásy's story is definitely presented as tragic and his suffering is not in question. But his is not the film's only tragedy. Even given the inevitability of the affair and the resultant death of Geoffrey, Katharine could still have been saved, as could Madox and Almásy himself, had he only accepted the context of war in which they found themselves and re-viewed himself from the point of view of the British soldiers on whose understanding he was so very dependent. The stunning simplicity and stupidity of this one mistake is his story's real tragedy.

The opening title sequence of the film has already been described as suggesting the importance of different stories, views and interpretations of events to the full narrative picture. Following this lead, however, the film goes on to present us with a constant array of images, pictures, representations and frames through which the characters view and understand things and events around them. The very opening image of the film is, of course, a painting. More than that, it is a painting that is a copy of another painting—a representation of a representation. Such representations are important, of course, as a means of knowing and understanding the world, a point made most emphatically by the central role played by maps and photographs in the fates of so many of the characters. The patient remembers his own life partly through the images that he carries within the book of Herodotus and his very first transition into the past moves from one of those images in the present to its own creation in the past. The very first flashback image, like the very first image of the film, is therefore also a picture.

Going further than the film's opening suggestion of the importance of imagery, however, this picture offers a representation of a representation of a representation. It is Almásy's artistic interpretation of the Arab man's description of one object according to their shared understanding of the appearance of another: "a mountain the shape of a woman's back."[98] Almásy is surrounded in the Cave of Swimmers, as are Hana and Kip in the church at Arezzo, by painted representations of figures from the past. In both contexts, in fact, these pictures become the object of romantic exchange in the form of gifts between the lovers. As the patient begins to explain his past to Hana he even refers to it, quite pointedly, as a "view" of the desert.[99] The connection of seeing to personal understanding, interpretation and meaning is then emphasized by the constant presentation of personal 'views' that are framed by particular elements of mise-en-scène. Every event, this suggests, means something different from every separate point of view.

The nature of the frame is important to the interpretation of the view that is seen through it, and as we progress through the film we see frames that obscure, fragment, unite and divide characters and, of course, frames that reveal and highlight important events and discoveries. Framing through frosted glass suggests but obscures the physical horror of the operating theater on the army hospital train and the social horror of Almásy and Katharine's liaison at the Christmas party. While this highlights the importance of images that are *not* seen by other characters, frames that fragment views suggest the partial understanding or complete misunderstanding of what *is* seen.

Hana sees her patient through the hole in her bedroom floor at the monastery, but the mystery of his true identity is reflected in the fragmenting of his image by the surviving wooden beams. Her first meeting with Caravaggio takes place through the frame of the iron gate and until she accepts his proof of identity so that he may pass through it, he remains fragmented by its harsh, cell-like vertical bars. In this case, of course, Hana would do well to heed the warning of the mise-en-scène and suspect Caravaggio's integrity. Similarly, the breakdown of Almásy's self-control and understanding of social codes after the end of his relationship with Katharine is reflected in the latticework frame through which he watches her dance with a colleague of Geoffrey's before accusing her of yet another affair (see the account of the role of diegetic music and dance in preparing for this scene in chapter 4).

Clear vision, however, often comes at a heavy price. The significance of Jan's death in Hana's emotional trajectory is reflected in its central framing through the clear window of her hospital truck, thus surrounding it, appropriately, in a halo of khaki canvas. This both symbolizes the iconic images of wartime carnage that are the cause of Hana's misery and emphasizes her physical distance from the event as it happens. These things combined are the source of Hana's misery and trauma. Geoffrey's view of Katharine's meeting with Almásy is seen, likewise, through the illicit frame of the taxi window. This reduces him to the undignified status of a private eye—as a man forced to spy on his own wife—and rather cruelly recalls Almásy's earlier accusation that, contrary to Geoffrey's preferred method, "you can't explore from the air."[100] Proving his point at last, Almásy certainly brings Geoffrey down to earth.

Almásy is also, however, brought down in symbolic terms by the clear framing of a particular image. In the hotel room where he and Katharine carry on their affair, a window onto the city places a minaret in the very center of its frame. This iconic image represents, in his view, the culture in which he feels he is allowed so much license. In fact, however, the minaret represents a religion that is intolerant of infidelity.[101] Through the significantly pointed frame of his bedroom window, he is therefore shown a potent indicator of his selective relationship with his surroundings. Finally, the patient's own last view of his past shows him carrying Katharine's dead body away from the Cave of Swimmers, framed within the wings and struts of the biplane, the mode of transport that both united and separated them. The significance of the image for the diegetic viewer is thus reflected in its framing, and the possible points of view on any one image may be numerous, a point which is emphasized at the Italian beach hospital. Here, the patient is interrogated by the British officer against a background of other verandas, forming in diminishing perspective one painted wooden frame after another containing infinite comparable scenes.

One of the most important recontextualizations of the patient's view concerns the film's critical revelation, for the eyes of the film audience only, of Geoffrey's emotional trajectory. From the moment of his arrival with Katharine in the desert to the moment of his crazed suicide, we are offered a privileged view of Geoffrey. This reveals to us alone the real personal and social destruction caused by his wife's affair and the danger that his resultant anger poses to the couple.

As Katharine tells the story of Candaules and Gyges to the explorers assembled around the desert campfire, we see Almásy's gaze become fixated on her. It is not his point of view, however, but an apparently objective view, that shows us Geoffrey's awkwardness as the end of the story suggests the death of the husband as a possible narrative outcome. Likewise we see Geoffrey struggle momentarily with his own obviously upset emotions both while Almásy dances with Katharine at the Shepheard's Hotel and after his wife pulls away from him at the Christmas party. After he has learned of their affair, we witness his barely contained anger in response to Almásy's shameful display at the farewell dinner of the International Sand Club. Even though the affair is now over and Geoffrey is relegated to the background of the shot in which Katharine glares in profile at her ex-lover, however, his continued and future importance is assured. Although out of focus, he sits in the very center of the image, driving a wedge, no matter how indistinct, between his wife and Almásy.

Perhaps the most poignant criticism of Geoffrey's treatment at the hands of the lovers, however, comes via the unconventional device of framing one of the patient's flashbacks as if through Geoffrey's point of view. This comes as a result of Caravaggio's question about the symbol for a first wedding anniversary, a question that, of course, means little to Almásy but everything to Geoffrey. In order to explain its significance, the flashback must therefore move out of the patient/Almásy's experience and allow Geoffrey to take a temporary lead. Most importantly, this allows a space in which Geoffrey can explain the circumstances of his marriage, a confession that perhaps allows us to realize the reason for his earlier insecurities whenever his wife is the focus of attention for other men. Katharine, he knows, *settled* for marrying him. He loves her so much, however, that he doesn't really mind.

We see him later that evening, waiting in anguish outside the old city, where he has seen Katharine disappear for her secret assignation. Now, the film hammers home the cruelty of events from his point of view. Almásy and Katharine languish in bed. Almásy shares a gramophone recording of a beloved song from his childhood, *Szerelem, Szerelem*, with his lover and finally claims ownership over her. She explains, in return, her reconfiguration of their situation as an 'alternative' reality, in order to excuse her adultery to herself. They kiss and the film cuts to Geoffrey, swigging the champagne intended for their surprise anniversary celebration and tearing hearts from the paper that signifies their time together as husband and wife. Katharine's "different life" as a "different wife"[102] with Almásy implies, by definition, an ordinary life as an ordinary wife—to the poor 'ordinary husband' that Geoffrey represents. The film is at pains to ensure that the audience, if not the couple, does not forget this.

It is through Caravaggio that we then come to understand the wider political implications of this very personal betrayal. His specific framing adds to the context already offered for the patient's flashbacks by the situation in and around the monastery. These surroundings evidence the hard, dangerous and filthy work of war to which Almásy was never party, the routine way in which ordinary people are expected to withstand personal wartime losses and the selflessness of Hana and Kip's mutually supportive relationship. Against this, Almásy's tortured emotions seem almost luxuriously and, with Caravaggio's intervention, dangerously self-indulgent.

Most of the flashbacks are shown to occur solely within the patient's own imagination, although we must suppose that some do involve conversation to which we are not party, particularly where the patient and his interrogator are concerned. Caravaggio's own flashback, for one, must involve a spoken narration of some kind in order for its place in and result on the narrative to make sense. Caravaggio immediately disrupts the air of secret reverie that has pervaded the patient's early flashbacks, which represent the early history of his meeting and relationship with Katharine purely in terms of their burgeoning personal and social betrayal. From the very outset, he casts doubt on the patient's avowed amnesia, suggests a significance to the connection between Almásy and Katharine that has yet to be explained and blames him openly for his torture and mutilation. What appears to be a simple story of forbidden passion becomes laced with a mystery of far greater magnitude. How, indeed, could the patient have been responsible for the loss of Caravaggio's thumbs? How are these apparently very different characters even connected to each other?

As the story progresses, we receive clues and information in a fragmentary fashion that both casts an increasingly dark shadow over the flashbacks and leads, eventually, to the answer to Caravaggio's question. We learn from Katharine that Geoffrey is in fact working as a spy for the British government, taking aerial photographs of Africa. We then see, in the Paper Wedding Anniversary flashback, that Caravaggio and Geoffrey worked together in Cairo. Caravaggio is thus recontextualized in both past and present as a spy, rather than the small-time thief that he has presented himself as at the monastery.

Still, however, the connection between their acquaintance and Caravaggio's as yet undefined torture remains unclear. This is remedied by the only flashback that belongs solely to Caravaggio, through which we learn everything as he understands it. Fenelon-Barnes (Clive Merrison) tells him, as Moose, how Almásy gave the Royal Geographical Society maps to the Germans, thereby allowing them to get their spies into Cairo. As a result, Almásy's closest friend Madox has committed suicide. We then learn that photographs taken by the Germans in Cairo are the cause of Caravaggio/Moose's capture and torture.

The connection between the characters is thus explained, as is the reason for Caravaggio's hunt for the patient. As he accuses him, the patient's memories return to those very maps and an angry conversation with Madox about the need for security during the onset of war. By now, of course, we know that poor Madox, who has been presented as the epitome of English politeness and reserve, and who has been so tolerant of Almásy's personal misdemeanors, will die as a result of these very maps and the rank naïveté that Almásy stubbornly persists in exhibiting during this exchange. Madox tries to explain the significance of the desert to the impending war, to which Almásy responds by asking if he knows the name of the hollow "at the base of a woman's throat."[103]

We therefore share Caravaggio's position of knowledge, at this point, in knowing the facts of what Almásy went on to do. Although we are beginning to realize that he refused to acknowledge the war, however, we still do not know exactly why or how someone so opposed to national allegiance could have come to offer so much help to the German army. Furthermore, although Caravaggio's flashback contained the news of Madox's death, this same news now comes as a shock to the patient in the present. He contests in horrified tones the assumption that he was a spy and remembers his final parting from Madox, who warns him directly about the danger of the suspicion of espionage attached to anyone who is "remotely foreign."[104] The fact that this warning goes completely unheeded by Almásy is the ultimate cause of both their deaths. Realizing, as a result of this, that he is also responsible for Geoffrey and Katharine's deaths, he finally breaks down and presents the final piece of Caravaggio's puzzle. Once his motivation for helping the Germans has been revealed, Caravaggio disappears from the story until after the patient's death.

Although his remaining flashbacks return purely to the realm of the personal, the tragedy of the loss that he had already acknowledged on his own terms is now compounded by the new knowledge of his own culpability and the other related deaths. Caravaggio's intervention signals, therefore, that the comprehensive veracity of the patient's subjective account is definitely open to question. He is not an unreliable narrator as such, but his view is tragically narrow. Without Caravaggio and the wider view of the film, his story would be very different.

The whole question of the patient's subjectivity must therefore be considered with the greatest possible care. When, for example, we momentarily witness Katharine's or Geoffrey's point of view, does this merely represent the freedom of the flashback mode to move away from its primary narrator once it has been established, or does it represent scenes that the patient imagines must have happened in order to make sense of later events of which he was a part? In a film where subjectivity is so important, whose subjectivity are we experiencing?

## Romantic Emotion and the Patient's Subjectivity: Men, Love and Music in Film

The dichotomy of subjective and objective views is also crucial to understanding the use of music in the film, particularly the placement and development of the non-diegetic score in connection with the patient/Almásy. In broad terms, of course, the score adheres to the kind of melodramatic model discussed in chapter 2, whereby it reveals the emotional truth of characters in support of, or despite their outward appearance or behavior. It also, of course, represents a level of emotion that is in excess of what can be adequately expressed through words, actions or other more tangible textual elements. In a film that deals almost exclusively with this kind of emotion, this function is at a premium. As Hana struggles to contain her sense of emotional isolation over the personal losses she has suffered and the countless other deaths she has witnessed, her themes reveal the depth of her pain and loneliness even when she hides behind typically stoic behavior. Likewise the score ensures that the way forward that she discovers through Kip is a genuine road to recovery.

For the patient, the non-diegetic music that introduces and accompanies many of his flashbacks indicates their intense privacy and separation from the persona that he presents to the others at the monastery. Behind his rather wry wit, the music suggests, are emotions that he could never share. Once within the flashbacks, however, the non-diegetic score presents a rather more complex problem. In the strictest terms, we may suppose that all the music we hear within his flashbacks reflects his own present-day emotions in considering his past. He is, after all, the implied narrator of almost all the flashbacks whether or not he is speaking. Alternatively, we may suppose that the film slips into a representation of his emotions as they happen in the past. As a third possibility, similar to the earlier consideration of shifting points of view within the flashbacks, it may be argued that the music also sometimes represents the emotions of other characters. It is certainly true, however, that the music within the flashbacks seems primarily associated with Almásy's own emotions and always at the very least with emotional situations in which he is involved.

This focus is particularly telling in its apparent marginalization of Katharine's emotions. As Almásy carries her injured body along the cliff edge to the Cave of Swimmers, for example, she is denied a full emotional stake in her climactic admission of love by the concealment of her face behind his and the resultant focus on his sorrowful reaction. Furthermore, any theme that does accompany her has already originated with either Almásy in the past or the patient in the present. She therefore lacks a distinctive musical identity or a sense of individual musical representation. Seen first through the patient's and then through Almásy's point of view, she is subsumed musically into their more romantic and less responsible view of their emotional involvement. We never see Katharine completely alone, and on the one short occasion that we see her only with Geoffrey, her emotional plea to return home remains unaccompanied by music. When she is accompanied by non-diegetic music we therefore tend to forget, as does Almásy, the more complicated feelings for her husband that inform many of her comments and actions.

This greater focus on Almásy's emotions seems further compounded by the very tone of many of the non-diegetic cues. Even in those moments that should be Almásy's happiest, the score appears to suggest the frame of his present-day view as the patient in its underlying tone of sadness and regret. This could also, of course, be considered part of the intervention of the wider voice of the film, commenting on the impossibility of his future with Katharine. Whichever seems most likely, the fact remains that the patient and his alter ego share an unusually and intriguingly close relationship to the non-diegetic score that has a considerable effect on their characterization.

The nature of the patient's story, and his emotional centrality as its primary narrator, place him in an interesting position in relation to the conventional male love story protagonist. On one hand, *The English Patient* exhibits the same tendency as the 1940s love story, as described by Doane, in seeking to protect the male protagonist from the feminizing effect of involvement in a love story and its over-investment in music, by making him a musician by profession. In this way, the male character can remain masculine while still enjoying a prevalent association with music. Although Almásy is not a musician as such, he does utilize music as a significant and actively controlled aspect of his own characterization. As is noted on at least two occasions, for example, he "sings all the time,"[105] a tendency that appears to signify a certain introspection and a related desire for privacy and the silence of those around him. He also actively chooses to circumscribe his romance with Katharine within the terms of a recorded song. Even though he is clearly not the author of this music, he 'rewrites' it as descriptive of their shared emotional trajectory and thus transfers the apparent profundity of his bond with his childhood *"daijke"*[106] onto his adult romantic attachment.

The comparative relationship of Almásy and Katharine to *Szerelem, Szerelem* then mirrors, to some extent, the conventional musical-gender divide of the 1940s love story. The male musician plays music within the diegetic space, much as Almásy plays his gramophone record, and the transferal of this music into the non-diegetic score signals the transferal of its emotional affect onto the trajectory of the female protagonist. The male character, although emotional is, as a result, rarely shown in the non-diegetic terms of excessive and, moreover, vulnerable emotionality. The non-diegetic music that accompanies the female character, however, continues to bear the trace of the male musician's diegetic performance.

Although Almásy's song is both sung by a woman and associated with another woman, therefore, its function at the non-diegetic level remains connected, to a significant degree, with Almásy himself. This means that when it returns, in stylistic terms at least, it represents Katharine's emotions as a 'product' of Almásy's behavior and emotional investment in her. Most importantly in this respect is the accompaniment of her death scene with the *Lullaby for Katharine*, a piece that is highly reminiscent of *Szerelem, Szerelem*.[107] By extension of the meaning attributed to the music by Almásy, Katharine's death is represented as the result of her lover's romantic, childlike nostalgia for a time and place with no borders.

While this may suggest the patient/Almásy as a rather strong character both narratively and musically, he also shares many of the attributes that would usually, in this genre, be expected to appear in association with the female protagonist. At both the overall structural level and the level of narrative minutiae, for example, it is Almásy who endures what Doane refers to as a "feminine relation to time," which she defines as a relation that emphasizes "repetition, waiting [and] duration."[108] It is the woman, in the 1940s love story, who waits for the man and resigns herself, often, to a secondary social position in relation to his legitimate wife. "Adultery is allowable," Doane suggests, only "insofar as it itself mimics the matrimonial bond."[109] It is usually the man, however, who is actually married and the woman who gives up all else for the sake of the little time he can offer her.[110] The waiting woman lives, as a result, "in a state of expectation which is never fulfilled or fulfilled only in imagination."[111] According to Doane, therefore, "[i]f, by chance, it is the man who waits, he is, as Barthes points out, 'feminized' by this relation to time and the other and suffering."[112]

Clearly, in *The English Patient*, it is Almásy who waits, and Almásy whose suffering in the absence of the other that we witness. It is Almásy, furthermore, who is subjected to the painful and fateful repetitions of scenarios involving the arrival of Geoffrey's plane in the desert, the dance floor of the Shepheard's Hotel, the plant in the desert whose heart can be cut out to produce a sweet liquid and the crucial phrase: "Yes. Yes. Absolutely."[113]

Most notable in this respect, however, is his musical representation. Apart from the function of *Szerelem, Szerelem*, the patient/Almásy is a rather unconventional musical male. Firstly, music is so much a part of his own subconscious that he even professes to being unaware of his own singing. Believing himself to be silent, no doubt, like the other characters around him, this may suggest a certain loss of masculine self-awareness and self-control to the kind of private reverie and introspection more conventionally associated with female characters. Whatever he is dreaming about has its own integral soundtrack, although, from his point of view, it seems to remain non-diegetic and 'unheard.'

Secondly, he is also the primary subject of non-diegetic musical-emotional representation, much of which is concerned with the revelation of intensely vulnerable and conventionally 'feminine' emotions.

The surging passion of the non-diegetic score therefore becomes the evidence that the heart beating within his seemingly icy chest is indeed "an organ of fire"[114] and the musical equivalent of his unheard tears as he finally and unequivocally breaks down with grief. His relationship to the musical score overall is therefore by turns conventionally masculine and feminine. Even in the context of contemporaneous trends toward the more emotional representation of masculinity, such excessive musical emotionality, particularly in connection with feelings for a woman, remains rare for a male character. The most relevant model in this respect may, in fact, be one of the 'great' love stories to which the film is often compared—*Dr. Zhivago*. In this film also, we witness the genuine emotional sensitivity and vulnerability of the hero, as well as his profound attachment to his illegitimate lover, through the transferal of a melody originally associated with a maternal figure—in this case his late mother—onto his feelings for his lover. Like the patient/Almásy, he remains throughout the film the only character whose emotions we know so intimately and who seems so destructively in thrall to those very emotions that real men are supposed to control.

This may go some way to explaining the popularity of the patient/Almásy, despite his many faults, as a romantic hero. Doane suggests that a major element of male characterization in the love stories of the 1940s may be "that men in the love story are what women would want them to be, and what they want them to be is like themselves."[115] In terms of the love story, Almásy loves like a woman rather than like a man. This may go nowhere in excusing his political actions, but it does lend his weaknesses and motivations a romantic veracity with which it is hard to argue.

The result of re-viewing the patient's story as one particularly subjective rendition of history, is that the rank romanticization of which the film has been accused may be reconfigured as belonging very pointedly to the patient/Almásy alone. When his passionate, adulterous encounters with Katharine are accompanied by surging romantic music, this does not necessarily imply that the film considers their genuine emotions to be a justification for their adultery. Rather, it is seeking to represent both their shared *subjective* experience of the moment and the way in which the patient *remembers* his affair. As the screenplay says as Almásy makes love with Katharine on Christmas Day:

> It's as if the world has stopped and there's only their passion, overwhelming reason and logic and rules.[116]

If, therefore, we are to understand Almásy's perception of events in relation to the attitudes of the other characters and the wider voice of the film itself, we must realize the truth, in his eyes, of his emotions. Only then can we fully understand the horror of his ultimate realization, a horror that may even be so strong that Caravaggio considers it the best possible punishment for his wartime betrayal.

# 4

# THE NARRATIVE SOUNDTRACK

Given his background in music and radio drama and his use of music as described in chapter 2, it is hardly surprising that Minghella wanted *The English Patient* to "sound as interesting as it looked."[1] With acknowledged master of the narrative soundtrack, Walter Murch, he spent "sixteen or seventeen hours a day" absorbed in the film's complex process of editing and sound design.[2] The result is a fully integrated diegetic and non-diegetic soundtrack that is both intricately designed and dense with thematic function and meaning. To discuss the musical score without first placing it within this wider aural context would therefore be both nonsensical and impossible.

## The Creative Process

The level of integration between the sound and music tracks is a reflection of the intensely collaborative working process of Minghella, Yared and Murch. Yared's collaboration with Minghella began at the very outset of the project, when Minghella approached him with both the script and the musical parameters within which he felt the score should work. According to Yared, in introducing him to the song *Szerelem, Szerelem*, Minghella explained its attraction as a musical sound without clear roots—atypical of any particular national style of folk music and sounding by turns Arabic, Hungarian, Turkish and Bulgarian.[3] Minghella wanted the musical world of the film to be inhabited by this song, alongside music in the styles of Puccini and J. S. Bach; the *Aria* from the *Goldberg Variations* was already specified as diegetic material.[4]

With these three principal musical touchstones, Yared began composing while Minghella was shooting.

His compositional process was further aided by visits to sets to see
the scenes of the church at Arezzo, the patient's make-up, and to act as
musical director for the Cairo hotel scenes involving the diegetic jazz
dance band. For these particular scenes, Minghella and Yared collaborated over the choice of diegetic music for the band and Yared, feeling
he lacked sufficient expertise in popular music of this style and period,
collaborated in turn with specialist arranger Ronnie Hazlehurst.[5]

This musical process fed into Yared and Minghella's mutual collaboration with Murch. Minghella was particularly concerned that the
editing process should avoid a sense of fragmentation that would dis-
orient the audience. In approaching the multiple temporal transitions,
he wanted to achieve the feeling that they were "urgent and necessary
and inexorable so that the audience didn't feel rocked round between
two disparate stories and two locations. It had to be one story, one
tense, that could somehow lasso several time periods."[6] He felt that
"one way to soften those transitions was . . . to cue the transitions always with sound as much as with image and with dissolves."[7] Murch's
expertise in both fields enabled them to "design those transitions together both aurally and visually."[8]

While Yared worked only with the script in his initial creation of
the main musical themes, this stage of the collaboration turned his attention to the pictures themselves and the minute detail of integrating
his music into each scene. Before he had seen anything of the film, he
delivered several recordings of his themes to Murch. Minghella and
Murch cut these themes into the film in rough form and returned the
relevant scenes to Yared, who then adapted each cue to its particular
scene. Decisions about how and where the music should be placed
were made mutually, so much so that Yared feels it is impossible to say
who actually made the final decisions. As a result, he maintains that he
wrote the score as music rather than as film music, with the process of
making it into a score being led primarily by Minghella and Murch.[9]

# The Sound and Music Tracks

## An Overview

From the film's outset, sound is identified as a very particular carrier of meaning. Under the opening titles, before the appearance of the first enigmatic image, our introduction to the narrative comes in faint and sporadic voices, speaking in Arabic, and the sound of tinkling glass and grunting camels. These sounds bear no obvious relation to the slow and careful painting of a figure or the first non-diegetic music that follows. Rather, they are contextualized and identified retrospectively as the opening desert narrative gradually unfolds. The foregrounding and peculiarity of these opening sounds, however, reveal many of the vital narrative roles that both sound and music will play throughout the film.

The design of the sound and music tracks in relation to the images and multiple temporal shifts offers a constant reflection on the emotional states and trajectories of the central characters. On a structural and thematic level, sound and music are crucial in recreating the various worlds of the interweaving stories through what might be termed the 'filter' of character subjectivity, so that we are encouraged to understand each world as its principal inhabitant understands it or relates to it. At the same time, aspects of the sound and music design also encapsulate the film's central concern with the constant negotiation between present and past and life and death, which is so vital to the formation and development of these subjectivities. For both the patient and Hana in particular, it is often the unique qualities of sound and music that open doors between the past, present and future, ushering in knowledge, memories or even new characters in a way that ultimately leads to routes away from the limbo state of the monastery.

The non-diegetic score, conventionally enough, privileges the representation of those characters whose subjectivity and emotions are most central to the narrative. This involves only a small number of characters, primarily the patient/Almásy and Hana, but also to some extent Katharine and Kip and even momentarily Caravaggio, by virtue of their various associations with the two principal characters. Diegetic music, however, is a constant feature of all the characters' lives as they sing, play instruments, dance, talk about and listen to music in a wide variety of contexts throughout the film. Although there is nothing unusual in a score that combines non-diegetic and diegetic music in this way, this score actually uses their respective connotations of the private and the public to thematicize the opposition of personal emotion and social convention that permeates the narrative.

As such, at its most general level, the diegetic music provides a powerful and constant reminder of everyday, social life against which the very private melodrama of the main protagonists is set. Many instances of diegetic music could in fact easily be re-termed 'community' music, as they demonstrate the variety of ways in which music can signify distinct national, cultural and religious identities and the associated rituals of social bonding and cohesion. Making diegetic music such a powerful element of the mise-en-scène, however, places it in an interesting position with regard to the non-diegetic score. As was outlined in chapter 2, one of the key roles of non-diegetic music, which is particularly pertinent to the work of Minghella and Yared, is to represent or express the otherwise inexpressible depths of individual character interiority. The communal values of this particular diegetic score and the individual priorities of the non-diegetic score are therefore immediately at odds.

As part of the narrative's construction of multiple points of view and layers of meaning, the oppositional operation of the score becomes yet more complex as the relative values of the public and the private are mirrored between the past and the present. Whereas for Katharine and Almásy the diegetic music contests the emotional representation of the non-diegetic score with a sometimes pointed commentary on their social transgression, for Hana it suggests the salvation of a coherent and civilized society as a way forward from the solitude of grief.

## The Patient: The Passage of Time and the Simultaneity of Past and Present

As the Bedouin rescue Almásy from the wreckage of his plane, they cover his face with a protective mask, which is only removed much later by the healer whose glass bottles identify the sound of tinkling glass from the opening of the film. Although we see Almásy's full rescue entourage progressing through the desert, his only point-of-view shot shows an indistinct image, seen through this mask, of some surrounding figures, the sky and glaring sun. The lack of a visual source for the sounds that open the film may therefore be recontextualized, in retrospect, as Almásy's mainly aural perception of this desert journey. While the opening visual sequence tells us to con-

sider our interpretation of events and information, the initial foregrounding of sound is therefore confirmed as an indication of the centrality of hearing to the narrative. In both actual and symbolic terms,
'hearing' proves to be a vital mode of perception, a motivation for investigation and discovery and a means of survival. In the monastery, it
becomes crucial to the patient's re-viewing of his past as a now completed story, and therefore, eventually, to his understanding of it. His
insistence to Hana that he can "*see* all the way to the desert" [my ital-
ics][10] is contingent upon the fact that sound is one of the most important portals through which he gains that view.

In terms of sound and music, almost all the patient's movement between, or confused merging of the past and present—as described in
chapter 3—involves a transition from one diegetic plane to another via
the mediating space of the meta-diegetic realm.[11] This means that the
patient's private perception of sound and music, unheard by other
characters but often shared by the film audience, provides the aural
route from one time and place to another. Once the full aural and visual
transition has taken place, of course, the sound and music become
diegetically sourced once more.[12] In very broad terms, this temporal
movement happens in three ways, which can be differentiated through
the relationship of visual to sound editing and the particular way in
which sound is placed and designed, at each point of transition.

First, on two occasions, the motivation for the patient's movement
into the past comes from the evocative power of sounds in the present
to recall qualitatively similar sounds or music from quite different
sources in the past. Such is the case, for example, when the motivation
for the patient's second flashback comes from Hana's game of hopscotch in the monastery courtyard. First we see the game for a sufficient length of time to absorb how it sounds close up and then from the
approximate distance of the patient's window, before we move inside
to see the patient listening.

The patient's solely aural perception reduces the game to a series
of banging noises. As we watch him, these sounds are already merging
at the meta-diegetic level, through a spatially impossible increase in
volume and a doubling of their rhythm, into percussive Arabic music in
the past of the patient's imagination. The explanatory visual cut to the
Arab musicians on the desert expedition follows immediately. A similar transition occurs later as Kip taps the top of a tin of condensed milk
and the patient is recalled to the noises of a Cairo street. The use of
particular words can also trigger memories and as the patient's past

story gathers momentum, particularly as Caravaggio begins to politicize his otherwise purely romantic rendition, his memories are motivated more frequently by key names, accusations or direct questions.

The second way concerns the stimulus for his return from these flashbacks to the present, which also often comes through sounds, words or music from the present. This time, however, they sharply interrupt the visualization of his memories, appearing incongruous at first but being contextualized as they drag him back to the visual world of the monastery. This introduces a new fluidity of sound between spaces whereby the patient can evidently still hear sound from the present when his consciousness appears otherwise to be in the past. Rather than one sound reminding him of another, these sounds enter his mind unexpectedly, without the context of private memories to explain their appearance, so that there appears to be a clash between his consciousness as Almásy in the past and as the patient in the present.

Perhaps more so than the transitions from present to past, therefore, this fluidity expresses the constant hovering of the patient's consciousness between what might be seen as his two lives, or his life and death. He is unexpectedly drawn out of his second flashback, for example, by the apparently incongruous sound of Hana's voice over a shot of Almásy sitting in the desert, asking whether or not he is asleep. Only the subsequent cut back to the monastery makes sense of her words as we realize, of course, that she is being heard by the patient rather, as it were, than by Almásy. In much the same way later in the story, Hana's piano playing in the monastery cuts across the desert just as Almásy is left alone with Katharine, and her question about his baby photograph ends his frustration at offending his new lover with his avowed hatred of ownership.

Such instances of direct movement nevertheless operate within an overall schema of the patient's generally amorphous state of consciousness. This third form of temporal movement is perhaps the most important and intriguing aspect of the patient's 'soundworld' and is attributed early on by Hana to the effects of morphine. It is in this state that the patient, through his perception of sound, constantly confuses or conflates the present and the past to such an extent that it is impossible to pinpoint where his consciousness lies at any one time. This aural confusion may or may not be shared by the film audience and may or may not be articulated by the patient.

During the second flashback, for example, as Katharine tells the story of Candaules and Gyges, a birdcall is heard, apparently part of the diegetic soundtrack of the desert evening. After the patient has been drawn back into the present, however, the same birdcall is heard twice in the nighttime space of the monastery. The source of the birdcall is therefore confusing. Its volume remains constant between the two spaces, suggesting that unless the same bird happens to inhabit each country, the subjective soundtrack of the patient is crossing freely between the two worlds. If this is the case, although we still see the patient in the present context of the monastery, we may assume that his thoughts have moved back once again, unseen by us, to his past in the desert. Since the patient does not articulate any confusion, we are therefore left to wonder to what extent we are being absorbed into his meta-diegetic experience of sound.

On another occasion, however, the patient does in fact voice the limitless potential for aural overlap between the worlds. He is returning to the present from a flashback that has included events that he could not have witnessed, namely, the only private conversation that we ever see between Geoffrey and Katharine. Katharine tells Geoffrey that she longs for rain and would go home at any time if he so wished. As Geoffrey explains that they cannot go home and she leaves his side, the faint sound of thunder cuts across the searing heat of Christmas Day in Cairo. The following dissolve to the patient lying behind his net curtain and being woken by Caravaggio, however, reveals the thunder to be outside the monastery. The patient says that he heard Caravaggio's breathing and thought it was the rain. He says that he is "dying for rain."[13] Both the thunder and Caravaggio's breathing therefore appear to have permeated his dream—the thunder as an actual sound and the breathing as the related idea of rain. A complex series of associations thus connects the thunder and Caravaggio's breathing in the present with Katharine's imagined desire for rain in the past and the patient's subsequent desire for rain in the present.

The overall structure of the patient's narrative, however, places the two episodes in which the patient listens simultaneously to the voices of Hana and Katharine as the apotheoses of all such aural fluidity. As the moments that mark the beginning and mortal end of the couple's relationship, these go beyond movement or confusion between the present and the past. Instead, they come painfully close to collapsing the two planes into absolute simultaneity. This kind of aural transition finds a purely visual equivalent as the patient recalls being trapped in the desert sandstorm with Katharine, and her fingers, pressing against the window of their truck, appear to reach through time to touch his

face as he lies in the monastery. It is through the written word and
reading, however, that Katharine sends her two most important mes-
sages, firstly to Almásy in the past and secondly to the patient in the
present.

Hana reads to the patient on two occasions, once from his own
book and once from the final letter that Katharine writes to Almásy
before she dies in the Cave of Swimmers. On the first occasion, the
patient is returned to a simultaneous visual and aural memory of
Katharine as he watches and listens to Hana. On the second occasion,
however, Hana's voice gives way to Katharine's even in the present,
and removes the patient to a realm of memory from which he will
never return.

It is during the patient's second flashback to the desert that
Katharine tells the story of Candaules and Gyges from Herodotus' *The
Histories* as her contribution to a game of Spin the Bottle. This rendition begins with a sudden cut back to the monastery and a close-up of
the pages of the patient's copy of the book. Hana is reading aloud and
hesitates over the pronunciation of the name "Candaules."[14] The patient gives her the correct pronunciation and continues to watch her as
he repeats the name more thoughtfully for a second time. With the following cut to the desert, we see and hear Katharine say the same name
as she continues with the story. Five consecutive statements of the
name therefore transport us from the present to the past and between
the different voices heard by the patient and Almásy. The storytelling
returns once more to Hana, in apparent response to which the patient
moves his gaze towards her. The reverse shot of what he sees and presumably hears, however, returns us to Katharine in the desert, who
goes on to complete the story and thereby communicate her romantic
interest to Almásy. By the time Katharine finishes the story, the patient
has lost all consciousness of the present.

At the same time as this indirect mode of communication begins
their relationship, however, it also rehearses for the communication
across time of Katharine's directly intimate final message. Almásy carries her body from the Cave of Swimmers, heavy with the knowledge,
gained too late, of her continued love for him. For this most painful
moment, we are left to his imagination alone. He is ready to die and
rejoin his lost love and after he has wordlessly persuaded Hana to ad-
minister a fatal morphine overdose, she agrees to "[r]ead [him] to
sleep" from Katharine's final letter from the cave.[15]

The two temporal spaces are now completely collapsed as the patient loses consciousness for the last time. Even as we watch him watching Hana read in the space of the monastery, it is Katharine's voice that we hear. By alternating in the present between an objective view of Hana and this suggestion of the patient's auditory point of view, we realize that as far as he is concerned, Hana's voice has disappeared altogether and now acts only as a vehicle through which to hear Katharine.[16] This overlap of sound and visual editing means that rather than it being Hana's voice that *sends* the patient back into the past, it is Katharine's voice that *draws* him back and provides a smooth continuity between the two visual planes. The visual past does not show Katharine speaking the words since, of course, she never did, and the precise sound of her speech is now purely a figment of the patient's imagination. As he grants her wish by carrying her out of the cave, the whole soundworld of the film is raised to the non- and meta-diegetic levels, leaving her voice as the only thing that the patient hears as he dies. Even his own roars of grief, so graphically represented in visual terms, remain unheard as he is gradually removed from diegetic life.

The ability of sound to transcend temporal, spatial and visual boundaries is crucial to the patient's preparation for death. It offers a portal through which he can eventually be returned to Katharine in eternity, freed by her love and her final words from the national and social barriers that fettered them in the past and from the guilt of his failure to save her life.

The function of the patient's soundworld therefore extends beyond sound and music merely providing a gateway to the past. Rather, the passage through time that they open up is a practical means to a therapeutic end, a way of helping the patient to face up to and come to terms with his past actions and their consequences. In facing his past he faces nothing less than himself. Thus as he returns to the point at which his story began, flying with Katharine's dead body in Madox's biplane over the war-torn desert, he is ready to face death for the second time in full knowledge of what his life has meant both to himself and to others.

## Almásy and Katharine: The Private and the Public

> I once travelled with a guide, who was taking me to Faya. He didn't
> speak for nine hours. At the end of it he pointed to the horizon and
> said, "Faya!" That was a good day.[17]

Considering the opening title sequence once more, it is possible to
see that there is even more at stake than the actual and symbolic modes
of hearing. Also crucial is the question of precisely *what* is heard and
how that can reflect a very subjective relationship to the environment.
The foregrounding of the particular sounds that open the film, for example, gives an immediate impression of the desert that is later contextualized as Almásy's view. The aural landscape of the patient's
flashbacks then becomes a definitive element of his personality. His
interpretation of his surroundings, the desires that he projects onto
them and the way in which he sees himself as part of that landscape,
can all be traced to a significant extent through the sounds and music
that inhabit his world and the way in which he responds to them.

The voices of the opening titles transpire most immediately as belonging to the Bedouin who save Almásy's life and carry him out of the
desert. Their motives, however, are unclear, so that unlike the Bedouin
of the novel who preserve the patient's life in order that he may identify their cache of guns and ammunition, these men appear merely benevolent and unconcerned with world affairs. This suggests a thematic
link to their initial positioning on the soundtrack. As the patient returns
in his memory to Cairo and the desert, the surrounding Arab culture
and even individual Arab characters appear first of all sidelined, in the
service of the putative "*International* Sand Club," [18] [my italics] and
later, little short of invisible in the face of invading armies and World
War II.

Arab speech remains untranslated, although we witness it being lis-
tened to, understood and spoken by Almásy and other club members.
In visual and narrative terms, the frequent relegation of Arab characters
to the backgrounds of shots reflects their position at the margins of the
explorers' lives. They remain comparatively anonymous, being made
to entertain themselves in a separate group in the evening and to ride
precariously on the roofs of the trucks during the desert expeditions.
Even their mid-expedition prayers, presented initially in such prominent visual and aural terms, are ignored by Almásy and presumably
interrupted by his discovery of the Cave of Swimmers.

This does not mean, however, that Arab culture offers nothing more than a 'neutral' background to the story. On the contrary, it is Almásy and Katharine's particular interpretation of their surroundings that provides the necessary context for their romantic melodrama. The preconceptions and desires that they each bring to Cairo, the desert and their relationship are reflected in many ways in the design of their own particular soundtrack. One of the most notable indications of this subjective reconfiguration of sound is the way in which the call to prayer is employed as a very particular kind of love theme, which allows illegitimate passion to cast off its social conscience. Seen in its proper context in the desert, but appearing on the diegetic track of Cairo without any attention to its visual source or religious function, the call to prayer draws the couple together with the perceived promise of a world of 'Otherness.'

It is heard for the first time as they meet in the Cairo marketplace. Their conversation is stilted and Almásy apologizes for his abruptness, attributing it with pointed sarcasm to being "rusty at social graces."[19] The call drifts across the awkward silence that follows, before continuing in sharp contrast to their poisonous exchange and Almásy's tart references to social etiquette and tourism. Its softly musical line connotes the Otherness of ancient culture and religion. It suggests both the couple's common distance from 'home,' and a connection between their personal desires that undermines their somewhat brittle and superficial avowal of difference. As it continues to reappear in leitmotivic style, its recollection of these connotations seems to draw the couple together. It renders their liaison not only permissible, but, moreover, driven by a depth of mutual recognition that transcends the codes of their ordinary, everyday life.

The call's evocation of a world of Otherness thus allows Almásy's conception of the desert's timeless suspension of reality (see chapter 3) to be extended, significantly, to the old part of the city where he stays. As he sleeps in his room after he and Katharine have returned from their vital isolation in the desert, the call connotes the important difference between this space and the luxurious, westernized hotel inhabited by the others. It therefore suggests the room as an appropriate locus for their marital and social infidelity. So much license do the perceived connotations of this sound give the couple, in fact, that its later appearance during the Christmas party introduces their most passionate and audacious lovemaking, taking place literally and cruelly within sight of the as yet unsuspecting Geoffrey.

Tellingly, of course, Katharine can only deal with the Otherness of her newfound passion by reconceptualizing it as an alternative 'normal' life.[20] She is still essentially bound by social codes and as soon as she reawakens to the responsibilities of her real life and realizes the falsity of the cultural license that they assume in the old city, she ends the relationship. This decision is reflected in the call's permanent disappearance from the Cairo soundtrack.

As the story quoted at the head of this section makes clear, Almásy desires control of his own sonic environment so that he only needs to hear, both physically and metaphorically, what he wants to hear. Katharine's effective removal of the call to prayer from the soundtrack is not the only instance, however, when this desire is catastrophically denied. On the contrary, the whole diegetic soundtrack of the patient's flashback carefully rehearses the trajectory of his possession and loss of both self and social control, leaving him more impotent in the end than perhaps even he realizes.

Katharine's very first appearance in the desert demonstrates his potential weakness in this respect as, despite his impressive ability to understand Arabic, he fails to hear the more important approach of her plane, and turns to see it only because of the greater awareness of the old man with whom he is speaking. Like his rejection of adjectives in his writing, he assumes that he hears what is important and therefore dismisses everything else as superfluous. Hence his annoyance when Katharine reveals his propensity for singing and he is forced to admit that he is not even fully aware of the sound that he himself makes.[21]

Their exchange over his singing is, in fact, particularly important, since it is through music in general that the issue of the patient/Almásy's narrative and emotional control is most strongly represented and contested. He is the character most intimately associated with and characterized by music. In general, both non-diegetic and diegetic music relate him to the past rather than the present, and non-diegetic music usually only accompanies him in the monastery as a mode of transition from one temporal space to the other. As was discussed in chapter 3, this means that most of his non-diegetic scoring is contained within a highly subjective framework, inflecting the representation of his memories with a romantic view that not even Caravaggio's dramatic recontextualization of events can affect. This view concerns the unfathomable and often uncontrollable emotional excesses that confound both Almásy and the patient alike: namely his emotional identification with Katharine and the desert. His music is the most

dramatic and excessive in the score and is, by its very independent nature, not prey to the threat that undermines his equally important relationship to diegetic music.

Almásy is literally *identified* by diegetic music—by other characters and himself—in the desert, Cairo and the monastery. So close is
his relationship to diegetic music, in fact, that his entire emotional trajectory can be charted through his behavioral interaction with it. Mirrored scenes foregrounding music—on the dance floor of the Cairo
hotel and in the desert—chart his movement from complete control to
loss of control, over both himself and the course of the desert narrative.
Crucial to this loss of emotional and narrative control is Caravaggio's
ability, halfway through the story, to remove the patient's symbolic
mastery over diegetic music by his appropriation of its mechanical
means of reproduction within the monastery. After this point, the
diegetic music that so readily supported Almásy's emotional cause in
the past turns on him to such extremely "anempathetic" effect that the
result is almost ghoulish.[22]

Music is one of the first means by which we see the possibility of
community between the explorers in the desert, and the means by
which we understand how that community is to be defined. Whereas
during the patient's first flashback Madox argues with Almásy over his
antagonism toward newcomers Geoffrey and Katharine, by the time of
the second flashback they are all happily ensconced in a musical game.
Against the backdrop of the Arab group's own musical activity, we see
D'Agostino (Nino Castelnuovo) complete a Puccini aria, before Geoffrey performs a comic rendition of *Yes! We Have No Bananas*. Everyone seems to know the song and a humorous multi-lingual chorus follows Geoffrey's performance.

This overt show of internationalism, however, also reveals an
overall conventional Western bias in the group's cultural identification.
Despite their current setting, and their English, Egyptian, German, Italian and Hungarian nationalities, they choose to unite over an American
song and show no interest in the Arab music behind them.[23] This
shared investment in American popular song then contributes to their
further identification according to a particularly urbane mode of internationalism. Its cultural cache is confirmed by its repeated appearance
in the ballroom of the exclusive Shepheard's Hotel in Cairo. As a mark
of the hotel's modern sophistication, this music removes its residents
temporarily from their actual locality and returns them to a Western
'society' atmosphere.

It is precisely this atmosphere, however, with which Almásy seems most uncomfortable. Whatever pretences may inform it, his preference is certainly for the old part of the city. Perhaps accordingly, his relationship to the musical identity of the group is somewhat problematic and his musical tastes are notably hybrid. For him, interaction with or through music has little or nothing to do with cultural or social signification and everything to do with intense personal feelings. Since music is so personal to Almásy, it makes sense that it should reflect his fluid sense of identity. He lives against the backdrop of Cairo's 'old city' soundtrack and the only gramophone record he plays is his beloved Hungarian *Szerelem, Szerelem*, which Katharine mistakes for an Arabic song. His private performance repertoire, however, appears to consist almost entirely of American popular song. Although he sings incessantly, he does so apparently unconsciously and does not join in with the flippant chorus during the game of Spin the Bottle. His relationship with music is not about performance. He sings 'to himself,' not for the entertainment of those around him.

This detachment from an engagement with music as an element of cultural and social ritual enables a starkly dichotomous representation of the development of Almásy and Katharine's social transgression. From the ballroom to the Christmas party, his hotel room and the final dinner of the International Sand Club, the relationship of Almásy's behavior to diegetic music charts his move from disregarding, to completely misunderstanding, the social codification and sanitization of something so personal. Katharine, meanwhile, having been drawn away from the social-musical codes that have informed her life so far, returns to them as the most effective and painful way of proving her eventual fidelity to Geoffrey.

The first point at which Almásy's interest in Katharine is registered comes as they dance to Rodgers and Hart's romantic classic *Where or When*. The dance floor provides an interesting interim space between social and intimate interaction, with each dancing couple presenting a closed, and yet still public, unit. The act of dancing as a couple offers a sanctioned space for private interaction, but social convention assumes that the nature of this interaction is determined by the legitimate relationship of the couple. Almásy and Katharine may dance, therefore, as members of the same social group and as his mark of his respect for his colleague's wife.

He maintains such an acceptable relationship during the initial stages of their conversation, claiming to have followed her on an earlier occasion in the street purely out of concern for her safety as "the wife of one of [their] party."[24] As this apparent neutrality is replaced by his intense "predatory" gaze,[25] however, he transgresses the dance floor code of conduct. At the same time, he appears to take possession of the music so that it becomes a vehicle for his intimate feelings rather than a harmlessly romantic dance for the whole room. The clarinet which has been playing the melody gives way to the solo violin which, as Almásy stares alarmingly at his prey, seems to fill in for the words that he would like to say. As Geoffrey looks on, therefore, Almásy actively disregards his socially assured innocence, using the sanctioned romance of dance floor music to transgress the accepted boundaries of decency.

The audacity of this encounter, however, is as nothing compared to that of the Christmas party. Here, the soundtrack, diegetic and non-diegetic music are vital, foregrounded elements of a highly contradictory mise-en-scène. The non-diegetic music, together with our proximity to the couple, emphasizes the passionate fulfillment of their stolen moment rather than its danger or destructive capacity. It must battle, however—and in an extremely pointed way—with the diegetic music of the social, cultural, religious and national rituals of Christianity, Islam and Britishness that continue, unheeded, around them.

The couple's arrival in the hidden room is accompanied, as was their previous encounter in Almásy's hotel room, by the distant sound of the call to prayer. This therefore evokes the same sense of Otherness that has permeated their romance on earlier occasions. As Almásy explores Katharine's throat and shoulder, however, there is a crucial change in their cultural backdrop as the partygoers outside begin singing *Silent Night* to a bagpipe accompaniment. The calm, homely sound and contemplative lyrics of the carol are immediately incongruous with the adulterous and deceptive nature of their encounter. Furthermore, the evidence of cultural community offered by this particular type of singing, and its implication of the tenets and commandments of the Christian religion, place the couple firmly and finally apart from the coherence and acceptable cultural codes of their social group. The transgression of their behavior is doubled when taking place in such a ritual social and familial context, away from the "different life" that they imagine in the old part of the city.[26] Yet, in sympathy at the same time with a completely different point of view, the mood of the music is well matched to Almásy's reverent and focused contemplation of Katharine's body. As their encounter progresses and the battle between the diegetic and non-diegetic music begins, personal desire and social obligation are placed in violent opposition (a full analysis of this can be found in chapter 5).

The pivotal scene in their adulterous relationship sees Almásy introducing Katharine to his childhood song in his hotel room and relating it humorously to their relationship, while Geoffrey waits in the street to discover his wife's infidelity. As was described in chapter 3, as soon as Almásy has transferred the emotional bond of *Szerelem, Szerelem* from his childhood *daijke* onto Katharine, 'claimed' her as his 'territory' and closed the gap between public music and private emotions, the film steps in to remind us of Katharine's obligation to Geoffrey and the cruelty of her deception. Not content with just the visual reminder provided by the edit to Geoffrey, however, the film hammers home the sheer smugness of their actions through the soundtrack.

As Almásy reassures Katharine, in a phrase that rhymes with their earlier experience in the desert sandstorm, that they will be alright, the exuberant strains of *Cheek to Cheek* burst onto the soundtrack with the words "Heaven, I'm in Heaven." As Geoffrey sees his wife and dissolves into distraction before our very eyes, the romantic words of the song continue, appearing to mock his desperate and confused grief. It is only with the following dissolve that we realize that the song represents the patient's subjective view of the events. Caravaggio has put a record on the gramophone to test the patient's musical knowledge and it is this that breaks into his dream and casts its unfortunate spell over Geoffrey. [27] Neither the actual source of the music, nor the fact that the patient could not possibly have known about Geoffrey witnessing the scene, however, prevent its acid commentary on how cruelly Geoffrey is being treated. Caravaggio, bitterly critical of the patient's past, has taken control of the diegetic music in order to turn the patient's own passion back on him as a means of failsafe identification. As the episode with Geoffrey demonstrates, however, an apparent consequence of this is that the music *itself* becomes a means of commenting on and undermining Almásy rather than supporting or justifying him.

On the evening that Katharine ends their relationship, she awaits Almásy at the outdoor cinema. The cinema newsreel tells us, in a commentary that is simultaneously flippant and ominous given the events we are about to see, that "never have the British been so much of one mind." [28] The newsreel reminds Katharine of her very Britishness and, by extension, of everything that this entails in terms of her social and marital identity. When Almásy arrives, she tells him she can no longer go on with their relationship. An abrupt edit follows, bringing us face to face with the broad grins of Busby Berkeley's chorus girls in *Golddiggers of 1933* on the cinema screen. They sing a cheery song admonishing a fictitious "bad girl" and "bad boy" for "[p]ettin' in the park," and the song continues in the background as Katharine takes her leave of Almásy. The couple's sadness is lampooned by this awful juxtaposition, gaining revenge on Geoffrey's behalf for his own musical humiliation.

Almásy's gradual loss of control over diegetic music and the role that it plays in his life then turns into an abject anger at, and a willful misunderstanding of, the contrived nature of social music and dancing. He arrives drunk at the final dinner party of the International Sand Club and announces that he has invented a new dance, "the Bosphorus Hug."[29] The private reference that this contains to his naming of the hollow at the base of Katharine's throat as "the *Almásy Bosphorus*"[30] renders it an attack on Katharine that contrasts the social propriety of dancing with the genuine passion that Almásy believed existed between them. As the dinner party dance band begins playing *Manhattan*, he then recites what he explains sanctimoniously are the original, precensorship lyrics, pointing their racy insinuations squarely at Katharine. Having undermined the façade of social propriety and cohesion that he sees as corruptive of music's real meaning, he then proceeds to lose control over his understanding of the musical-social ritual of dance. Witnessing Katharine's innocent dance with Rupert Douglas (Raymond Coulthard) through the latticework frame, discussed in chapter 3 as suggesting his incomplete understanding of what he sees, he makes his distracted accusation of a further affair.

This complete loss of control both musically and emotionally leaves Almásy and Katharine no future in a social-musical context. The next time they meet, however, they are unexpectedly removed from that context by Geoffrey's death and their isolation once again in the desert. Sadly, only now can Almásy's emotions be fully expressed by the non-diegetic score, free at last from the nagging voice of diegetic music's social conscience.

While Caravaggio's adoption of control over diegetic music has a catastrophic effect on Almásy, however, it proves to be a driving force in Hana's salvation. Prior to the moment when Caravaggio first plays his purloined gramophone records, the only diegetic music that has sounded in the monastery has been the patient's indistinct singing and

Hana's solitary piano playing—followed by her joke on the irrelevance of musical nationality as she suggests that playing the German J. S. Bach's music may protect you from the wartime attacks of his countrymen. Now, however, diegetic music bonds the disparate Italian household into a cheerful unified whole, permeating its physical boundaries to allow everyone to hear and respond to the same music at the same time. It echoes the perceived internationalism of the dance music in Cairo, but suggests the supportiveness of commonality rather than its restrictions.

## Hana: The Impermanence of Life and the Permeable Monastery

While the patient has been learning to face his past, Hana has been learning to face her future. Her grief over the loss of both her sweetheart and her best friend has led to her desire to deny the very fact of death through a dedication to prolonging the life of the patient indefinitely. In order to move forward from the patient and the monastery, she must learn that this desire to halt death can no more change the 'rules' of World War II in the present, than Almásy's desire to transcend boundaries could change the rules of society and nationality in the past. Hana's own soundworld, operating in conjunction with that of the patient, plays an equally vital symbolic role in her therapeutic process. The ultimate aim of this process, and therefore of the soundworld, however, is quite different. It seeks to release Hana into life and the future rather than death and the past.

In many ways, Hana's soundworld operates according to the same main principle as the patient's. Her knowledge also comes from the ability of sound to move freely and irrespectively of visual and physical boundaries and to precede or preclude sight. The route to knowledge that sound offers also brings her as much bad news as good. Unlike the patient, however, Hana's soundworld exists purely in the present, with sound traversing the spatial and physical, rather than temporal boundaries of both her army hospital unit and the monastery. This reflects the fact that whereas the answers to the patient's questions lie only in the past, Hana's are to be found only in the present. In order to move into the future, she must accept the inevitable passing of time and of life.

In a similar way to Almásy, Hana's first appearance sees her contextualized through sound before sight. We hear the train engine and voices before the darkness lifts to reveal her as a nurse on an army hospital train. As the film introduces and unites her journey with that of her patient, she undergoes two character-defining moments that preclude any further need for representation of her history. Both involve the loss of someone close to her and both come to her, initially at least, through sound.

The first involves her in an exchange with a dying soldier, from whom she learns that her sweetheart has been killed. The way in which she learns, however, defines the way that she will learn many things throughout the rest of the film. Hana does not speak directly with the soldier and it is unlikely that she can see him, at least not properly. Their exchange passes through the intermediary of a doctor who moves between the soldier and Hana and bends closely over the soldier to hear him speak. The curtains that separate them are partially drawn by the doctor, but since Hana and the soldier are both lying down she is, like Almásy on his stretcher in the desert, almost completely dependent on her hearing. The soldier imparts the news of her sweetheart's death to the doctor who, hoping she has not heard, attempts to deceive her. Hana has heard just enough, however, to realize the truth. Later, as her hospital unit moves along the road, Hana is summoned noisily from inside the back of her truck by the calls of her best friend Jan and the beeping horn of her jeep. Jan affectionately cadges money for the luxuries that are promised in the next town and drives away with her friends. Hana's attention returns to the patient until the sound of Jan's jeep exploding as it drives over a landmine draws her attention swiftly back outside.

As Hana subsequently ensconces herself in the monastery with the patient, she enters a limbo world that reflects her desire to defer death indefinitely in order to compensate for these deaths that happened, as it were, while she was not looking. As was discussed in chapter 3, the physicality of the monastery reflects Hana's emotional state, caught as it is between its own life and destruction. Its walls are half destroyed and there are holes between rooms, in floors and in ceilings. In short, the monastery has become a permeable space, the assumed permanence and solidity of its ancient walls disproved by the ravages of war and the reclamation processes of nature.

The ability of sound to pass freely through such a space, without even the necessity of a visible source, becomes a constant reminder of this physical permeability and, by extension, impermanence in general. Thus sound becomes a vital part of the way in which Hana's space is

created, but also an important factor in her escape. Sound from outside
the monastery is a constant conscious or subconscious reminder of another space, ready to open up before Hana as a literal 'way out' any-
time she chooses. At the same time, and in order to help her eventually
make this choice, the sound that travels within the monastery offers a
means for Hana to 'listen in' to the life experience of the patient, sometimes by means of conversation but also through overhearing things
that are not necessarily meant for her ears. Now, by listening and overhearing, she can learn from the patient's story and the emotional journey that leads to his eventual desire for death. Hana comes to accept
the transience of life, therefore, through a combination of the monastery's and the patient's encapsulation of physical impermanence.

Early episodes in the monastery emphasize the ability of sound to
traverse what is left of its physical boundaries. As Hana first enters the
library in her initial investigation, the sound of birdsong follows her,
consistent in volume to that heard outside. As she cuts her hair and
changes out of her army uniform, she sees and hears the patient
through a hole in the floor that opens into the ceiling of his room. He is
singing breathily to himself in Arabic, lost—we may assume from later
evidence—in a memory of the desert. She closes the window, shutting
out both the sight and the sound of the hospital convoy disappearing
into the distance, and proceeds to mend the broken staircase with
books from the library. Her first exchange with the patient in the monastery begins with a reference to both the pervasiveness and the indis-
tinctness of the sound she makes in doing this. He has heard the banging noises, but has misconstrued their possible source.[31]

Hana's soundworld finds an equivalent to the temporal transitions
of the patient's world in a series of key points at which its specific
qualities are foregrounded. Just as the patient progresses through his
continual moves into the past, Hana's progress through her own story
and therapy can be measured by these moments. The first occurs when
she plays the half-upturned piano in the library. The sound of the music
binds together the spaces in and around the monastery and gives the
scenes accompanied by her playing a firm sense of continuous time,
which is the very opposite of the patient's relationship to temporality.
As we cut to the patient and Caravaggio in the patient's room, the music's diminished volume and unbroken continuity signal its continued
diegetic status. Likewise, over the cut to a view of the monastery from
the surrounding countryside, the music remains constant, although appropriately altered in volume and tone to reflect its now distant source.

It is this latter view that is most important to Hana's progress. Through playing the piano, Hana is reversing the usual pattern of her soundworld. Rather than sound coming in from the outside, she is sending a sound signal, as it were, from the inside to the outside. The view from the countryside, ostensibly Kip's point of view as the music draws him to the monastery and Hana's side, demonstrates the absolute power of sound, or music, to permeate space and to form relationships between different spaces and the people within them. As Hana subsequently tells the patient: "My mother always told me I would summon my husband by playing the piano."[32] Although said in a light-hearted way, there is much truth in her mother's prediction. Hana may not end up marrying Kip, but as her lover he will unwittingly take on a vital role, in conjunction with the patient's more passive influence, in drawing her out of the monastery and back into life.

The permeating sound of diegetic music also draws the monastery and its community together in order to mark the second important stage of Hana's development. Caravaggio's gramophone record of *Cheek to Cheek* has just drawn the patient back from a memory of Cairo and we find that, as well as crossing the patient's two spaces, it is also crossing Hana's. After asking, in a parallel question to Katharine's in the past, whether the patient realizes that he is always singing, Hana attributes the same habit to Kip.[33] She looks out of the window and hears him, from some distance across the garden, humming a harmonizing line to the song. She continues listening to him as Caravaggio puts on a record of *Wang Wang Blues*, and then sets off on the spurious premise of taking him some olive oil for his hair. En route, she meets Sergeant Hardy and remembers him bringing her back from her reckless walk into the minefield that had killed Jan. She tells him she felt like a toddler next to him and, as he walks off, she laughs at his comic imitation, in time to the music, of a toddler's gait. Kip is humming along to the record, which is audible throughout the whole episode, as she reaches his encampment in the garden.

Although she has been out into the garden before, Kip's arrival has changed the nature of her relationship to this outside space. His singing acts as a response to her earlier piano playing by reaching back into the monastery with a sound that attracts her out to a greater degree than the usual birdsong. He makes her begin to want to leave the monastery, even if only within the confines of its garden walls, in order to be closer to him. Now Hana begins to look actively out of the windows and, instead of closing them onto the world as she did when she first arrived, she actually goes out willingly in response to what she hears and sees.

The key scenes that finally unite Hana and Kip, of course, begin as she finds the trail of tiny torchlights that he has left to lead her from the monastery to the barn. This trail offers a visual equivalent of his singing and, indeed, his very presence. As she follows it and enters the barn, Kip's voice emerges from the darkness behind her and she turns to find him, rehearsing once again the pattern of sound preceding sight and understanding. He has drawn her willingly from her shell, so that the following morning he can take her away from the monastery completely, to their own painted cave: 'their' church at Arezzo. When she is tested immediately after the beginning of this relationship, as Kip is called to deal with an unexploded bomb, she is therefore able to reverse the pattern of her past by leaving the monastery without a second thought. In seeking to actively *see* before she *hears* and to be with Kip as he possibly faces death, she lays to rest the ghosts that have plagued her character. Now that she has learned to face the prospect of death and loss, it only remains for her to accept their occasional inevitability.

This final stage in her therapy is offered, appropriately, by the patient. Hana has been shut out by Kip following the unexpected death of Hardy, which happened, true to form, when Kip was 'not looking.' She returns to the monastery and, as the sound of cooing doves retains the thought of the permeable structure and the outside world, she overhears the beginning of a conversation between Caravaggio and the patient. Through this, she hears her idealized Englishman confess his unwitting guilt of the crimes that Caravaggio has leveled at him from the outset. She also comes to understand, however, the sheer depth of his love for Katharine and his all-consuming grief at her death and, even more so, his culpability in failing to save her. In the end, she recognizes their dilemmas as one. Neither could save the people they loved from death.

As Hana contemplates the awful end of Almásy and Katharine's story, the cooing of the doves breaks through the silence once again. Kip leaves and the patient decides that it is time to die. Hana, still filled with grief in the face of loss, nevertheless now accepts its inevitability. By reading Katharine's letter to the dying patient, she overhears the intimate words of another voice from another space and time. As she hears, she finally understands the richness of life that cannot be overshadowed by death.

It is fitting, after all this, that Hana's final move from the monastery should be motivated once again by sound. She gazes nostalgically around the patient's now empty room until Caravaggio's insistent call from outside rouses her into action. She grabs the copy of Herodotus that holds a whole life's worth of lessons and guidance for her and runs out of the monastery and into her future.

# 5

# THE SCORE

## Introduction

As with any film score, it is impossible to consider the narrative role and signification of the score of *The English Patient* in isolation from the particular nature of the film's narrative structure, mode of narration, themes and issues. The construction, placement and development of themes and the relationship of the original score to the precomposed music, diegetic music and other elements of the soundtrack, reflect an enormous range of complex narrative concerns. These include overarching ideological questions, issues of individual subjectivity, memory and identity, and human commonality and connections across time and space.

The highly subjective nature of the diegetic sound and music tracks considered in chapter 4 is also relevant to a consideration of non-diegetic musical themes. Particularly in the case of the patient/Almásy, this plays a significant role in facilitating the narrative ambiguity discussed in chapter 3, whereby his emotions are placed within a wider context that allows the film to be simultaneously sympathetic and critical. Perhaps as a result of such overall narrative, sonic and musical complexity, however, the associations of themes in this score are not immediately and easily identifiable. In order to approach analysis, therefore, it is first of all necessary to consider an appropriate methodology.

# Yared's Approach

When Yared was first approached by Minghella with the musical parameters for the score, he did not realize that he would eventually have to write a piece to replace the *Aria* from the *Goldberg Variations*. While Minghella was shooting, he worked on the themes for which Minghella had originally evoked the idea of the style of Puccini.[1] His work on the 'Bach' theme then began during the editing process. He does not feel that he looked to the film itself in order to find his themes, but acknowledges that he looked at it very carefully when he reached the stage of fitting his cues to particular scenes.[2] He began by listening to *Szerelem, Szerelem* and, although he considered composing a piece to replace it, he eventually decided against it. For the themes composed during shooting, he wanted to do something "very simple." He sees the result as a group of four connected themes.[3]

Although he cannot say exactly how he arrived at the B minor cor anglais theme (called the *Desert Theme* in the analysis), his Eastern roots make the sound "something that is in his skin."[4] With this, there is an F minor theme (called the *Love Theme* in the analysis), a short theme referred to as the *Passage of Time Theme* in the analysis, and a strumming motif using the sampled sound of the quanoun (called the *Oriental Theme* in the analysis).[5] He feels, he says, that he could "build a symphony with these four themes, . . . so it's like as if in one piece of music [there was] all the material and potential to make it work."[6]

The second area of the score concerned the replacement of J. S. Bach. Yared saw this challenge as "the most fantastic and the most poisonous" for his confidence as a composer; nobody but Minghella, he says, has ever "brought him to try to replace Bach with a little prelude in G major."[7] In association with this G major theme (called the *New Life Theme* in the analysis), he composed a further B minor theme (called the *Mortality Theme* in the analysis). Yared sees almost the entire score as being based on these two groups of material, with everything else constituting variations thereon. The musical unity implied by such a conceptualization of the score is clear.

# Analytical Methodology

As this account of Yared's approach makes clear, he did not create his musical themes, initially at least, according to specific narrative events. His aim was rather, as is characteristic of his style, to capture the spirit of Minghella's narrative. It was Minghella and Murch who decided to a large extent how and where each theme should be deployed. Yared then worked on adapting and differentiating each cue according to its own particular circumstance. In the written score, therefore, it is the cues rather than the separate themes that are named.

This poses a problem in terms of analysis and makes it necessary to find some way of referring to the thematic links that exist and are developed between these cues. Yared did, of course, conceive the grouped themes, although connected, as distinct in themselves. Furthermore, as he himself points out, the separate themes of each group are dominant by turns in the score. During the process of deciding how the themes would be deployed and their subsequent rewriting, specific narrative connections have been made and developed in a normal thematic manner. Analysis would therefore be rendered extremely difficult without allocating a name to each of the themes.

In response to this, as a necessary part of analyzing the narrative role of the score, I have allocated names to the themes according to their most prevalent narrative associations as I perceive them. Before this analysis begins, I must therefore admit the possible subjectivity of my own reading, since the result of this method is, clearly, that themes will be named according to my own comprehension of the film. While it is surely true that all analysis must be subjective to a certain extent, I have nevertheless tried to remain as objective as possible by constantly challenging my own assumptions and decisions about the meanings of themes.

In a narrative that courts emotional and moral ambiguity and makes so many connections between apparently disparate characters and spaces, it is likely that the emotional connotations of the score will be broad. It soon became apparent, for example, that a conventional attachment of themes to individual characters or places made no sense whatsoever. In order to understand the full significance of each theme, it was necessary to account instead for its whole narrative context. This included the circumstances and the way in which it first appeared, how it operated in relation to character subjectivity and the point of view on events that it appeared to encourage. Added to this, was a consideration of how its meaning was altered, developed or enhanced as it moved through its various narrative contexts. Furthermore, I was able to incorporate Yared's own grouping of the themes. Since certain themes are musically related, it may be fair to assume that they will also be narratively related. Although I have eventually settled on

names for each of the themes that I hope are indicative of their narrative significance, these names are intended to be as broad and in some
cases as metaphorical as possible.

# The Score

> The world's musicians celebrate our differences . . . Gabriel Yared
> had the difficult task of unifying these differences into a coherent
> musical statement.[8]

> Added to that there is one of those musical scores . . . that swirls
> around you like an enveloping mist.[9]

## An Overview

Considering Yared's career as a whole, the score of *The English
Patient* does indeed offer a pivotal point between an old and new
working style. As was suggested in chapter 2's consideration of the
scores that followed this one, the basic methods of composition are
typical of those already in use in his previous work. The richness of
meaning in his themes, as well as his characteristic techniques of lyrical and sequential melodic construction, wide-ranging instrumental
color, foregrounding key melodic lines in solo instruments, ostinato
and drone basses, contrapuntal and interlocking textures and the eerie
and spiritual sound of the synthesizer are all present.

He did not author the whole score; it encompasses, overall, two
Hungarian folk songs, Arabic music, various American popular songs
and jazz classics, a Christmas carol, the British national anthem, an
operatic aria and, of course, J. S. Bach's *Goldberg Variations*. Yared's
original work, while unifying all these pieces into a nostalgic whole, is
nevertheless eclectic in its own right and reveals, as did his score for
*L'Amant*, his desire to combine his own Eastern and Western cultural
influences.

His instrumental palette encompasses a full symphony orchestra
with the addition of piano, harp, synthesizer, the sampled sound of the
quanoun and, occasionally, the improvisatory female voice of the
Hungarian folk song, and the range of his instrumental variations is
easily as impressive as any of his earlier scores. His score absorbs the
'Eastern' sound of the song into a largely nineteenth-century Romantic
idiom and, although the themes are distinctive in their own right, they

are unified in both musical and narrative terms through the sharing of particular features and motifs. They encapsulate meaning at a profound and extremely subtle level, often connoting ideas, themes and conundrums that are never explicitly worked out anywhere else in the filmic text. Even the integration of the non-diegetic score with the diegetic music and sound is typical, although in this particular case, this was also the work of Minghella and Murch (see chapter 4 and specific instances later in this chapter).

In other ways, however, the score reveals itself as developmental of Yared's style. Although, as I explained above, I have made certain decisions about the signification and related naming of themes and motifs, it is nevertheless the case that the themes in this score are used a great deal more fluidly than is typical of previous scores. While the extraction of short motifs enables the extremely meaningful scoring of very brief moments in time, a tendency to combine themes and motifs across cues also begins to appear, thus allowing for the fluidity in temporal and spatial transition that Minghella desired.

Finally, of course, the shaping of the score to dialogue and action is a notable development. The working method already described involved Minghella and Murch allocating cues to scenes in order that Yared could rewrite them to fit more precisely. As a result, Yared's music is often married at a level of minute detail with the scenes that it accompanies. Combined with the powerful emotional and narrative connotation of the music itself, this makes for an unusually intimate and involving score.

## Themes

Before considering their placement, full narrative significance and development, this section will introduce the themes of the score in terms of basic musical patterns and connections with other themes. While the themes can be grouped in the film very generally according to the temporal spaces in which they belong or the character to whose subjectivity they are most closely linked, they will be presented here in the order that they first appear, with the exception of the *Mortality* and *New Life* themes. These are presented together because of their particularly close narrative and musical relationship.

The musical examples, however, do not necessarily show the form in which the themes first appear. The nature of thematic development in this score means that, firstly, many of the themes do not appear in their fullest and most representative form until some way into the score. Secondly—and typically of Yared's technique as described in chapter 2—following the complex courses and interrelationships of the characters' emotional trajectories as closely as they do, some themes undergo such constant development and change that it is virtually impossible to identify typical examples. In such cases, the examples used are representative of the themes in terms of what appear to be their most consistent features.

*The Hungarian Theme*
The film opens with the Hungarian folk song *Szerelem, Szerelem*, the distinctive style and vocal sound of which return throughout the film in the form of improvisation around other themes and in the *Lullaby for Katharine* that appears for Katharine's final living scene in the Cave of Swimmers. Although these are, strictly speaking, independent musical pieces and improvisations, the fact that they share a distinctly recognizable relationship in terms of general idiom and sound suggests that they may be considered, in terms of their narrative function, as a 'themed' group. Given Almásy's explanation of the origins of the piece, and for clarity of reference, this grouping will be named collectively as the *Hungarian Theme*. Although it is not developed in a conventional thematic manner, the original song will be used as an example of the theme's characteristic features (figure 5.1).[10]

Figure 5.1: *The English Patient* (1996).
*Szerelem, Szerelem* (The *Hungarian Theme*): Minor third bracketed.
Words and Music by (Traditional) arranged by Márta Sebestyén.
© Copyright 1998 Ryko Music (100%).
Used By Permission of Music Sales Limited.
All Rights Reserved. International Copyright Secured.

Eventually designated as a source of comforting nostalgia from Almásy's childhood, this song has a gentle, rhythmically and harmonically fluid improvisatory sound. The pitch range is limited largely to one octave and the melody is freely and elaborately ornamented. Its ambiguous 'Eastern' sound, as outlined in chapter 4, contains the essence of the film's thematic concern with nationhood and identity. As Minghella says: "It's part of the mystery of the story; it becomes a puzzle to find the music. It's not from a Western or European background. . . . [I]t does have strong Arabic influences, but it's mostly from old Hungarian traditions."[11]

## The Desert Theme

The instrumentation, melodic pattern and ornamentation of this theme place it halfway between the Eastern sound of the *Hungarian Theme* and the solidly Western orchestral sound of the *Love Theme*. It contrasts in turn the poignant voices of the cor anglais and the clarinet with the mellow female voice of the *Hungarian Theme*, in a melody which is usually accompanied and which has a less fluid rhythm and a more regular sense of meter and phrasing. The influence of the *Hungarian Theme* remains, however, in several features. The pitch range is similar, as is the basic melodic style, particularly with the adoption of a freer improvisatory style as the *Desert Theme* progresses.

This new theme casts an initially darker shadow by adopting the contour of *Szerelem, Szerelem*'s descending perfect fifth anacrusis, but narrowing it to recall the overall minor third span of the song's first phrase. This minor third interval then becomes a structural motif of the *Desert Theme*'s opening phrase and a recurrent motif of the theme as a whole. The slow pace and steady rhythm, together with the doleful solo voice, minor tonality and the temporary tension caused by the sustained seventh note (figure 5.2, bar 5), suggests a deep sadness and longing.

The small hint of ornamentation in the second phrase, however, prepares for the much freer elaboration and chromaticism of the third and fourth phrases, which open with a sudden temporary shift into a brighter major tonality. The melody now becomes much more constricted in its range, emphasizing increasingly ornamented approaches to sustained notes over minor and diminished seventh harmonies. This introduces an element of growing tension, which is then dispelled, if only slightly, as the melody line falls again to end unresolved in anticipation of either its own repetition or transition to another theme.

Figure 5.2: *The English Patient.*
The *Desert Theme* Melody: Minor thirds bracketed.
Written by Gabriel Yared.
Used by permission of Tiger Moth Music/Fantasy, Inc.
All Rights Reserved.

### The Oriental Theme

This theme epitomizes the ornamental approach to connoting 'Eastern' narrative elements that characterizes the *Hungarian* and *Desert* themes. It is used to suggest Almásy's romantic vision of the desert as a space of Otherness. It features the distinctively oriental sound of the quanoun and has a basic 3-note melody, extended by the repetition of each note and their decorative introduction by glissandi (figure 5.3). The first semitone interval of the melodic ascent is then inverted in the 2-note descending figure that ends the line. If the theme is repeated it raises the highest pitch of the melody by a further minor third.

Figure 5.3: *The English Patient.*
The *Oriental Theme.*
Written by Gabriel Yared.
Used by permission of Tiger Moth Music/Fantasy, Inc.
All Rights Reserved.

*The Mortality Theme and the New Life Theme*

Both the *Mortality Theme* (figure 5.4) and its later counterpart the *New Life Theme* (figure 5.5) are based in broad stylistic and formal terms on the music that Hana plays at the piano in the monastery. The development between the themes and the way in which this reflects on Hana's narrative and emotional development, is predicted in her own diegetic musical movement from the slow, pensive *Aria* of Bach's *Goldberg Variations* into an extract of its more buoyant first variation.

The strong narrative link between Hana's preoccupation with mortality and her decision to retreat into the monastery is reflected musically in the structure of the *Mortality Theme*. It adopts the same prevailing minor tonality as the *Desert Theme*, which accompanies her discovery of the monastery, and the same minor third interval as the principal structural element of its opening phrase. The descending minor third of the *Desert Theme* is inverted, however, into an ascending pair of notes decorated with a Baroque turn. After being repeated a tone higher, it is expanded and momentarily brightened into a major third at the beginning of the following phrase (figure 5.4, bars 9–10), and although this more positive sound is countered to some extent by the phrase's offbeat, unsettled meter, it does end with a modulation into major tonality. There may be hope, this suggests, in the midst of Hana's despair.

Figure 5.4: *The English Patient.*
The *Mortality Theme*: Opening minor third pattern and offbeat rhythm.
Written by Gabriel Yared.
Used by permission of Tiger Moth Music/Fantasy, Inc.
All Rights Reserved.

The following sequential chromatic descent, however, darkens the tone once again with its tortured twists and turns, and although the final phrase juxtaposes two sequentially ascending melodies in counterpoint, a final descending scale defeats their rising optimism and leads to a minor key resolution.

The *New Life Theme* replaces the minor tonality and the hesitant, offbeat rhythms of the *Mortality Theme* with fluid, perpetual motion and a bright major key. The initial smooth upward sweep through a clear major arpeggio cuts through the tortured chromaticism of the previous theme like the positive tonic that Kip's presence becomes to Hana.

Figure 5.5: *The English Patient.*
The *New Life Theme.*
Written by Gabriel Yared.
Used by permission of Tiger Moth Music/Fantasy, Inc.
All Rights Reserved.

The melody progresses easily, separating momentarily into two contrapuntal voices before being reunited for a final cadence that once again emphasizes major over minor tonality.

*The Love Theme, the Loss Motif and the Passage of Time Theme*
    It is not only Almásy's relationship with the desert that begins with the opening titles. As the film progresses, the mysterious opening image is contextualized as pivotal to his relationship with Katharine. The painting takes place in the Cave of Swimmers—the reflection of both the monastery and the church in the present and the place where Almásy will eventually bring his lover to die. Katharine is the artist, and this and her other paintings become the means of final connection between the couple, as the objects of exchange through which she gains her vital access to Almásy's book and his notes about "K."[12] It is to Katharine alone that Almásy reveals the opening song's diegetic identity and their relationship to which he humorously relates it.

    Musically, the growth of Almásy's passion for Katharine is also expressed by the development of the *Love Theme* from a fragment of the opening song. The theme borrows the lilt of the anacrusis beat to lead into a simplified version of the structural minor third of the song's first phrase. This pattern becomes the *Love Theme*'s principal structural motif (bracketed in figure 5.6) and as such, carries a multitude of meanings.

It is absolutely appropriate that the phrase of the song from which this theme derives, translates, at least according to Almásy, as "love, love."[13] At the same time, however, the minor third interval creates a link with the *Desert* and *Mortality* themes that imbues the *Love Theme*, throughout the score, with an inherent sense of sadness and even foreboding that can only be deepened with the additional knowledge of the song's particular signification for Almásy. The motif is repeated in sequential descent, which counters its own constant striving toward ascent. The second repeat heralds the end of the theme, which takes one of two forms: either a short 3-note descending variation on the anacrusis beat, which leads to a repeat of the whole theme, or an extension of the main motif's ascent that either leads into a repeat of the theme or acts as its conclusion (figure 5.6). The latter is the most prevalent and even enjoys some independent appearances, not least as the very first introduction to the *Love Theme* within the score. The nature and placement of these independent appearances, as well as the particular meaning that seems to be contained within the motif, make it worth singling out and naming in its own right as the *Loss Motif.*

The *Loss Motif* begins with the pattern of the basic *Love Theme* motif (figure 5.6). As it reaches the usual final note, however, it continues the ascent, increasing its pace and sense of fluidity through the use of triplet crotchets. This suddenly excited, anticipatory ascent is interrupted as the melody hesitates momentarily on the dotted rhythmic pattern of the *Love Theme*'s anacrusis figure, which, although still on the final beat of the bar, is now incorporated into the melodic line. This provides a last rhythmic drive toward the final cadence, which in turn suggests the problematization of eventual resolution. The sighing appoggiatura of the final cadence is so dominant that, even when resolving into a major key, it is sufficiently strong to overpower any positive connotations with a sense of intense regret and loss.

The culmination in the yearning sound of the appoggiatura links this theme strongly to the *Passage of Time Theme* (figure 5.7), with which it appears in close juxtaposition as the patient moves back into the past for his first meeting with Katharine. The *Passage of Time Theme*'s sighing melodic contour, high pitch and the breathy timbre of its string and flute orchestration give it an ethereal feel appropriate to the ideas of movement backward and forward in time and the irretrievability of history. Its sustained first note followed by a descent in tight semitones, together with its major and minor shifts, suggest turmoil, pain and sadness. This feeling is emphasized by the sudden ascending phrase that ends with a regretful sighing appoggiatura over an unresolved minor seventh chord. A short accompaniment figure moving in contrary motion against the contour of the appoggiatura and ending tantalizingly on the seventh note, emphasizes the sense of anticipation and therefore the eventual thwarting of resolution (figure 5.14, bar 2).

Figure 5.6: *The English Patient.*
The *Love Theme*: Alternative theme endings and the *Loss Motif.*
Written by Gabriel Yared.
Used by permission of Tiger Moth Music/Fantasy, Inc.
All Rights Reserved.

Figure 5.7: *The English Patient.*
The *Passage of Time Theme.*
Written by Gabriel Yared.
Used by permission of Tiger Moth Music/Fantasy, Inc.
All Rights Reserved.

This musical-narrative juxtaposition creates a powerful association of love, loss and the irretrievability of the past. This then inflects every repetition of the *Love Theme* in particular with the patient's recollection of the couple's eventual fate—even in their most ecstatic moments and even when their meetings are deeply embedded in the more extensive flashbacks.

## Overall Musical Unity and Narrative Connections

As well as the narrative-musical connections linking specific themes, there are also a number of musical ideas that perform more pervasive, overarching functions across the score as a whole. The ornamentation that links *Szerelem, Szerelem* to the *Desert* and *Oriental* themes, for example, can also be seen to extend into the present world of the monastery and Hana's emotional trajectory. Although in quite a different style, the Baroque ornamentation of the Bach *Aria* and the *Mortality Theme*, and the free, fluid perpetual motion of the *New Life Theme*, echo their oriental counterparts. This is emphasized by the *Mortality Theme*'s initially fragmented appearance at the point of Jan's death, where it is linked through the similar sound of the oboe to the *Desert Theme*'s cor anglais (figure 5.11). As the film comes to a close, as if to ensure that this point has not been missed, the *New Life Theme* and the improvisatory voice of the *Hungarian Theme* finally merge together in the amorphous space offered by the closing titles. The idea of racial and national boundaries that the film is at such pains to both present and break down, is therefore reflected in an overall musical scheme that compares, contrasts and unites two apparently very different musical worlds.

The breaking or denying of boundaries is a positive feature of both the score and the soundtrack as a whole. It is evoked in turn by particular compositional techniques, the merging of diegetic music and sound effects and the passing of musical themes between characters and temporal spaces. Yared uses tied notes and his characteristic interlocking contrapuntal textures, for example, not only to undermine the hierarchies of meter, barline and melodic voice leading, but in the case of counterpoint, also to emphasize the interdependence of otherwise individual lines.

The first example of this comes with the freedom of *Szerelem, Szerelem*, but the techniques are used both separately and together throughout the score to many different effects that reflect the range of uses across several films identified in chapter 2. These include the sheer violence of Hana's shock at Jan's death (figure 5.8), her sense of hope and freedom on discovering the monastery (figure 5.9), the

oneiric quality of the planes flying above the desert and a first memory
of love (figures 5.14 and 5.15), the desperate exhaustion of Hana's
grief and the lightness of spirit that comes with the beginning of her
new life (figure 5.20).

Figure 5.8: *The English Patient.*
Cue title: *Jan's Death* [as Hana runs toward the burning jeep].
Written by Gabriel Yared.
Used by permission of Tiger Moth Music/Fantasy, Inc.
All Rights Reserved.

Equally pervasive is Yared's hallmark use of the pedal note or
drone. This has a strong narrative link to the sound of the airplane engine that is heard so constantly throughout the story, heralding many
pivotal narrative events. It is heard for the first time as the opening
titles move into the shot of Almásy and Katharine flying over the desert and often fulfills a similar role in aiding the transition from present
into past, as if the sound of the engine is a constant element of the patient's memory. The eerie density and depth of this initial musical
drone was, in fact, created by processing a chorus of male voices
through a synthesizer. The drone of the airplane engine was then tuned
to the same tone in order to emerge seamlessly from the end of the
cue.[14]

Throughout the score, drones and pedal notes are used to a typically wide range of effects. They are layered to increase the sense of suspense as Almásy discovers the Cave of Swimmers; building gradually from low to high pitches into a whole texture of sustained notes, they reflect his growing anticipation of what he may have found. Their sense of stasis is also used to underline a different kind of suspense in the moment when Hana looks out of her army truck and realizes what has happened to Jan (figure 5.11). The same technique also, however, supports a sense of freedom of movement in other voices—such as the underpinning of the *Desert Theme* at the opening of the film and as Almásy carries Katharine to the Cave of Swimmers—or helps ground melodies in a sense of calm (figure 5.9).

The most important boundaries that the film seeks to erode—those between past and present and the stories of its principal characters—are expressed in the crossing between temporal and geographical spaces of the *Desert* and *Mortality* and to some extent the *Oriental* themes. In particular, the *Desert* and *Mortality* themes' fluid disregard for the conventional fidelity of theme to character allows them to evoke broader conceptual associations and connections. The progress and development of each of these themes plays a major role in the effective collapsing of Almásy and Hana's worlds.

## Thematic Placement and Development

*The Hungarian Theme*

It's a folk song.
Arabic?
No, no, it's Hungarian.[15]

Although *Szerelem, Szerelem* appears in its original form only once more after the opening titles, and then diegetically, it is continually recalled through the weaving of the female voice around the *Desert* and *Passage of Time* themes, as well as in the *Lullaby for Katharine* in the Cave of Swimmers. These musical instances, looking backward and forward from Almásy's explanation of its origins, cast the shadow of his romantic evocation of an irretrievably lost past over particular events in the desert. His use of the song to encompass himself and Katharine in a legitimate relationship, furthermore, echoes her evocation of her "different life"[16] and, considering the song's own ambiguous identity, also suggests it as a signifier of their shared fantasy of fluid national, social and marital boundaries. The romanticization of both a lost past and a war-torn present and the failure of the world to live up to the couple's unworldly ideals, contributes to the almost childlike loneliness of Katharine's death.

## The Desert Theme

We are the real countries.[17]

This is the only theme that occurs across all the temporal spaces of the narrative, appearing in various forms in the stories of Almásy and Katharine in the desert, Hana and the patient at the monastery and Caravaggio in Tobruk. Such flexibility suggests a broad meaning that connects the characters' experiences. It is the first fully non-diegetic theme to be heard in the film, appearing as a bridge during the title sequence between the song that will later be located diegetically and the opening desert scene. While this first appearance suggests a link to the desert as a place, however, later appearances also suggest the possible significance of the desert in a wider metaphorical sense. The theme appears most frequently in association with particularly fateful moments in Almásy and Katharine's relationship that occur specifically in the desert rather than Cairo. This suggests the connection of the theme to both the physical and metaphorical role of the desert in the course of their relationship.

The theme first appears as the final detail of the opening painting reveals its human subject. The solo cor anglais introduces an immediately melancholy and plaintive tone, emphasizing the melody's minor mode with its opening descending minor third. The contour of the melody and its ornamentation are imitative of the opening song, but the instrumentation, slow pace and minor mode invest it with a heavy sense of sorrow. The drone accompaniment of lower strings and a mixture of synthesizers and male bass voices ensures the prominence of the solo instrument. Then, as the painted figure dissolves into desert dunes and the shadow of a small plane flying above them, this accompaniment blends evocatively and imperceptibly into the sound of the airplane engine. As the desert sands appear, the melody is embellished first by the quanoun playing descending pairs of notes and then by the reintroduction of the female voice of the opening song weaving wordlessly around the melody.

As we learn more about Almásy and his childhood song, the full reflection of his character and his relationship to the desert in this opening arrangement become clear. The quintessentially English pastoral sound of the cor anglais appears in the midst of a song that we later learn is Hungarian. Rather than taking us to the English countryside, it summons up an image of the desert as its sound is transformed by its partnership with the quanoun and its own free, chromatic ornamentation. When the voice returns, we are faced with a musical melting pot of Hungarian, English and Middle Eastern identities. Almásy and Katharine, seen for the first time flying over the desert, are presented through the doleful sound of this international blend, which maintains the emotional tone of their flight despite the subsequent violent assertion of national boundaries by the German army.

The arrangement suggests that the theme represents more than just the desert itself, but rather Almásy's stubborn and fateful projection of his personal needs and desires onto its geography, physicality and culture. As the various consequences of his actions transpire, it recalls his belief in the borderless purity of the desert and renders his dogged romanticism increasingly tragic. Transported to both Hana and Caravaggio's stories, it then suggests the narrative parallels and connections that bind them all together. Hana's retreat is introduced through the same theme, suggesting her monastery and Almásy's desert as parallel conceptual spaces. Later, as Caravaggio reaches the conclusion of his story, a variation of the theme in combination with the *Oriental Theme* marks his torture and mutilation as a fateful result of Almásy's naïvely selfish actions in the desert.

As the theme moves into Hana's world, it undergoes a major transformation. It appears as she approaches the monastery for the first time, seeking a place of refuge from the evidence of human mortality that she can no longer stand, and thus linking her emotional trajectory and its reflection in the monastery to the patient's opening scenes in the desert. A harp ostinato, maintaining rhythmic regularity and a sense of tranquility, introduces and accompanies the melody in the solo clarinet (figure 5.9). While clearer and less melancholy in timbre than the cor anglais, this solo voice still strikes a dolefully solitary tone. Muted strings underpin the texture with sustained pedal notes and, in the second statement of the theme, a slightly more prominent interlocking counter melody that offers a resolution to the final hovering note of the first melodic phrase. The clarinet takes advantage of the regular ostinato bass to play in a fluid rhythm, subverting the sense of meter with anacrusis beats, long tied notes and smooth triplet semiquavers. The mood of the cue is therefore one of peaceful tranquility, with the suggestion of a partnership between the instruments offering both freedom and resolution.

Figure 5.9: *The English Patient.*
The *Desert Theme*: Hana discovers the monastery.
Written by Gabriel Yared.
Used by permission of Tiger Moth Music/Fantasy, Inc.
All Rights Reserved.

The tone of her 'monastery' arrangement changes, however, as Hana is at last left alone with her patient. He asks why she is so determined to keep him alive. Her answer, "[B]ecause I'm a nurse,"[18] and her sad facial expression, remind us of the reason for her retreat. The following cut to her solitary game of hopscotch and the reappearance of the clarinet melody, alone at first and then interspersed by the fractured appearance of the harp ostinato, therefore link her sad words and facial expression back to her discovery of the monastery, emphasizing the loneliness of her trauma with its tentative solo voice.

Returned to the world of the patient's flashback, the development of the theme continues in a different vein as Katharine tells the story of Candaules and Gyges. Her rendition appears heavy with insinuation in Almásy's direction and the theme punctuates the story at the points that appear to resonate most powerfully between them. This variation returns to the cor anglais and rearranges the three principal notes of the theme into a highly ornamented descending pattern that emphasizes its stylistic and thematic relationship to both the *Hungarian* and *Oriental* themes (figure 5.10).

Figure 5.10: *The English Patient.*
The *Desert Theme*: Katharine tells the story of Candaules and Gyges.
Written by Gabriel Yared.
Used by permission of Tiger Moth Music/Fantasy, Inc.
All Rights Reserved.

Played unobtrusively over a drone accompaniment, this figure casts its ominous shadow as the Queen sees Gyges watching her and as her ultimatum causes her husband's murder. Musically, it looks both backward and forward in the narrative. It recalls both the title sequence, with the mysterious artist who later transpires as Katharine, and the opening scenes in the desert. Combining the music from these scenes at this precise point suggests their resonance with the Candaules and Gyges story and extends the story as a likely pattern for the future of the couple. It is indeed from this point in the patient's reminiscences that both the *Hungarian* and *Desert* themes begin to mark the most fateful moments in their romance.

The theme reappears, once again in juxtaposition with the voice of the *Hungarian Theme*, as Almásy discovers the Cave of Swimmers and calls the others to see it. As we watch him smiling at the sight of the swimming figures that we have yet to see, the *Desert Theme* begins at its halfway point, the cor anglais sounding over a sustained string and synthesizer drone. It continues with string orchestral accompaniment as he runs outside and calls the others, and its return to a more regular, less fluid rhythm than at the monastery casts a heavy, fatalistic tone over their hurried movements. As we see the painted figures illuminated by torchlight, the *Desert Theme* gives way to the improvisatory line of the *Hungarian Theme* interspersed with the *Oriental Theme*. A cut to a close-up of a painting in progress then rhymes with the opening titles, before opening out to resolve the mystery of the artist's identity as the music ends. The Cave of Swimmers is thus musically bound into Almásy and Katharine's romantic trajectory, linking it already to both the beginning and the end of their story.

Although it remains as yet unconsummated, a key point in the beginning of their romance comes when Katharine confronts Almásy with the question of whether she is "'K' in [his] book[.]"[19] The *Desert Theme* now appears in its sparest form, with the solo clarinet of Hana's monastery arrangement playing completely unaccompanied. This suggests both the passion and tragedy of the forthcoming romance. The shared theme draws them together and the solo instrument suggests intensity and intimacy. It also, however, evokes the idea of loneliness. Hana's isolation at the villa is projected by the theme's arrangement onto Katharine and Almásy's potential relationship. Drawn together though they are, they can have no future as a couple.

Although the theme does not reappear in the context of the desert until after the end of the relationship, it does, in the interim, accompany Caravaggio's torture and mutilation in Tobruk. The rapid editing of the scene, intensified by the visible distress of the German soldiers and Caravaggio's screams, is underpinned by the same variation of the *Desert Theme* that punctuated Katharine's fateful rendition of the story of Candaules and Gyges (figure 5.10). The use of the *Oriental Theme* before and after this variation consolidates the association of this event with Almásy. Not only is this torture a direct result of Almásy's selfish actions in the desert, but it is also determined according to the Islamic punishment for adultery. Katharine and Almásy's concurrent naïveté in presuming the Otherness of Cairo and the desert—as well as the historical precedent offered by Herodotus—as a license for infidelity, is therefore thrown into stark and portentous relief.

Once the secret of their connection is known, the patient is compelled to justify his actions from his own point of view. The appearance of the theme's 'desert' instrumentation in the monastery, as he breaks down at the final realization of his role in Katharine's death, signals the catching up of the past with the present and the closure of the presumed gap between the two. The patient can no longer see his own past as something completely separate from his present experience—something over which he had no control or something completely discrete from the experiences of others. Caravaggio acts as an agent from that past, reconfiguring it from the point of view of a firsthand witness, living proof of an aspect of his past that the patient had never considered and does not really understand.

The patient's realization returns us once more to the past and Geoffrey's fatal plane crash. As Almásy realizes that Katharine is in the wreckage, the score recalls their earlier fateful moments and in particular—through the similarity of the arrangement—their first appearance flying over the desert. Once again it begins with the solo cor anglais over a gradual layering of pedal notes in the strings. The melody is returned to its stricter rhythmic pattern, leaving behind the fluidity of its clarinet version to return to its former weighty sense of tragedy.

The second statement of the theme then begins on the cut to Almásy carrying Katharine along the cliff edge toward the Cave of Swimmers. The dramatic visual change from intimate to epic scale is mirrored in the music, as the first two phrases of this statement are also suddenly expanded into the theme's fullest and most complex arrangement. The move back to the intimate scale of the couple's conversation is then reflected once again in the reduction of the musical texture, the solo cor anglais reemerging for the third phrase with the melody over a predominantly pedal note accompaniment in the strings and woodwind. As this second statement comes to an end, its final note sounds a tone higher than usual and is played over a sparse orchestral texture. The sudden change in texture and melodic line is striking, and the underlying timpani roll anticipates a tense accumulation of fragmentary phrases across the whole orchestra in preparation for the *Desert Theme*'s climactic resolution, after Katharine's dramatic confession, into the *Love Theme*.

As Almásy prepares the cave for Katharine and gives her the copy of Herodotus as "a good read"[20] to keep her company, the film and its music once again looks backward and forward in time. The parallel story of Candaules and Gyges is recalled through reference to the book, particularly now that its prophecy has been fulfilled. At the same time, looking forward, it reminds us that by the time we return to the present space of the monastery, Katharine and, in effect, Almásy, will also be dead. The increasing proximity of past and present, and the gradual revelation of how one has led to the other, is reflected in the movement of the music of the monastery, in two stages, into the space of the past. Firstly, the harp ostinato that gave Hana's retreat its steady basis accompanies the cor anglais, thus suggesting the parallels between her and Almásy's experiences. He too will try to save someone from the moment of death in order to fulfill his own desires and needs, to prove that his love for Katharine can overcome all worldly barriers and borders. The cave, the monastery, Almásy, Katharine and Hana are collapsed together. As the score then transfers Hana's complete 'monastery' arrangement to Almásy's three-day trek across the desert, their bleak emotional landscapes are fully united.

This union continues in the present with the patient's final admission of the culpability of his name and his love in Katharine's death. The theme appears once again in the solo clarinet, recalling both Hana's emotional loneliness in her retreat and the first point of no return between the lovers in the desert. Coming full circle as a theme that connects the emotional experiences of the patient and Hana, the solo clarinet now signifies the patient's desolate realization of his tragically naïve role in his own fate. Likewise, the 'desert' arrangement of the theme appears as Hana, being driven away from the monastery after his death, looks back one last time at her disappearing retreat. This is the first time since her game of hopscotch that the theme has accompanied her experience and the first time at all that the 'desert' arrangement has been related to her point of view. Just as the patient's dilemma was revealed as so close to Hana's, so perhaps Hana now realizes how much her monastery reflected his desert and his cave.

*The Passage of Time Theme*

Are you remembering more?[21]

This short theme is introduced as a conclusion to the *Desert Theme*'s first statement, as Almásy attempts to free Katharine and then himself from his burning plane, before the image is engulfed in flames. This suggests that the theme's transitional musical qualities are being used to represent the pivotal nature of this moment for Almásy. It is the point, in effect, at which his life ends. It is therefore only his life up to this point that will have to be reckoned with before he can be allowed to complete his extremely lengthy death process.

The theme appears at many of the patient's transitions between past and present and emphasizes moments of particular proximity between the temporal spaces, such as when Hana and Katharine tell the story of Candaules and Gyges and as Katharine's hand reaches from the midst of the desert sandstorm to touch the patient's face at the monastery. Thus, as Almásy first discovers the Cave of Swimmers, the theme suggests its portentous symbolic status as a pivotal space between past and present, life and death, water and aridity. In this particular context, the cave's fateful role is compounded with the appearance of the *Desert Theme*. Both themes and their connotations eventually coincide as Almásy carries Katharine into the cave after the plane crash. This is a space where life becomes a memory and, accordingly, the final appearance of the theme comes later as Almásy lies next to Katharine's dead body and speaks the name that she can no longer hear.

This theme does not undergo the same level of variation as the *Desert*, *Mortality* and *Love* themes, but is often used in conjunction with the *Desert* and *Love* themes as a means of emphasizing the subjective narrative framework of the patient's memory. Particularly in its final appearance, its usual string orchestration combines with the female voice of the *Hungarian Theme* and the cor anglais of the *Desert Theme* to unite aspects of Almásy's identity, romanticism, self-delusion and deception in Katharine's death.

### The Oriental Theme

Own the desert.[22]

This theme is heard in its entirety for the first time as we move back from Hana with the army hospital train to Almásy's injured body being carried across the desert, although it has already been prepared for by the incorporation of its distinctive instrument, the quanoun, in the *Desert Theme*'s first appearance. Despite not being specifically associated with the patient's point of view in this first instance, it does appear to reflect his subjectivity. Its place in the sound and music world of the film is with those sounds that mark Cairo and the desert as a place of Otherness, contrasting starkly with the Western sounds of the orchestral score, popular songs, jazz music and the hotel dance band.

Indeed, the extremely distinctive sound of the quanoun means that only a few notes, independently or in conjunction with another theme, can evoke Almásy's view of Eastern Otherness. Such Romanticism can then be contrasted with the greater pragmatism and worldliness of the other characters or the very real events happening under Almásy's nose—often as a consequence of his own naïve actions. It appears, for example, as Caravaggio is about to be tortured according to traditional Muslim law in a modern political context as a result of Almásy's exchange with the Germans. It also appears, finally, as Hana listens unseen to the end of the patient's narration of his story, as he admits his own very particular social and national culpability in Katharine's death.

*The Mortality Theme*

I'm in love with ghosts. So is he. He's in love with ghosts.[23]

This theme is first introduced as Hana reacts to the sudden death of her best friend Jan. It marks the first time that any music has been heard in connection with her character and remains the theme with which she is most closely associated throughout the film. Its relatively infrequent use, however, together with the very particular placing of its appearances, raises the question of its fuller narrative significance. For, like the relationship of the *Desert Theme* and Almásy, rather than expressing 'Hana' as a personality, this theme encapsulates her equation with a particular narrative theme and its development. This allows a more flexible movement of the musical theme between her character and others as the issues that she represents also touch them. The theme thus serves to suggest the paralleling and even interdependence of her story and the emotional trajectories of both Kip and the patient.

Hana is defined from the outset as being traumatized by personal loss and her own powerlessness to prevent such loss. This is reflected in her retreat into the monastery, her desire to prolong the moment of the patient's death and her narrative rhyming with the monastery in terms of both its physical state and its parallels with the desert. Hana and the patient must each accept that personal emotions and individualist principles are tragically misplaced in the face of war. Hana must accept that she can no more prevent death than bring back those already dead and the patient must accept responsibility for the deaths caused by his own obstinate naïveté. Kip, on the other hand, must learn to acknowledge the unavoidable presence of love in war, and the necessity of pain in a context where death cannot always be cheated and emotions cannot be shut out at will for the sake of professionalism. All three characters have to come to terms with the relationship of love and death in different ways and this theme becomes a key reflection of this common trajectory.

Despite this commonality, however, the theme remains most significantly associated with Hana and reflects principally on her emotional development. Its first appearance represents her interiority and narrative positioning in a very precise way. Later appearances then link it to her piano playing in the monastery library, when she gives a joyous rendition of the *Aria* and part of the first variation of Bach's *Goldberg Variations*. This music seems out of kilter with her emotional state, suggesting instead a temporary escape to the pleasure of musical expression and perhaps the memory of childhood piano lessons, just as Almásy recalls the childhood comforts of his *daijke*'s voice through his Hungarian folk song. The non-diegetic score, however, always the site of emotional truth, takes Hana's diegetic musical language as a means of expressing her true interiority. The *Mortality Theme*, written in the style of Bach, is slow and melancholy, expressing a terrible sense of loneliness and fragility and, until the very end of the film, a hopeless sense of suspension and the absence of a proper resolution.

The first appearance of the theme combines a sense of Hana's desperate fear of loss with the full force of her grief. As she looks in the direction of the explosion that has killed Jan, it begins in the minor mode with an oboe line marked *libre* over a drone bass in the first violins (figure 5.11). The short phrases of the theme's melody are thus momentarily suspended like little disjointed fragments over a texture of sustained notes, interspersed with soft supporting notes in the horns and a plaintively extended appoggiatura note in the clarinet.

Figure 5.11: *The English Patient.*
The *Mortality Theme.* Cue title: *Jan's Death* [as Hana realizes what
has happened to her friend].
Written by Gabriel Yared.
Used by permission of Tiger Moth Music/Fantasy, Inc.

As Hana realizes what has happened, she runs toward the burning
jeep. The music switches suddenly to a strictly *a tempo* 12/8 rhythm
underpinned by a jagged interlocking pattern in the strings (figure 5.8).
Over this the first violins play a 4-note motif incorporating dramatic
leaps and ending unresolved on a sustained note as the driving pattern
in the strings dies away. As Hana is caught by a colleague and is seen
crying desperately in long shot beside the site of her best friend's
death, this sustained note provides a drone under a repetition of the
two melodic phrases that opened the cue. In her apparently unending
grief, Hana cuts as small and isolated a figure as these disjointed melodic fragments.

As it reappears throughout the film, the theme reflects Hana's
gradual emotional development and the relationship of this development to other characters and their own predicaments. The full melodic

line and form of the theme become clear as Hana is woken from an upsetting dream by the patient and leaves him to sleep while she washes in the kitchen. The theme is orchestrated on this occasion for a faintly echoing, muted string quartet—a timbre that adds to the wistfulness and ancientness suggested by its now clearly Baroque style and slower and more regular pacing.

The melody begins with a slow sequential ascent from its tonic note of B, ornamenting its minor third steps with turns. The accompaniment is sparse and its accented, separated, regularly paced notes give a labored feel to the theme's movement. The faltering ascent of the melody continues into the beginning of a phrase based on the 4-note violin motif from the moment of Jan's death. Built on an interlocking texture, it is now transformed from the drama of the *Jan's Death* cue into a delicate and tentative structure. The melodic intervals are much narrower than the corresponding phrase of the previous cue and after an initial strain to continue its ascent, it settles at a lower pitch. The meter of the phrase is disrupted by the use of anticipatory notes tied over the barline and the accenting of weak beats that drag at the pace of the melody and delay harmonic movement. The ending of the phrase on a rare major chord is then immediately countered by its semitonal slide into a diminished seventh chord. This heralds a slow sequential descent accompanied by a countermelody in the second violin that once again delays harmonies through extended appoggiatura patterns and the confounding of anticipated resolutions by further diminished seventh chords. The final phrase sees a desperate sequential climb to the highest pitch of the theme, with a countermelody in the viola seeming to force the first violin line upwards. All is lost, however, as the melody descends from this highest point back to its originating tonic, all accompaniment fading away to leave the first violin alone on its single note B.

The theme thus takes on the air of Hana's dilemma. Her emotional constraint seems reflected in the restricted and constantly thwarted ascent of the melody. She is dragged down by tragedy, disjointed and displaced, just as the interlocking structure of off-beat accents, delayed harmonies and undermined resolutions leads only to the further sad anticipation of diminished seventh chords and appoggiaturas. And she is trapped, just as all the efforts of the music to move away from its beginnings and to develop in scale eventually return it to its original minor mode and its lonely and isolated beginnings. The theme represents the quiet profundity of her grief away from the immediacy of a new loss and, in tandem with the image that she sees of herself re-

flected in her bowl of water, locates her problems as being within herself, stemming from her own particular personality and emotionality.

As it ends with her denial of Caravaggio's accusation of her love
for her patient, however, it is clear that she already recognizes the
same dilemma in her patient. Such recognition of her own emotions in
others, particularly Kip and the patient, is vital to her emotional development. Through the patient and his story in particular, Hana will finally accept both the inescapability of fate and the potential powerlessness of death in the face of love. Love, despite the end of physical
life, continues unchanging—to accept and embrace this is to deny
death its dominion and so to stop fearing life. The theme's last two
appearances bond Hana's emotions to her two major influences, Kip
and the patient, and thus provide a therapeutic influence on the course
of the narrative itself.

The first clear stage in Hana's cure comes as she finds herself in
the role of therapist to her primary emotional savior, Kip. Kip has
shown Hana the way back to life through their romance and the timeless beauty of the church at Arezzo. With him has come a light, delicate and playful Baroque style of non-diegetic scoring that restores
some of the joy of Hana's original piano playing to the score. He has
demonstrated the possibility of cheating death and spends his life actively hunting out unexploded bombs and defusing them. Such is the
symbolic role he has played in Hana's life, until he himself has his
back turned when Sergeant Hardy falls foul of a booby trap bomb during a celebration to mark, most ironically of all, the end of the war.
The effect on both Kip and Hana, caught out in the midst of their celebratory mood, is salutary. Through witnessing and clarifying Kip's
grief, Hana realizes that she is not alone in her own losses. Kip's self-
imposed isolation reflects her own, and through this and his subsequent confusion Hana realizes the naturalness of grief and the necessity of facing up to the love still felt for the dead.

As Kip is seen in solitary contemplation, refusing Hana the right
to comfort him, the *Mortality Theme* undergoes an important transformation. This reflects the developments that both Kip's habitual sense
of life and his current grief have effected in Hana. The theme is now
heard in the piano—Hana's own instrument—for the first time. Hana
is, as she says, a nurse, and she defines herself by her ability to help
and save others. In trying to comfort Kip, whether or not he is initially
receptive, she begins to exercise a new strength through helping someone else to accept the connection of love and grief. In reflection of this,
her strong diegetic musical voice takes ownership of her tragic non-

diegetic theme and begins to clear the path towards her own eventual acceptance of both death and life. This development is expressed through an arrangement that combines what might be seen as 'negative' and 'positive' musical factors.

Apart from its narrative significance as a representation of Hana's emotional voice, the use of the piano also alters the sound quality of the theme. Its timbre is brighter and clearer than the plaintive solo oboe or muted string quartet and the melody is pitched a fourth higher. Despite this, the arrangement retains a sense of loneliness and sadness by setting the ornamentation and strain toward ascent of the first two melodic phrases against the relentless contrary descent and almost depressing rhythmic regularity of arpeggiated chords in the bass. These arpeggios, however, establish a much less dissonant harmony than before, suggesting a new sense of resolution underneath the endless yearning of the melody. As the third phrase begins its descent, the almost unheard drone of the celli present from the beginning opens into a more prominent accompaniment that also draws in the second violins and violas. Although the delay of harmony through appoggiatura notes is still present, there is a greater sense of dissonances and leaning notes leading to real resolution. This suggestion gains momentum through repeated resolution onto major chords and through subsequent new material comprising light, constant, quaver movement— firmly fixed in the major mode.

The continuing doubt over Hana's future nevertheless prevents the theme's full resolution. On this occasion the positive quaver movement leads to two figures that suggest a kind of musical question mark. This rises in sequence, absorbing to some extent in its final expanded repetition the previously sad and hesitant effect of the turn decoration (figure 5.12, bar 3). The thinning of the texture through the loss of the lower strings and the piano bass line recalls the gradual thinning to a single note at the end of the string quartet arrangement. This conclusion is more forward-looking, however, ending as it does with a sense of tentative anticipation, rather than sadly sparse and lonely resolution.

Figure 5.12: *The English Patient.*
The *Mortality Theme*: The possibility of hope for Hana in Kip's grief.
Written by Gabriel Yared.
Used by permission of Tiger Moth Music/Fantasy, Inc.
All Rights Reserved.

The connection of Hana's experiences with those of her companions reaches its most significant point as she helps the patient to die. Kip has left and Caravaggio has led the patient to the end of his memories, re-presenting them to him in such a way that the patient now desires nothing but death. As Hana prepares his regular morphine injection, he indicates his wish for a fatal overdose and asks to be read to sleep.[24] Hana and Katharine's voices then interchange in reading Katharine's dying thoughts as a voice-over to the patient's dying memories.

Hana's compliance with the patient's wishes thus enables four simultaneous acceptances of death: Katharine's acceptance of her own, the patient's acceptance of both hers and his own, and Hana's acceptance of her actual losses as well as the fact and meaning of death. The weight of this moment for the characters and the narrative is reflected in the extreme poignancy of the theme's arrangement and its role in uniting the two key temporal spaces and character trajectories. As Hana holds the key to allowing all their stories to be laid to rest, it is her musical theme that first binds them together in their common love and loss and then allows them to go their separate ways.

The theme reappears as the patient knocks over the box of morphine ampoules and pushes them toward Hana. It is stated three times continuously, with each repeat marking a new stage of the patient's dying moments. The first stage concerns the patient's request and Hana's decision, the second introduces Katharine's final thoughts on life and death, and the third returns the patient completely to the desert and the past as he finally carries Katharine from the Cave of Swimmers. We slip once again into the patient's visually and aurally disjunctured experience of events past and present, with the editing and design of the soundtrack in particular being motivated purely by his perceptions and emotions. With the visual and aural tracks so out of step, the non-diegetic music becomes the only constant holding together the experiences and words of the living and the dead, and the only means of expressing such a purely emotional moment.

As Hana watches the ampoules being pushed toward her, the slow, tentative piano arrangement of the theme reflects the pain of finally reaching a moment that was always inevitable but always deferred. The piano stands completely alone for the first time on the non-diegetic track. The pitch is lowered to place the theme back in the B minor key of its first two statements and the pace seems the slowest that it has ever been. The texture is spare and delicate, the harmonies simple and the rhythm regular and pedestrian, with the potential flourish of the theme's Baroque ornamentation being tightly controlled (figure 5.13). The bass line moves away from and back toward a B pedal note in such a way that emphasizes stasis and restraint alongside separation and reunion. The air of dignified loneliness offers a complete contrast to the unrestrained excesses of the *Love Theme*, bringing the patient's emotions at last into alignment with Hana's in their shared need to leave behind escapism and accept reality.

Figure 5.13: *The English Patient.*
The *Mortality Theme*. Cue title: *"Read me to sleep."*
Written by Gabriel Yared.
Used by permission of Tiger Moth Music/Fantasy, Inc.
All Rights Reserved.

As Hana begins to open the extra ampoules, the strings enter gradually below the piano, the full string section finally coming into place for the beginning of the theme's second statement—just as the patient asks her to "read [him] to sleep."[25]

The orchestral texture continues to fill out as she reads and the patient's thoughts regress to Katharine's voice and his return to the cave.

As the theme comes to an end for the second time, its further repeat is delayed by a bridge passage with more fluid quaver movement in the piano which eventually pauses in anticipation of the third section of the patient's dying thoughts. Diegetic sound has been barely a part of the patient's experience of dying, but the foregrounding of diegetic silence as he carries Katharine from the cave suggests not only his final removal from reality, but also a grief too deep to be conveyed in such normal expression. Only her voice and the final statement of the non-diegetic theme accompany the violent grief that racks his whole body as he carries her toward their final flight.

Hana reappears on both the sound and visual track in time to finish the letter with the line that unites Katharine's moment of death with the patient's: "The lamp's gone out . . . and I'm writing in the darkness."[26] As the sequential ascent of the theme's final section reaches its highest point, Hana smiles at the patient's release into death. Tears then fill her eyes, accompanied by the descent of the theme to the final, full cadence that has evaded it throughout the film. As this particular narrative theme is resolved, so is its musical theme.

*The Love Theme*

I can see my wife in that view.[27]

The final word, however, is given not to death but to the love that lives beyond it. This theme is introduced in connection with the patient's memories of his relationship with Katharine. As was described in chapter 4, all the non-diegetic music associated with the patient circumscribes his all-important memories of past events and Other places. This very particular contextualization must always be kept in mind, since the narrative pivots on both Almásy's and the patient's highly subjective points of view. In the past, Almásy's view is defined by his Romantic idealism and his social and political naïveté. In the present, it is further clouded by a combination of grief and regret, as well the selectivity and obscurity of his memories that give rise, for example, to his contention that Katharine was his wife.

Despite the inclusion in his flashbacks of a certain number of scenes to which he clearly could not have been party, a consideration of the patient's unique subjectivity is therefore crucial to an interpretation of his musical themes and their placement. As we understand his ahistorical, apolitical perception of the desert partly through the exotic styles of the *Oriental* and *Desert* themes, so we understand his view of his adulterous affair as a real love that transcends social boundaries through the placement and development of the *Love Theme*.

The theme first appears, with a sense of the sadness of hindsight, as the patient succumbs to the draw of his book of Herodotus—the only surviving physical link to his mysterious past. The book has been presented as a clue from the beginning of the film, its loose contents having been seen fleetingly after the plane crash before being concealed once again within its leather covers. Now, with the patient seen alone for the first time in the film, a medium close-up of his face as he contemplates the book on his bedside table reveals a hitherto unseen grief and vulnerability that frames his first flashback with a sense of intensely private sorrow and regret. The introduction of the *Loss Motif* into this particular scene therefore invests the motif with narrative emotion that mirrors its musical pattern of unfulfilled longing.

The slow glide of the patient's hand into the frame and toward the book, his turning of its pages and its fall to the floor, seem almost choreographed to the non-diegetic music. The smooth sweeping ascent of the melody is emphasized by a fluid rhythmic pattern of tied, triplet and dotted notes. It begins with a long appoggiatura that leads into the continued harmonic forestalling of a half diminished seventh chord. As the melody reaches its highest point, it strains against the harmony once more with a prepared appoggiatura that finally resolves onto the G major tonic chord.

The romantic dynamism of the melodic movement therefore gives way to prolonged yearning. The potential brightness of the final major chord is undermined by the heavy leaning of the appoggiatura, an affect emphasized in the immediate echo-like repeat of the cadence and a segue into the pensive *Passage of Time Theme*. The tension created by this theme remains unresolved, however, as the strumming of the quanoun over the characteristic ominous drone returns us to Almásy's desert and his first meeting with Katharine (figure 5.14).

Figure 5.14: *The English Patient.*
The *Passage of Time Theme*: The final appoggiatura leading into the
first flashback, the drone motif and the *Oriental Theme.*
Written by Gabriel Yared.
Used by permission of Tiger Moth Music/Fantasy, Inc.
All Rights Reserved.

As the *Love Theme* appears in full within the flashback, it is removed from the pain of hindsight and imbued instead with a lighter,
more positive mood that reflects the patient's removal into a more optimistic past. The initial, tentative hints of a connection between
Almásy and Katharine are reflected in the subtle introduction of the
main body of the theme as they fly above the desert taking aerial photographs with Madox and Geoffrey. In line with the graceful, balletic

movement of the two planes, the cue is calm, measured and soothing
in tone. It begins with the regular rhythm of an arpeggiated harp figure over soft, sustained notes in the lower strings. Over this, a melody
emerges from a delicate interlocking texture in the upper strings. The
melody destabilizes the regular meter of its harp accompaniment
through the use of anacrusis and tied notes and an emphasis on weak
beats which, together with its appoggiaturas and languorous overlap-
ping phrases, invests the melody and the scene with a timeless, oneiric
quality (figure 5.15).

Figure 5.15: *The English Patient.*
The *Love Theme.* Cue title: *Two Planes.* Ostinato bass and variation of
melody.
Written by Gabriel Yared.
Used by permission of Tiger Moth Music/Fantasy, Inc.

This initial melody offers a variation on the *Love Theme* that delays its first full appearance until the precise moment that Almásy
waves to Katharine. At this point, the theme appears in fragmented
form, with the first phrase of the melody leading straight into a variation on the *Loss Motif*. The appearance of the theme does, however,
pull the orchestral texture together by marking the end of the interlocking texture and a move to a clear leading voice in the first violins accompanied by a slower, imitative rising pattern in the second violins
(figure 5.16).

Figure 5.16: *The English Patient.*
Cue title: *Two Planes*. The first fragment of the *Love Theme*.
Written by Gabriel Yared.
Used by permission of Tiger Moth Music/Fantasy, Inc.
All Rights Reserved.

This leads straight into a long ascending sequence, marked *crescendo* and underpinned with tremolando strings and woodwind that
lend a somewhat ominous tone, as Geoffrey shows off his flying
prowess by performing a barrel roll in his Stearman. The first phrase of
the theme diffuses this potential tension, however, returning in a high-
pitched arrangement for strings and woodwind and falling from its
highest point to resolve comfortably in to E flat major as the two
planes fly away from each other and a slow visual dissolve returns us
from the desert dunes to the folds of the sheet on the patient's bed.

The development of the theme continues to reflect Almásy and Katharine's relationship as two crucial scenes are paired by the use of a new arrangement. Although these scenes appear quite distinct in the stages of the relationship that they represent, they are similar to some extent in their emotional undercurrents. In the first scene, Katharine finds Almásy's baby photograph as she pastes her paintings from the Cave of Swimmers into his book. Although his interest has been made clear prior to this scene, the interest with which she now gazes at him is the first tangible sign of her feelings. As she looks down again at the book, however, she is visibly unnerved by her discovery of the observations about "K" that she rightly assumes refer to her.[28] As Almásy calls to her, she smiles awkwardly at him and hurriedly returns his notes to his book. In the second scene, Almásy and Katharine bathe together after making love for the first time in Almásy's hotel room. Asked to say what she loves and hates the most, Katharine cites her husband and "[a] lie" respectively.[29] When asked in return to say what he hates the most, Almásy replies: "Ownership. Being owned."[30] Disgusted at his assertion that she should therefore forget him as soon as she leaves, Katharine pushes him away and climbs out of the bath.

Each scene therefore contrasts the exciting possibility of new love with its dangers in this particular situation: unwelcome and illegitimate feelings, the reality of betrayal and the vulnerability resulting from involvement with the unknown and potentially destructive. Rather than mapping the physical progress of their affair, this arrangement of the theme charts its continuing emotional sticking point—the conflict between personal emotions and social boundaries that defines the couple's increasingly dangerous and insoluble relationship. Delicate coherence and jarring disruption are combined and developed to ominous effect, until both music and narrative reach a point of uneasy irresolution.

The theme is heard in its entirety for the first time, the instrumental texture is light, the dynamic soft and the pace moderate, with the clear voice of the piano leading with fragile delicacy over a gentle string accompaniment. This melodic coherence and simple soundworld are undermined, however, by a permeating sense of vacillation, as the piano accompaniment and strings reflect the pattern of the melody in rocking figures that create both harmonic and rhythmic instability. The accompaniment in the piano rocks constantly between a pedal note and a rising and falling scale, while the violas build a 2-note ostinato from a reflection in contrary motion of the theme's opening 3-note motif (figure 5.17). The unsettling affect of this arrangement is exacerbated

in the second half of the theme by the filling out of the string accompaniment. The first violins double the melody while the second violins
parallel the 2-note ostinato pattern of the violas, now also throwing
emphasis onto weak beats through the use of tied notes. The lower
strings complete the texture throughout the cue by doubling the piano
with a sustained pedal note, thus creating a major-minor tension with
the semitonal oscillation of the upper strings.

Figure 5.17: *The English Patient.*
The *Love Theme.* Cue title: *"Go on all day."*
Written by Gabriel Yared.
Used by permission of Tiger Moth Music/Fantasy, Inc.
All Rights Reserved.

While this reflects the precarious stasis in which the couple currently exist, the scalic line of the piano accompaniment, although partially obscured by the interspersing pedal note, nevertheless introduces
a fragment of a further narrative-musical development. Under the first
phrase of the theme, this line develops the accompaniment pattern of
the *Two Planes* cue (figure 5.16) into a coherent phrase, which doubles
the melody before continuing an ascending line under its final sustained note. This compacts the theme by layering its first phrase over a
variation of its final phrase, the *Loss Motif,* in the style of a stretto answering phrase. Although still in embryonic form, this arrangement of

the phrases, together with the constantly stymied striving toward ascent of the melody itself, suggests the inflection of the whole theme with the simultaneous passionate anticipation and sad regret of the *Loss Motif*. As the difficult reality of the relationship replaces the previous excitement of its possibility, the question of how things will end presents a new problem. Each of these two cues ends with a move between two sustained dissonant chords that suggest the possibility of resolution through appoggiaturas in the piano and strings, only to deny this potential with further dissonance. The sense of looming threat left in the narrative by this hovering discord is tangible.

Both the musical development and narrative significance of the theme come to full fruition at the Christmas party, where the equal depth and destructive potential of the couple's passion are finally realized. The representation of this surreptitious encounter contrasts Almásy's/the patient's purely emotional view of events with a rather more objective commentary through elements of music, mise-en-scène and editing. This invests the relationship with contrasting heights of passion and horror and, crucially, begins to separate Katharine's view of events from Almásy's.

Katharine feigns illness to absent herself from the party, while Almásy pens in timely fashion his poetic thoughts on the oblivious destructiveness of new love. As they hide away from the party and make love, the frantic nature of their first encounter is replaced with languorous eroticism. We are much closer to the couple than before, with the editing focusing us on intimate detail, particularly of Katharine's body as Almásy reveals it, and her face as they make love. We also remain with the couple to witness their most passionate moments, rather than cutting away soon after their first embrace.

This style of representation, together with the non-diegetic music, gives an emotional validation to the couple's actions that contrasts starkly with the film's somewhat critical framing of the scene. They make love in a room with a frosted glass window, actually visible, if they and their friends did only realize it, to the carol-singing group outside. As the singing ends, we cut to the figure of Santa Claus walking toward the room where the lovers have been and accosting Almásy as he hurries back to the party. We share Almásy's apparent shock as the figure asks after Katharine, before emerging from beneath the outfit's disguise as Geoffrey. Katharine's greater pragmatism becomes clear as we now realize why she watched and waited for the anonymous Santa Claus figure to disappear from sight before she pretended to faint. We have shared what appears to be Almásy's ignorance of

Geoffrey's presence at the party, perhaps even with the lovers in his sight, until in the midst of his good-hearted duties as children's entertainer he becomes innocently concerned for his wife's welfare.

Chapter 4 considered the diegetic music with which this scene begins in terms of its place in the trajectory of Almásy's interaction with its representation of social and cultural codes. The opposition of personal desire and social obligation established in the first few moments of the encounter is emphasized by the subsequent introduction into the scene of non-diegetic music. With this, Almásy's emotional view of events—and Katharine's despite her more careful approach—breaks through any suggestion of incongruity. His initial contemplation of her throat and shoulder, to the simultaneously critical and sympathetic accompaniment of the diegetic carol singing, is replaced by a shot of his hand reaching down to her leg. At this point, the non-diegetic score completely drowns the singing as it reintroduces the *Love Theme* with the repeated heavy sigh of a string appoggiatura. The theme then begins on a cut to the singers outside and the resurgence of their carol alongside the non-diegetic score.

As we move past the singers, however, and see the partially obscured sight of the couple through the window behind the bagpiper, the arrangement of the first half of the theme reemphasizes their social dissonance through musical dissonance. The melody is dominated by an accompaniment of repeated, accented, off-beat notes in the bassoons and lower strings, that weigh it down and obscure its potential beauty with an uncomfortably static harmony and a leaden beat. As we approach the second half of the theme, however, we cut back to the lovers and our previous view of events 'from the outside' is obliterated by a dramatic change in the musical arrangement that once again offers the experience as one of pure passion. The singing disappears completely, giving way to a *crescendo* emphasized by a timpani roll in the non-diegetic score, which leads into the most fully orchestrated version of the theme so far.

The second half of the theme is now declaimed in loud doubling between the strings and woodwind, underpinned by the variation on the *Loss Motif* introduced in the previous two cues and now expanded to its full effect. Its role is strengthened by changes in its notation and instrumentation and by its extension beyond the first phrase of the theme. It now forms a smooth uninterrupted line, appearing most noticeably in the French horns but also doubled in the strings and woodwind. This immediately renders it more prominent, particularly as it continues independently in-between each melodic phrase (figure 5.18).

Its compacting, exciting effect is heightened as it crosses briefly with the beginning of the second melodic phrase—its continued ascent pushing against the melody's initial descent. Although its overall contour is also one of sequential descent, it continues to push upward past the end of the second melodic phrase before taking its place as the final phrase of the theme.

The potential for resolution is undermined, however, with a sudden diminuendo and thinning of the orchestral texture, leading to a repeated sighing appoggiatura that denies the potency of the final G major chords and allows the return of the diegetic singing outside. Despite the initially triumphant sound of the theme's full orchestration and its sheer volume, both metaphorically and literally, in drowning out the diegetic musical background, its attempts toward resolution remain heavy with yearning. The stretto layering of the phrases compounds the sense of striving toward conclusion, while also constantly stymieing its possibility.

Figure 5.18: *The English Patient.*
The *Love Theme*. Cue title: *Christmas Party*. Countermelody.
Written by Gabriel Yared.
Used by permission of Tiger Moth Music/Fantasy, Inc.
All Rights Reserved.

By the time the lovers are next accompanied by this theme, their situation has changed dramatically. Katharine, having ended the affair, has been brought back to Almásy by Geoffrey's grief-stricken murder and suicide bid. As Almásy carries her from the wreckage of the plane crash to the Cave of Swimmers, Katharine finally admits her love for him. The overwhelming emotional culmination of this moment for Almásy is reflected in the dramatic preparation for the theme. The end of the *Desert Theme* hovers, waiting for Katharine's final admission. A fragment of the *Love Theme*'s opening motif appears, ending on a sustained note under which a line ascends using the same rhythmic pattern. Together with a long timpani roll, this leads to a loud declamation of the whole *Love Theme* as her words are finally spoken. It is notable at this point that her face is then obscured behind his neck, so that the visual focus is thrown pointedly and entirely onto his sobbing face.

The arrangement of the theme that follows is much more homogenous, emphasizing the melodic line in the strings and high-pitched woodwind. The heavily accented and repeated stretto accompaniment figure from the Christmas Party cue is smoothed into a more continuous and much less prominent ascending line in the French horn. Finally, ecstatic glissandi in the clarinets and harp give the theme a feeling of elation—and a removal from frantic yearning—that it has never enjoyed before. The tragic sense of the melody is momentarily lightened, and even the sighing appoggiaturas are denied their usual final word by the appearance of the *Passage of Time Theme* as the couple enter the cave.

The couple's happiness, of course, is extremely short-lived. Once Almásy knows that Katharine must be dead as a result of his failure to return to the cave in time, the theme becomes one of abject sorrow. After he escapes from his British captors by jumping from their train, the heavy, leaden, offbeat that plagued the theme as it first appeared at the Christmas party returns in imitation of his limping walk. He then returns, as promised, to the cave. In a transition that mirrors his very first flashback, we see the patient alone in the monastery for the second and final time and travel back into the past to the accompaniment of the *Loss Motif*. Almásy lies down next to Katharine's dead body and all the earlier power of the *Love Theme* is lost. The texture is sparse and the rhythmic dynamism of the dotted opening motif relaxes into smooth quavers. Most of the orchestra doubles the melody line over a sustained drone, although the third phrase sees a sad attempt at the ascending accompaniment motif, not in the strong voice of the French horns, but the more delicate tones of the strings and woodwind (figure 5.19).

Figure 5.19: *The English Patient.*
The *Love Theme.* Cue title: *Almásy returns to the Cave of Swimmers.*
Countermelody.
Written by Gabriel Yared.
Used by permission of Tiger Moth Music/Fantasy, Inc.
All Rights Reserved.

As the film's publicity says, however, "In memory, love lives forever,"[31] and as soon as the patient has come to terms with Katharine's death and his culpability, his only desire is to die himself. The end of his mortal life with Katharine is then replaced with the infinitely less problematic and more fittingly romantic idea of the couple's reunion in the afterlife. As Hana finishes reading Katharine's letter and realizes that the patient has died, the final cadence of the *Mortality Theme* segues into the *Love Theme* as we see the plane take off over the desert. The theme is presented in a simple arrangement, dominated by the melody in the violins and a drone accompaniment that once again blends with the drone of the plane's engine. Where the *Loss Motif* would ordinarily have appeared, however, it is replaced with two rising intervals, the second of which reverses the opening minor third descent of the score (figure 5.20). This musical inversion of the film's sad opening hovers in anticipation as the desert scene fades back to the now empty bedroom in the monastery.

This suggests two entirely separate ways forward in accordance with the film's tagline. Perhaps in death, first of all, Almásy and Katharine will achieve what they could not in life. Perhaps also in life, however, "the Hanas and Kips of this world" will indeed reverse the patterns of the past.[32] The ascending minor third is, of course, the opening interval of the *Mortality Theme* and the questioning pattern of these two rising intervals repeats the earlier hint of possible happiness contained in the rising figures of figure 5.12.

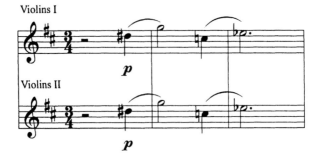

Figure 5.20: *The English Patient.*
The *Love Theme*'s final notes.
Written by Gabriel Yared.
Used by permission of Tiger Moth Music/Fantasy, Inc.
All Rights Reserved.

The promise of such shared, but nevertheless separate ways forward seems confirmed as Hana is driven away from the monastery and looks back momentarily in contemplation of all that happened there. The *Desert Theme* leads once again into the *Love Theme* as we see a rhyming scene to the film's opening—with Katharine and Almásy once again ensconced in their plane, now appearing to fly away unencumbered across the desert. Although the theme still ends with its characteristic sighing appoggiatura, this new narrative context has a dramatic influence on its affect. With the couple removed from the impossibility of their relationship in life, the appoggiatura seems stripped of its ability to override the positive effect of the final major tonality. The sight of the plane disappearing toward the horizon now seems bathed in the positive resolution of the final G major chord. Almásy and Katharine's posthumous reunion then gives way to the bright G major key of the *New Life Theme* as the film returns to Hana.

*The New Life Theme*

I'll always go back to that church.[33]

This theme only appears three times in the score but is extremely important, reflecting the means by which Hana learns to look forward, beyond the monastery, and to allow both herself and the patient to leave their pasts behind. It appears for the first time as Hana leaves the patient and finds the trail of improvised oil lamps that will lead her to Kip. The piano leads tentatively with an introductory passage, doubled by the celesta and harp harmonics over an accompaniment of sustained notes in the upper strings. The theme that follows has a bright, delicate sound. Its clear major tonality and diatonic harmony, constant melodic movement and fluid sense of meter afforded by anacrusis and tied notes, return a refreshing sense of simplicity and lightness to Hana's characteristic association with Bach. Now, however, the non-diegetic status of the music marks its lightness as a genuine reflection of her emotions, rather than a temporary nostalgic release into prewar happiness. As she and Kip arrive at the church the next morning, this first cue comes to an end with a clear resolution into G major, emphasized by a magical shimmer of synthesizer and celesta.

The uplifting role of this theme is literalized in its reappearance as Kip lifts Hana up into the painted ceiling of the church. As was discussed in chapter 2, Yared rarely employs the technique known as *mickey-mousing* in his scores, only doing so when the emotional 'movement' of the action matches its physical movement. In this case, it is Hana's emotional uplift, rather than her physical trajectory, that Yared emphasizes.[34] The first violins give the melody a sweeping fluidity and its contrapuntal arrangement with first pizzicato violas, then also tremolando second violins, celli and divisi double basses, emphasizes the fluidity of the meter. The violas, in particular, in emphasizing the offbeats, lend a gentle rocking sensation to the music that matches Hana's gliding twists and turns (figure 5.21). The proximity of the music to her movements and the magical feel of the moment are then underlined as Yared matches her sudden swings from one side of the church to the other with magnificent harp glissandi. Once again the music maintains its major tonality and diatonic harmony, ending with clear resolve in G major.

Figure 5.21: *The English Patient.*
The *New Life Theme.* Cue title: *The Church.*
Written by Gabriel Yared.
Used by permission of Tiger Moth Music/Fantasy, Inc.
All Rights Reserved.

The theme's final appearance comes as Hana is driven away from the monastery. It follows directly after Almásy and Katharine are seen for the last time flying over the desert and takes the film out of its final narrative images and into the end titles. The desert lovers have been given their chance of happiness and by replacing the *Mortality Theme,* the *New Life Theme* takes Hana to her own future. She turns her head from the monastery and looks forward. Now, the female voice of the *Hungarian Theme* integrates for the first time with the *New Life Theme* to end on an optimistic note. Perhaps Hana will see more of the borderless world of which her patient could only dream.

## Conclusion

Although, as is so often the case with film scores, the structure of this score is determined largely by the flow of the narrative, the connections that Yared creates between his themes mean that their narrative implications will echo wherever they are placed. The "little prelude in G major" that Yared wrote to replace Bach's *Goldberg Variations,* however, also seems to point to a final, more chronological, overall narrative project within his music. Just as the appearance of Kip offers hope within the film, so the bright, G major key of the *New Life Theme* brings a glimmer of light to the score. It acts most immediately as an antidote to the somber minor tonality of the *Mortality Theme* and indicates a change, accordingly, in the course of Hana's life. Its positive tone also seems, however, to throw a retrospective lifeline to the efforts of the *Love Theme* to cadence into that very key as the patient remembered his past. In the end, as Hana leaves the monastery, the *New Life Theme* seems to replace the *Passage of Time Theme* in its direct emergence from the end of the *Love Theme*. The aural and musical ambiguity that opened the film seems to be settled on one level, at least, and the bright sound of the *Hungarian Theme*'s improvisatory voice as the film ends suggests that internationalism may be part of this new clarity.

The intimacy of the score with the emotional trajectories of the film's characters may offer one reason for the contention that arose over the film. It absorbs us, most specifically, so deeply into the patient's/Almásy's view of events that we are infected by the character's own urge to forget the significance of the all-important contextual frame of events. At times, the music that represents his emotions recalls the epic scale and lyricism of Romanticism, and saturates his experiences to such an extent that he seems constituted of pure emotion. At other times, however, such as his final walk from the Cave of Swimmers, its simplicity is devastating. Yared's skill in adapting his music to the film's images, learned from working with Minghella and Murch, means that in certain instances, the patient/Almásy's movements go so far as to enjoy an almost balletic relationship with the score. The scene in which he pensively lifts his hand to his copy of Herodotus on the bedside table, for example, can easily be seen as a precursor to the kind of intricate music-narrative relationship and the musical 'structuring' of scenes that was demonstrated in chapter 2's analysis of a scene from *City of Angels*. Not only are his simple movements given shape by the music, but the fluid movement between themes and motifs also draws us into the most intimate depths of his imagination. The sheer and unexpected joy of Hana's ascent into the rafters of the church at Arezzo, by the same virtue, is perfectly contained in the brightness and parallel ascent of her accompanying arpeggio.

On these and other occasions, the combination of complete or near diegetic silence and non-diegetic music is particularly convincing of the story's emotional depths. Since such musical-emotional representation is unusual for a male character, and indeed since such a depth of vulnerability is also not common, it can be hard to resist reacting with sympathy. Perhaps, however, that is how we should react, for the film certainly loves its main character, whatever his faults. Nevertheless, we must remember its opening warning and constantly pay attention to those other stories, points of view and interpretations that drag the romantic patient/Almásy kicking and screaming back into the everyday world.

*The English Patient* marks a turning point in Yared's career, from which he emerges intact as a composer, while also re-formed as a film composer. As a result of this project, he is able to match the intricacy of the image as closely as he always could the intricacy of character and drama. In order to achieve this, he has compromised neither his musical integrity nor the integrity and unity of his scores. Musically, they are as meaningful as they ever were. Now, however, that meaning may travel further back into its own source and become more a part of the narrative world that first inspired it.

# APPENDIX A

# FILMOGRAPHY

1980    *Sauve qui peut la vie* (Jean-Luc Godard)
      *Malevil* (Christian de Chalonge)
1981    *L'Invitation au voyage* (Peter del Monte)
1982    *Interdit aux moins de treize ans* (Jean-Louis Bertuccelli)
1983    *Les Petites guerres* (Maroun Bagdadi)
      *Sarah* (Maurice Dugowson)
      *La Scarlatine* (Gabriel Aghion)
      *La Java des ombres* (Romain Goupil)
      *La Lune dans le caniveau/The Moon in the Gutter* (Jean-Jacques Beineix)
1984    *Tir à vue* (Marc Angelo)
      *La Diagonale du fou* (Richard Dembo)
      *Némo* (Arnaud Sélignac)
      *Hanna K* (Costa Gavras)
1985    *Scout toujours* (Gérard Jugnot)
      *Adieu Bonaparte* (Youssef Chanine)
      *Le Téléphone sonne toujours deux fois* (Jean-Pierre Vergne)
1986    *Désordre* (Olivier Assayas)
      *Flagrant désir* (Claude Faraldo)
      *Zone rouge* (Robert Enrico)
      *37°2 le matin/Betty Blue* (Jean-Jacques Beineix)
1987    *Gandahar contre les hommes machines* (René Laloux)
      *Agent trouble* (Jean-Pierre Mocky)
      *Beyond Therapy* (Robert Altman)
1988    *Camille Claudel* (Bruno Nuytten)
      *La Romana* (Giuseppe Patroni Griffi)
      *Une nuit à l'assemblée nationale* (Jean-Pierre Mocky)
      *Clean and Sober* (Glenn Caron)

*L'Homme voilé* (Maroun Bagdadi)
*Les Saisons du plaisir* (Jean-Pierre Mocky)
*Le Testament d'un poète juif assassiné* (Franck Cassenti)
1989    *Les Mille et Une nuits* (Philippe de Broca)
*Tennessee Nights* (Nicolas Gessner)
*Romero* (John Duigan)
1990    *La Putain du roi* (Axel Corti)
*Tatie Danielle* (Étienne Chatiliez)
*Vincent and Theo* (Robert Altman)
1991    *IP5* (Jean-Jacques Beineix)
*L'Arche et les déluges* (François Bel)
*L'Amant/The Lover* (Jean-Jacques Annaud)
1992    *L'Instinct de l'ange* (Richard Dembo)
*La Fille de l'air* (Maround Bagdadi)
*Le Premier Cercle* (Larry Sheldon)
*Map of the Human Heart* (Vincent Ward)
1993    *Profil bas* (Claude Zidi)
*Les Marmottes* (Elie Chouraqui)
*Des Feux mal éteints* (Serge Moati)
1994    *Wings of Courage* (Jean-Jacques Annaud)
1995    *Noir comme le souvenir* (Jean-Pierre Mocky)
1996    *The English Patient* (Anthony Minghella)
1997    *Hercule et Sherlock* (Jeannot Szwarc)
*Tonka* (Jean-Hughes Anglade)
1998    *City of Angels* (Brad Silberling)
1999    *Message in a Bottle* (Luis Mandoki)
*The Talented Mr. Ripley* (Anthony Minghella)
2000    *The Next Best Thing* (John Schlesinger)
*Autumn in New York* (Joan Chen)
2001    *Lisa* (Pierre Grimblat)
*Not Afraid, Not Afraid* (Annette Carducci)
*Possession* (Neil LaBute)
2002    *L'Idole* (Samantha Lang)
*Les Marins perdus* (Claire Devers)
*The One and Only* (Simon Cellan Jones)
2003    *Bon voyage* (Jean-Paul Rappeneau)

# APPENDIX B

# AWARDS AND NOMINATIONS

## (A) = Award; (N) = Nomination

1983   *La Lune dans le caniveau*
Grand Prix de la SACEM 1984 **(A)**

1984   *Hanna K*
Grand Prix de la SACEM 1984 **(A)**

1986   *37°2 le matin*
Victoire de la Musique 1986 **(A)**
César de la Musique 1988 **(N)**

1987   *Agent trouble*
César de la Musique 1988 **(N)**
Victoires de la Musique 1988 **(N)**

1988   *Camille Claudel*
Victoire de la Musique 1989 **(A)**
César de la Musique 1989 **(N)**

1991   *L'Amant/The Lover*
Victoire de la Musique 1992 **(A)**
César de la Musique 1993 **(A)**
International Musical Visual Award 1993 **(N)**

1992   *Map of the Human Heart*
Australian Film Institute Award 1993 **(N)**

1993   *Les Marmottes*
       Victoires de la Musique 1994 **(N)**

       *Des Feux mal éteints*
       Midem Award for all work **(N)**

1994   *Wings of Courage*
       Midem Award for all work **(N)**

1995   *Noir comme le souvenir*
       Victoires de la Musique 1995 **(N)**

1996   *The English Patient*
       Academy Award 1997 **(A)**
       Golden Globe 1997 **(A)**
       First Golden Satellite Award 1997 **(A)**
       Indie Award 1997 **(A)**
       BAFTA Award 1997 **(A)**
       Grammy Award 1998 **(A)**
       Victoire de la Musique 1998 **(A)**
       Grand Prix de la SACEM 1998 **(A)**

1998   *City of Angels*
       Film & Television Music Award **(A)**
       Grammy Award **(N)**
       Golden Satellite Award **(N)**

1999   *The Talented Mr. Ripley*
       Academy Award 2000 **(N)**
       Golden Globe 2000 **(N)**
       BAFTA Award 2000 **(N)**
       Broadcast Film Critics Association Award 2000 **(N)**

# NOTES

## Chapter One

1. This quotation is taken from an interview with Gabriel Yared by the author on 11 November 2001. The structure of this chapter and most of its material is drawn from this interview and subsequent correspondence between Gabriel Yared and the author. While it would be impractical to credit these as sources each time they are used as a point of reference, direct quotations will be footnoted. The term "interview by the author" covers both the interview itself and the subsequent correspondence.

2. Yared, interview by the author.

3. Yared, interview by the author.

4. Yared, interview by the author.

5. Yared, interview by the author.

6. Yared, interview by the author.

7. Because of this aversion to violence on screen, Yared has never, to date, seen the scene in *The English Patient* in which Caravaggio is tortured by the German officer. As told by Yared, interview by the author.

8. Yared, interview by the author.

9. Gabriel Yared in Mark Russell and James Young, *Film Music: Screencraft* (Switzerland: RotoVision, 2000), 109, 112.

10. Yared, interview by the author.

11. This working process is described thus by Gabriel Yared in both Juliette Michaud, "Gabriel Yared: Envoyez la Musique!," *Studio Magazine* no. 88 (June 1994): 103 and Russell and Young, *Film Music: Screencraft*, 112. Paraphrases of or quotations from interviews originally published in French appear within the chapter in translation

by the author. Direct quotations will be footnoted in their original form.

12. Michaud, "Gabriel Yared: Envoyez la Musique!," 102: "Et Gabriel Yared, lui, est un véritable orfèvre."

13. Yared, interview by the author.

14. Yared in Michaud, "Gabriel Yared: Envoyez la Musique!," 103: "Cette première expérience a été déterminante."

15. Yared, interview by the author.

16. Gabriel Yared in "Questionnaire adressé aux Compositeurs," *Cinémaction* no. 62 (January 1992): 89: "D'égal à égal, de novice à novice, de découvreur à découvreur."

17. Yared, interview by the author.

18. Yared, interview by the author.

19. This is discussed in Elisabeth Lesbats, "Profession: Compositeur—Gabriel Yared: 'Dans un film, moins il y a de musique, mieux je me porte!'," *Ciné Télé Revue* 65, no. 11 (14 March 1985): 45 and by Gabiel Yared in Kevin David and Emmanuelle Franck, "Musique de Films," *Film Français* no. 2282 (26 January 1990): 19.

20. Gabriel Yared in Lesbats, "Profession: Compositeur—Gabriel Yared: 'Dans un film, moins il y a de musique, mieux je me porte!'," 45: "Ecrire deux fois trente ou quarante minutes par an c'est déjà énorme. Je me suis préservé parce que d'abord je veux choisir les films, je ne veux pas prendre ce qu'on me propose sans avoir lu le scénario. Et puis ce sont avant tout les rapports humains que j'ai avec les réalisateurs qui comptent. Enfin je veux que mes musiques soient de vraies musiques, qu'on puisse entendre aussi sans le film."

21. Yared in Michaud, "Gabriel Yared: Envoyez la Musique!," 103.

22. Yared in Michaud, "Gabriel Yared: Envoyez la Musique!," 103: "J'ai alors vraiment vu l'impact de la musique sur le tournage."

23. Yared in Michaud, "Gabriel Yared: Envoyez la Musique!," 103.

24. Yared in Michaud, "Gabriel Yared: Envoyez la Musique!," 103.

25. Yared in Russell and Young, *Film Music: Screencraft*, 112.

26. The process of composing this piece in accordance with the actors' abilities is described in Russell and Young, *Film Music: Screencraft*, 112.

27. Yared in Michaud, "Gabriel Yared: Envoyez la Musique!," 103.

28. Yared in Michaud, "Gabriel Yared: Envoyez la Musique!,"
104: "Cela a aussi été, pour moi, l'occasion de revenir un peu au jazz."
29. Gabriel Yared in Vance Brawley, "The Talented Mr. Yared,"
http://www.scorelogue.com/gabriel_yared.html (22 August 2000).
30. Yared in Russell and Young, *Film Music: Screencraft*, 116.
31. Yared in Brawley, "The Talented Mr. Yared."
32. Yared in Brawley, "The Talented Mr. Yared."
33. Yared in Michaud, "Gabriel Yared: Envoyez la Musique!,"
105: "Annaud est comme Beineix, c'est-à-dire qu'il entend réellement,
et qu'il possède le gout du risque."
34. Yared in Michaud, "Gabriel Yared: Envoyez la Musique!,"
105: "'une tonne de papiers sur ce qu'était la musique au Viêt-nam
dans les années 30.'"
35. Yared in Michaud, "Gabriel Yared: Envoyez la Musique!,"
105.
36. Yared in Michaud, "Gabriel Yared: Envoyez la Musique!,"
104: "Ma collaboration avec lui a toujours été très bénéfique parce
qu'elle m'a permis de marier ma culture orientale à la musique
occidentale."
37. Yared in Michaud, "Gabriel Yared: Envoyez la Musique!,"
105: "j'ai eu envie de ce romantisme presque morbide."
38. Yared in Michaud, "Gabriel Yared: Envoyez la Musique!,"
105: "*Camille Claudel* reste une grande expérience."
39. Jean-Philippe Guerand, "Disques: Gabriel Yared, Profession:
Décolleur de Papier Peint," *Première* 142 (January 1989): 112: "une
bande originale qui a l'ampleur d'une symphonie."
40. Michaud, "Gabriel Yared: Envoyez la Musique!," 102: "l'un
des musiciens de cinéma les plus sollicités."
41. David and Franck, "Musique de Films," 19: "Gabriel Yared est
aujourd'hui 'le' compositeur de musiques de films."
42. Guerand, "Disques: Gabriel Yared, Profession: Décolleur de
Papier Peint," 112: "Gabriel Yared a ralenti une ascension qu'on lui
prédisait fulgurante mais il y a gagné une enviable aura."
43. Such sentiments are evident in articles such as Guerand,
"Disques: Gabriel Yared, Profession: Décolleur de Papier Peint," 112
and David and Franck, "Musique de Films," 19.
44. Yared in David and Franck, "Musique de Films," 19: "un
métier épicier."
45. Yared, interview by the author. Also alluded to by Yared in
"Questionnaire adressé aux Compositeurs," 89.
46. Yared, interview by the author.

47. Yared in "Questionnaire adressé aux Compositeurs," 89.

48. Yared continues to advocate this kind of musical training as a standard element of film school courses.

49. Yared, interview by the author.

50. Yared, interview by the author (through correspondence from Jean-Pierre Arquié).

51. Yared, interview by the author.

52. Yared, interview by the author.

53. Information taken from the YAD Music website, http://www. gabrielyared.com/ (23 May 2001).

54. Yared, interview by the author.

55. Yared, interview by the author. Yared also talks in similar terms about Minghella in Russell and Young, *Film Music: Screencraft*, 116.

56. Yared, interview by the author.

57. Yared, interview by the author.

58. Yared, interview by the author.

59. Yared in David and Franck, "Musique de Films," 19: "Je ne veux pas être ce compositeur esclave qui ajuste ses mélodies aux images."

60. Michaud, "Gabriel Yared: Envoyez la Musique!," 102: "Mais l'objectif de Gabriel Yared n'est pas de finir à Hollywood avec un Oscar!"

61. Yared, interview by the author.

62. Yared, interview by the author.

63. Jeff Bond, *"Message in a Bottle," Film Score Monthly* 4, no. 5 (June 1999): 44.

64. Yared, interview by the author.

65. Yared, interview by the author.

66. Gabriel Yared, "La Musique de Film, Éternelle Sacrifiée des Budgets Français," *Film Français* no. 2804 (3 December 1999): 19.

67. Yared, "La Musique de Film, Éternelle Sacrifiée des Budgets Français," 18.

68. Yared, "La Musique de Film, Éternelle Sacrifiée des Budgets Français," 19.

69. Gabriel Yared, YAD Music website: "j'ai tout d'abord lu le Clavigo de Gœthe, afin de m'imprégner de l'esprit de l'œuvre."

70. Yared, YAD Music website.

71. YAD Music website.

72. Yared, interview by the author.

73. Yared, interview by the author.

# Chapter Two

1. The term "non-diegetic music" is used to denote the score that exists outside of the diegetic space of the film; there is no on-screen source for this music—it is performed, rather, by an 'invisible orchestra' of which the film's characters are completely unaware. The term "diegetic music" refers to music which is sourced from within the story itself.

2. Peter Brooks, *The Melodramatic Imagination* (New Haven: Yale University Press, 1976; New York: Columbia University Press, 1984), 9–11.

3. The term "melodrama" is appropriated from the French term "*mélo-drame*" meaning, literally, "music-drama."

4. Robert Lang quoted in Caryl Flinn, *Strains of Utopia: Gender, Nostalgia, and Hollywood Film Music* (Oxford and Princeton: Princeton University Press, 1992), 133.

5. Defined by Claudia Gorbman as: "Music making actions on the screen explicit—'imitating' their direction or rhythm" in *Unheard Melodies: Narrative Film Music* (Bloomington: Indiana University Press; London: BFI, 1987), 88.

6. Gabriel Yared, "La Musique de Film, Éternelle Sacrifiée des Budgets Français," *Film Français* no. 2804 (3 December 1999): 19.

7. Anthony Minghella in Richard Stayton, "The Talented Mr. Minghella," *Written By* (February 2000), 35.

8. Anthony Minghella in John Preston, "Yuppie Love," *Time Out*, 2–8 July 1986, 26.

9. Minghella in Stayton, "The Talented Mr. Minghella," 35.

10. Anthony Minghella in Nick James, "My Bloody Valentine," *Sight and Sound* 10, no. 2 (February 2000), 17.

11. Gabriel Yared, interview by the author, 11 November 2001.

12. Anthony Minghella, "My Kind of Day," *Radio Times*, 2–8 August, 122.

13. Anthony Minghella in Jaap Mees, "Anthony Minghella," http://www.talkingpix.co.uk/Anthony%20Minghella.html (6 August 2001).

14. She protests to her sister that: "That's practically all I've got of him. It is him. . . . It's like asking me to give you his body." Anthony Minghella, *Plays 2: Cigarettes and Chocolate; Hang-up; What If It's Raining?; Truly, Madly, Deeply; Mosaic; Days Like These* (London: Methuen Drama, 1997), 184.

15. Anthony Minghella in Erik Floren, "Ripley's—Believe It!," http://www.canoe.ca/JamMoviesArtistsM/minghella_anthony.html (6 August 2001).

16. All excerpts of dialogue from *The Talented Mr. Ripley* are transcribed directly from the screen.

17. Anthony Minghella in David Gritten, "Behind the Eyes of a Killer," *Daily Telegraph: Arts & Books*, 12 February 2000, 1.

18. Minghella in James, "My Bloody Valentine," 17.

19. A berceuse is either a sung lullaby or any composition in compound duple time that is suggestive of a lullaby. In this particular case, the lullaby is sung.

20. Yared, interview by the author.

21. Yared, interview by the author.

22. The use of synthesizers in the recording of the fully notated scores for *37°2 le matin* and *Vincent and Theo* is noted in Mark Russell and James Young, *Film Music: Screencraft* (Switzerland: RotoVision, 2000), 111, 113.

23. Name assigned to theme by the author. This extract was transcribed directly from the film by the author; all other extracts from *37°2 le matin* used in this chapter are taken from the concert suite of the score.

24. No name is given to this theme in the concert suite; this name has therefore been chosen owing to the theme's association with moments in the film that suggest Betty's encroaching madness.

25. This and other cue titles and all the extracts used in this chapter from *The Talented Mr. Ripley* are taken from the concert suite of the score.

26. The cue titles are taken from the score and are translated from the original French. The extracts from *IP5* are shown as they appear in the named cue only. The cue titles in the original French are: *Palier Tony—Gloria* (figure 2.7), *Le jour se lève* (figure 2.8), *L'Ile aux Pachydermes* (figure 2.9), *Juke Box—Hôpital* (figure 2.10).

27. Yared, interview by the author.

28. See chapter 1, note 72.

29. The cue titles for *City of Angels* have been chosen by the author. This extract and figure 2.13 were transcribed by the author from the film, with reference to the concert suite of the score.

# Chapter Three

1. Nigel Reynolds, "'Rejected' Film in Line for 13 Bafta Awards," *Daily Telegraph*, 26 February 1997, 5.

2. Anthony Minghella, "Introduction," *The English Patient: A Screenplay by Anthony Minghella* (London: Methuen Drama, 1997), xiii.

3. David Thomson, "How They Saved the Patient," *Independent on Sunday*, 22 December 1996, 15.

4. Simon Braund, "'We Lost Fox Because We Wouldn't Go for a Big Name for Kristin's Part...'" *Empire* no. 100 (October 1997): 206.

5. The unusual nature of Ondaatje's involvement in the screenwriting process is remarked upon by several critics and writers. Alan Plater, for example, is quoted as saying that it is "unique in the history of movie-making. Most producers and directors just tell the writer to go screw himself," Sue Summers, "The Patient English Director," *Daily Telegraph Weekend Magazine*, 22 February 1997, 36.

6. Anthony Minghella in Harriet Lane, "Mr. Motivator," *Observer Life Magazine* (© Harriet Lane, *Guardian Newspapers Limited*), 9 March 1997, 22.

7. Anthony Minghella in Jonathan Coe, "From Hull to Hollywood: Anthony Minghella Talks about His Film, *The English Patient*, and Denies That He Is Turning into David Lean," *New Statesman*, 7 March 1997, 38.

8. Anthony Minghella in Sarah Gristwood, "Medical Miracle," *Guardian: Section 2*, 29 November 1996, 4.

9. Saul Zaentz in Coe, "From Hull to Hollywood," 38.

10. Michael Ondaatje, "Foreword," in *The English Patient: A Screenplay by Anthony Minghella*, viii–ix.

11. Gristwood, "Medical Miracle," 4.

12. "It's All Wight on the Night for Minghella," *Daily Telegraph*, 26 March 1997, 10.

13. "It's All Wight on the Night for Minghella," 10. *The Evening Standard* in fact reported three years later that cast and crew remained unpaid for their work on the film, "[d]espite [the film] earning almost £154 million worldwide." "*English Patient* 'in the Red'," *Evening Standard*, 21 March 2000, 4.

14. Anthony Minghella describes breaking his ankle in articles such as "The English Patient," *Premiere* 10, no. 2 (October 1996): 72 and Summers, "The Patient English Director," 36.

15. Minghella in Summers, "The Patient English Director," 36.

16. Minghella in Summers, "The Patient English Director," 38.

16. Minghella in Summers, "The Patient English Director," 38.

17. Minghella in Lane, "Mr. Motivator," 22.

17. Minghella in Lane, "Mr. Motivator," 22.

18. Minghella in Lane, "Mr. Motivator," 24.

19. Sourced from the Internet Movie Database, http://us.imdb.com/Business?0116209 (14 February 2003).

20. David Gritten, "The Brits Are Back in Hollywood," *Daily Telegraph*, 25 November 1996, 21.

21. Bruce Dorminey, "War's First Casualty Is Love," *Evening Standard*, 11 January 1997, 29.

22. Internet Movie Database.

23. Andrew Lloyd Webber in Bob Thomas, "*English Patient* Is Best Film," *Asian Age*, 26 March 1997, 14.

24. Steve Keenan, "Tunisia Aims to Cash in on Oscar Film," *Times*, 13 March 1997, 31.

25. Richard Owen, "Cinema's Invasion Irritates Tuscans," *Times*, 2 April 1997, 17.

26. Anthony Minghella in Bill Frost, "Isle of Wight Hails Cream of the Oscars," *Times*, 26 March 1997, 3.

27. "It's All Wight on the Night for Minghella," 10.

28. Morris Barton in Frost, "Isle of Wight Hails Cream of the Oscars," 3.

29. Ian Burrell, "Isle of Wight Honours Oscar-winner Minghella," *Independent*, 15 November 1997, 2.

30. "Film Role Suits Jaeger's Image," *Sunday Times Section 3*, 23 February 1997, 12.

31. Nigel Reynolds, "Nigel Reynolds Looks at How a Starring Role in a Movie Has Put the Classical Author Herodotus Back in the Spotlight," *Daily Telegraph*, 19 March 1997, 3.

32. Dan Glaister, "Film Revives a Classic," *Guardian*, 20 March 1997, 6.

33. Nigel Reynolds, "Rush to Cash In on Herodotus," *Daily Telegraph*, 28 March 1997, 1.

34. Nigel Reynolds, "Rush to Cash In on Herodotus," 1.

35. "Making History," *Time Out*, 7–17 May 1997, 6.

36. Anthony Minghella in Thomson, "How They Saved the Patient," 17.

37. Adam Mars-Jones, "A Deceptive Beauty: *The English Patient*," *Independent*, 13 March 1997, 6.

38. Thomson, "How They Saved the Patient," 17.

39. Jacqui Sadashige, "Sweeping the Sands: Geographies of Desire in *The English Patient*," *Literature/Film Quarterly* 26, no. 4 (1998): 249, 250.

40. "DNH Bends Own Rules to Claim Patient as British," *Screen Finance*, 23 March 1997.

41. Sebastian O'Kelly, "The Real Laszlo de Almasy [sic]," *Daily Telegraph Weekend*, 1 March 1997, 19.

42. O'Kelly, "The Real Laszlo de Almasy [sic]," 19.

43. Richard Brooks, "Real-Life English Patient Adored Africa, Cigarettes, Guns—and Men," *Observer*, 17 August 1997, 3.

44. Anthony Minghella in Brooks, "Real-Life English Patient Adored Africa, Cigarettes, Guns—and Men," 3.

45. Miramax Films and Michael Ondaatje in Kate Dunn, "Sandstorm over Desert Hero's Nazi Deal," *Independent on Sunday*, 12 January 1997, 4.

46. Gerald E. Forshey, "*The English Patient*: From Novel to Screenplay," *Creative Screenwriting* (Summer 1997): 91.

47. Stephen Amidon, "Romancing the Prose," *Sunday Times: Section II*, 26 January 1997.

48. Anne Billson, "Cinema," *Sunday Telegraph*, 16 March 1997, 9.

49. Janet Maslin in *The New York Times*, quoted in Amidon, "Romancing the Prose."

50. Quentin Curtis, "Passion Where Worlds Collide," *Daily Telegraph*, 14 March 1997, 26.

51. Sharyn Emery, "'Call Me By My Name': Personal Identity and Possession in *The English Patient*," *Literature/Film Quarterly* 28, no. 3 (2000): 210–13, Philip French, "Rich, Exhilarating, First-Class," *Observer: Review*, 16 March 1997, 12, and Douglas Stenberg, "A Firmament in the Midst of the Waters: Dimensions of Love in *The English Patient*," *Literature/Film Quarterly* 26, no. 4 (1998): 255–62.

52. Stenberg, "A Firmament in the Midst of the Waters: Dimensions of Love in *The English Patient*," 261.

53. Jamal Mahjoub, "*The English Patient*," *Wasafiri* no. 26 (Autumn 1997): 76.

54. Nick James, "*The English Patient*," *Sight and Sound* 7, no. 3 (March 1997): 46.

55. Sadashige, "Sweeping the Sands: Geographies of Desire in *The English Patient*," 248.

56. Lisa Rundle, "From Novel to Film—*The English Patient* Distorted," *Borderlines* no. 43 (April 1997): 9.

57. Michael Ondaatje, "Foreword," *The English Patient: A Screenplay by Anthony Minghella*, viii.

58. Minghella, *The English Patient: A Screenplay by Anthony Minghella*, 16, 48.

59. Minghella, *The English Patient: A Screenplay by Anthony Minghella*, 28.

60. Raymond Aaron Younis, "Nationhood and Decolonization in *The English Patient*," *Literature/Film Quarterly* 26, no. 1 (1998): 2.

61. Mahjoub, "*The English Patient*," 76.

62. Jonathan Margolis, "'Biggles Meets Barbara Cartland': Is There a Backlash against *The English Patient?*" *The Sunday Times: Section II*, 27 April 1997, 5.

63. Sadashige, "Sweeping the Sands: Geographies of Desire in *The English Patient*," 249.

64. Anthony Minghella in David Benedict, "Cutting to the Quick," *Independent Tabloid*, 6 March 1997, 4.

65. In discussing both the novel and the film, it is difficult to determine exactly how to refer to the eponymous character. The patient and Almásy are, of course, one and the same person. At the same time, however, the patient does not acknowledge his name until very late in the film and is in many ways quite a different character than his former self. Like the film audience and his fellow characters in the monastery, he is 'viewing' the story of the young Almásy with an increasingly clear sense of hindsight that, at certain points, divides his understanding of events quite dramatically from that of his alter ego. Collapsing the patient and Almásy into a single name therefore seems impossible. Accordingly, I have tried to remain specific to whichever manifestation of the character is most pertinent at any one time. On some occasions, however, this means that the term "the patient/Almásy" seems the most appropriate expression of a point where the knowledge or personality of each coincides.

66. Minghella, *The English Patient: A Screenplay by Anthony Minghella*, 159.

67. Michael Ondaatje, *The English Patient* (London and Basingstoke: Picador, 1993), un-numbered page.

68. Ondaatje, *The English Patient*, beginning on page 3.

69. Ondaatje, *The English Patient*, 27.

70. Ondaatje, *The English Patient*, 4.

71. Ondaatje, *The English Patient*, 97.

72. Almásy does not call Katharine by her first name until the morning after their first moments of intimacy during the sandstorm.

She discovers the notes about "K" later that day after he has entrusted her with his copy of Herodotus and accepted the gift of her paintings from the Cave of Swimmers. Minghella, *The English Patient: A Screenplay by Anthony Minghella*, 70 and 72 respectively.

73. Minghella, *The English Patient: A Screenplay by Anthony Minghella*, 152.

74. Ondaatje, *The English Patient*, 250–51.

75. Minghella, *The English Patient: A Screenplay by Anthony Minghella*, 93.

76. Ondaatje, *The English Patient*, 286.

77. Minghella, *The English Patient: A Screenplay by Anthony Minghella*, 154.

78. Ondaatje, *The English Patient*, 138–39.

79. Minghella, *The English Patient: A Screenplay by Anthony Minghella*, 110.

80. Minghella, *The English Patient: A Screenplay by Anthony Minghella*, 25.

81. Minghella, *The English Patient: A Screenplay by Anthony Minghella*, 159. A very similar speech, containing much of the content of Katharine's final letter to Almásy in the film, appears as the patient/Almásy's own thoughts at the site of his former lover's death on page 261 of the novel.

82. Apart from the centrality of the Cave of Swimmers to both the film and the novel, the patient begins to collapse the distinction between the desert and water as early as pages 18 and 19 of the novel.

83. Ondaatje refers to the page of a book as "skin" on page 7 and to Bagnold's description of a sand dune on page 136 of the novel. The reference to "a mountain the shape of a woman's back" occurs in the film, although not in the published screenplay. The patient tells Hana of the description of landscapes according to the features of women on pages 140 and 141 of the novel immediately before an enigmatic reference to the as yet unnamed Katharine. He then speaks of describing Katharine on page 235 in the same way that he might describe a geographical feature.

84. Ondaatje, *The English Patient*, 3–4.

85. The serial number of the bomb that Kip is called to defuse shortly after the beginning of his relationship with Hana is KK-iP2600. Minghella, *The English Patient: A Screenplay by Anthony Minghella*, 123.

86. Minghella, *The English Patient: A Screenplay by Anthony Minghella*, 24.

87. Sergeant Hardy in Minghella, *The English Patient: A Screenplay by Anthony Minghella*, 13. The second sentence appears only in the film and not in the published screenplay.

88. Minghella, *The English Patient: A Screenplay by Anthony Minghella*, 51.

89. Minghella, *The English Patient: A Screenplay by Anthony Minghella*, 134.

90. Ondaatje, *The English Patient*, 4.

91. Ondaatje, *The English Patient*, 5–6.

92. Minghella, *The English Patient: A Screenplay by Anthony Minghella*, 153.

93. Mary Ann Doane, *The Desire to Desire: The Woman's Film of the 1940's* (Bloomington: Indiana University Press, 1989), 96.

94. Doane, *The Desire to Desire: The Woman's Film of the 1940's*, 96.

95. George F. Custen, *Bio/Pics: How Hollywood Constructed Public History* (New Brunswick, N.J.: Rutgers University Press, 1992), 183.

96. Sarah Kozloff, *Invisible Storytellers: Voice-Over in American Fiction Film* (Berkeley, Los Angeles, London: University of Chicago Press, 1983), 43–44.

97. Kozloff, *Invisible Storytellers: Voice-Over in American Fiction Film*, 45.

98. This phrase appears only in the film and not in the published screenplay.

99. Minghella, *The English Patient: A Screenplay by Anthony Minghella*, 27.

100. Minghella, *The English Patient: A Screenplay by Anthony Minghella*, 25.

101. A report in *Asian Age* actually told how the film was temporarily banned in the United Arab Emirates on the grounds that it "violated Islamic morals." It was then rereleased after five scenes had been cut, one of which featured Almásy and Katharine making love against the backdrop of "the sound of the Muslim call to prayer." "Ban lifted on *The English Patient* after cuts in UAE," *Asian Age*, 1 May 1997, 6. A similar report appeared in *The Guardian*, "Dubai Cuts *The English Patient*," 1 May 1997.

102. See note 75.

103. Minghella, *The English Patient: A Screenplay by Anthony Minghella*, 110. Almásy also poses this question to Madox, in a different context, on page 162 of the novel.

104. Minghella, *The English Patient: A Screenplay by Anthony Minghella*, 135.

105. Hana makes this point in Minghella, *The English Patient: A Screenplay by Anthony Minghella*, 97, and Katharine makes the same point in very similar words on page 58. It is interesting to note that in the novel, Kip enjoys an equally prevalent engagement with American popular song. It is he, in fact, who uses this music and his radio, quite consciously, to shut out the outside world in order that he may concentrate on his work.

106. Minghella, *The English Patient: A Screenplay by Anthony Minghella*, 91

107. The title *Lullaby for Katharine* is taken from the soundtrack recording of the film. The original listed name of this traditional piece is *Én Csak Azt Csodálom*. As will be seen in chapter 5, the similarity in sound between this song, *Szerelem, Szerelem* and the instances of improvisation by the same female voice around other cues is such that I have grouped them under the name of the *Hungarian Theme*.

108. Doane, *The Desire to Desire: The Woman's Film of the 1940's*, 109.

109. Doane, *The Desire to Desire: The Woman's Film of the 1940's*, 109.

110. Doane, *The Desire to Desire: The Woman's Film of the 1940's*, 109.

111. Doane, *The Desire to Desire: The Woman's Film of the 1940's*, 107.

112. Doane, *The Desire to Desire: The Woman's Film of the 1940's*, 107.

113. Minghella, *The English Patient: A Screenplay by Anthony Minghella*, 68, 95.

114. Minghella, *The English Patient: A Screenplay by Anthony Minghella*, 82; Ondaatje, *The English Patient*, 97.

115. Doane, *The Desire to Desire: The Woman's Film of the 1940's*, 116.

116. Minghella, *The English Patient: A Screenplay by Anthony Minghella*, 85.

# Chapter Four

1. Anthony Minghella, "Meridian Feature: BBC World Service Interview, Barbican Theatre," *BBCi: Audio Interviews*, 4 December 1997, http://www.bbc.co.uk/bbcfour/audiointerviews/profilepages/minghellaa1.shtml (3 October 2001).

2. Minghella, "Meridian Feature: BBC World Service Interview, Barbican Theatre."

3. Gabriel Yared, interview by the author, 11 November 2001.

4. Yared, interview by the author. According to Yared, the music of Puccini was evoked by Minghella as a stylistic reference point only at the very beginning of their discussions. After this, it was largely forgotten and Yared feels that any influence remains only in the "'elegance' of the melodic lines and the harmonies."

5. Yared, interview by the author.

6. Anthony Minghella in David Benedict, "Cutting to the Quick," *Independent Tabloid*, 6 March 1997, 4.

7. Minghella, "Meridian Feature: BBC World Service Interview, Barbican Theatre."

8. Minghella, "Meridian Feature: BBC World Service Interview, Barbican Theatre."

9. Yared, interview by the author.

10. Anthony Minghella, *The English Patient: A Screenplay by Anthony Minghella* (London: Methuen Drama, 1997), 27.

11. In defining the passage of aural transition as occurring through the meta-diegetic realm of the patient's imagination, I am borrowing the term and its suggested definition from Claudia Gorbman in *Unheard Melodies: Narrative Film Music* (Bloomington: Indiana University Press, 1987), 22–23. Gorbman suggests that music may be defined as meta-diegetic if it represents a character's "musical thoughts," which the audience is permitted to hear.

12. Although it could be argued that all the sound and music in the flashback sequences is actually sourced from the patient's memory/imagination and is therefore also strictly meta-diegetic, I am defining it as diegetic since it is audible to the other characters within the space of the flashback.

13. Minghella, *The English Patient: A Screenplay by Anthony Minghella*, 88.

14. Minghella, *The English Patient: A Screenplay by Anthony Minghella*, 29.

15. Minghella, *The English Patient: A Screenplay by Anthony Minghella*, 157.

16. The term "auditory point of view" is used here to suggest that we are hearing what the patient hears, rather than the sound that we actually know to be present in the space of the monastery. We are therefore locked into the patient's meta-diegetic experience of sound.

17. Almásy in Minghella, *The English Patient: A Screenplay by Anthony Minghella*, 57.

18. Minghella, *The English Patient: A Screenplay by Anthony Minghella*, 23.

19. Minghella, *The English Patient: A Screenplay by Anthony Minghella*, 41.

20. See page 65.

21. Hana and Katharine's shared reference to Almásy's singing is quoted on page 85.

22. The term "anempathetic" refers to Michel Chion's definition of the term as an instance where the mechanically unstoppable nature of diegetic music and its innocence of the drama that it accompanies, leads to purposeful narrative disjuncture between music and emotion. In Gorbman, *Unheard Melodies: Narrative Film Music*, 24.

23. In this respect, it is interesting to note that the published screenplay describes events around the game of Spin the Bottle in a slightly different way. Here, Fouad (Hichem Rostom), the Egyptian member of the party, is described as contributing to the game with a dance that is accompanied by the Bedouin musicians. Minghella, *The English Patient: A Screenplay by Anthony Minghella*, 28.

24. Minghella, *The English Patient: A Screenplay by Anthony Minghella*, 46.

25. Minghella, *The English Patient: A Screenplay by Anthony Minghella*, 46.

26. See page 65.

27. The celebratory mood that appears to mock Geoffrey in this instance is reemphasized later in the film. The song reappears, apparently at the non-diegetic level, as a veritable anthem to happiness as Hana, Caravaggio, Kip and Hardy run the patient around the courtyard in the rain for which both he and Katharine have yearned.

28. Although these words are clearly heard in the film, they do not appear in the published screenplay.

29. Minghella, *The English Patient: A Screenplay by Anthony Minghella*, 114. This is also mentioned in the novel on page 109.

30. Minghella, *The English Patient: A Screenplay by Anthony Minghella*, 92. This is also mentioned on page 236 of the novel.

31. The ability of the patient to hear sounds that he cannot identify within the space of the monastery is also featured in the novel, for example on page 15.

32. Minghella, *The English Patient: A Screenplay by Anthony Minghella*, 55.

33. This is the only implication offered by the film of Kip's love of music (see chapter 3, note 105).

# Chapter Five

1. Following chapter 4, note 4, it should be clear that the designation of Puccini as a starting point should not be overstated. Reference to Puccini is used here only as a convenient means of denoting a particular group of themes.

2. Gabriel Yared, interview by the author, 11 November 2001.

3. Yared, interview by the author.

4. Yared, interview by the author. Yared in fact also feels that his opening theme in the cor anglais demonstrates a stronger reference to Wagner's Overture to *Parsifal* than Puccini.

5. The sampled sound of a quanoun is used in the score. Throughout this analysis, however, for ease of reference, it will be referred to on most occasions simply as a quanoun.

6. Yared, interview by the author.

7. His success in this challenge, however, was confirmed when the cue *Convento di Santa Anna* was played as part of a concert in Ghent in 2001. The orchestra leader, according to Yared, confessed that he did not know the piece and asked which of Bach's works it was. Yared, interview by the author.

8. Oscar Benjamin, "The English Patient," *Film Score Monthly* 2, no. 3 (May 1997): 25.

9. Derek Malcolm, "A Fiennes Romance," *Guardian Section 2*, 14 March 1997, 7.

10. Quotations are taken from the score of the film held by YAD Music, Rue Jean-François Gerbillon, Paris. A complete score as it appears in the film does not exist and so some cues are partly or entirely transcribed by the author from the film soundtrack. Although the score includes transposing instruments in their own keys, all quotations have been converted to concert pitch.

11. Anthony Minghella, "Anthony Minghella on . . . the Evocative Marta Sebestyen [sic]," *Evening Standard: Hot Tickets*, 24 April 1997, 27.

12. Anthony Minghella, *The English Patient: A Screenplay by Anthony Minghella* (London: Methuen Drama, 1997), 72–73.

13. Almásy translates the word "szerelem" as meaning "love" on page 91 of Minghella, *The English Patient: A Screenplay by Anthony Minghella*.

14. A similar technique is employed in merging the high clarinet note of *Wang Wang Blues* into the sound of a siren wailing in Caravaggio's flashback to Tobruk.

15. Almásy and Katharine in Minghella, *The English Patient: A Screenplay by Anthony Minghella*, 91.

16. As quoted on page 65.

17. Katharine, as quoted on page 60.

18. As quoted on page 56.

19. Minghella, *The English Patient: A Screenplay by Anthony Minghella*, 73.

20. Minghella, *The English Patient: A Screenplay by Anthony Minghella*, 145.

21. Hana in Minghella, *The English Patient: A Screenplay by Anthony Minghella*, 27.

22. Almásy, as quoted on page 67.

23. Hana in Minghella, *The English Patient: A Screenplay by Anthony Minghella*, 48.

24. As quoted on page 96.

25. As quoted on page 96.

26. Minghella, *The English Patient: A Screenplay by Anthony Minghella*, 159.

27. The patient in Minghella, *The English Patient: A Screenplay by Anthony Minghella*, 27.

28. See chapter 3, note 72.

29. Minghella, *The English Patient: A Screenplay by Anthony Minghella*, 80–81.

30. Minghella, *The English Patient: A Screenplay by Anthony Minghella*, 81.

31. This line appeared on publicity for the film and is featured on the front covers of the video and DVD of the film.

32. Jamal Mahjoub, as quoted on page 57.

33. Hana and Kip in turn, in Minghella, *The English Patient: A Screenplay by Anthony Minghella*, 156–57.

34. Yared says that much discussion surrounded his composition of this cue, with Minghella imploring him to "lift her" with his music. Yared, interview by the author.

# BIBLIOGRAPHY

## Gabriel Yared

Benjamin, A. K. "*Autumn in New York.*" *Film Score Monthly* 5, no. 7 (August 2000): 35.

Benjamin, Oscar. "*The English Patient.*" *Film Score Monthly* 2, no. 3 (May 1997): 25.

Bond, Jeff. "*Message in a Bottle.*" *Film Score Monthly* 4, no. 5 (June 1999): 44.

Brawley, Vance. "The Talented Mr. Yared." http://www.scorelogue. com/gabriel_yared.html (22 August 2000).

Brown, Royal S. *Overtones and Undertones: Reading Film Music.* California and London: California University Press, 1994. (Chapter 8: "Music as Image as Music: A Postmodern Perspective.")

David, Kevin, and Emmanuelle Franck. "Musique de Films." *Film Français* no. 2282 (26 January 1990): 19.

Guerand, Jean-Philippe. "Gabriel Yared, Profession: Décolleur de Papier Peint." *Première* no. 142 (January 1989): 112.

Lesbats, Elisabeth. "Profession: Compositeur—Gabriel Yared: 'Dans un film, moins il y a de musique, mieux je me porte.'" *Ciné Télé Revue* 65, no. 11 (14 March 1985): 44–45.

"Les Nominations: Gabriel Yared: Compositeur." *Film Français* no. 2131 (6 March 1987): 30.

"Les Nominations: Gabriel Yared: Compositeur." *Film Français* no. 2184 (11 March 1988): 28.

Levergeois, Bertrand. "Gabriel Yared." *Avant-Scène du Cinéma* no. 491 (April 2000): 209–19.

McLean, Jamie. "*Message in a Bottle.*" *Film Score Monthly* 4, no. 10 (December 1999): 20.

Michaud, Juliette. "Gabriel Yared: Envoyez la Musique!" *Studio Magazine* no. 88 (June 1994): 102–05.

"Questionnaire adressé aux Compositeurs." *Cinémaction* no. 62 (January 1992): 40, 89.

Russell, Mark, and James Young. *Film Music: Screencraft.* Switzerland: Rotovision, 2000.

Weinstein, Jesus. "*The Talented Mr. Ripley.*" *Film Score Monthly* 5, no. 1 (January 2000): 35, 37.

YAD Music Website, http://gabrielyared.com/ (23 May 2001).

Yared, Gabriel. "La Musique de Film, Éternelle Sacrifiée des Budgets Français." *Film Français* no. 2804 (3 December 1999): 18–19.

# Anthony Minghella

Argent, Daniel. "The Talented Mister: An Interview with Anthony Minghella." *Creative Screenwriting* 7, no. 1 (January/February 2000): 63–67.

Burrell, Ian. "Isle of Wight Honours Oscar-Winner Minghella." *Independent* (15 November 1997): 2.

Carroll, Tom. "The Patient Englishman: Getting Personal with Anthony Minghella." *Directors Guild of America Magazine* 22, no. 2 (May/June 1997): 44–51, 70.

Coe, Jonathan. "From Hull to Hollywood: Anthony Minghella Talks about His Film, *The English Patient*, and Denies That He Is Turning into David Lean." *New Statesman* (7 March 1997): 38–39.

Floren, Erik. "Ripley's—Believe It!" http://www.canoe.ca/ JamMoviesArtistsM/minghella_Anthony.html (6 August 2001).

Frost, Bill. "Isle of Wight Hails Cream of the Oscars." *Times* (26 March 1997): 1, 3.

Mees, Jaap. "Anthony Minghella." http://talkingpix.co.uk/Anthony% 20Minghella.html (6 August 2001).

Minghella, Anthony. "Back Bites." *Independent Magazine* (16 October 1993): 58.

——— "My Kind of Day." *Radio Times* 294, no. 3835 (2–8 August 1997): 122.

———. *Plays: 2: Cigarettes and Chocolate; Hang-up; What If It's Raining?; Truly, Madly, Deeply; Mosaic; Days Like These.* London: Methuen Drama, 1997.

Preston, John. "Yuppie Love." *Time Out* (2–8 July 1986): 26.

Stayton, Richard. "The Talented Mr. Minghella." *Written By* 4, no. 2 (February 2000): 32–37.

*Sunday Telegraph, 7 Days Magazine*, 29 April 1990, 8. Article by Clive Davis on Minghella's passion for Bach, and his film *Cello* (*Truly, Madly, Deeply*).

Wilson, Andrew. "Magical Journey from Page to Screen." *Daily Telegraph* (5 March 1999): 25.


# Melodrama and the Woman's Film; Flashback Narrative; Narration and the Voice

Basinger, Jeanine. *A Woman's View: How Hollywood Spoke to Women, 1930–1960*. London: Chatto and Windus, 1993.

Branigan, Edward. *Narrative Comprehension and Film*. London: Routledge, 1992.

Brooks, Peter. *The Melodramatic Imagination*. New Haven: Yale University Press, 1976; New York: Columbia University Press, 1984.

Cavell, Stanley. *Contesting Tears: The Hollywood Melodrama of the Unknown Woman*. Chicago: University of Chicago Press, 1996.

Chion, Michel, edited and translated by Claudia Gorbman. *The Voice in Cinema*. New York: Columbia University Press, 1999.

Custen, George F. *Bio/Pics: How Hollywood Constructed Public History*. New Brunswick, N.J.: Rutgers University Press, 1992.

Doane, Mary Ann. *The Desire to Desire: The Woman's Film of the 1940's*. Bloomington: Indiana University Press, 1989.

Fleishman, Avrom. *Narrated Films*. Baltimore: Johns Hopkins University Press, 1984.

Gledhill, Christine, ed. *Home Is Where the Heart Is: Studies in Melodrama and the Woman's Film*. London: BFI, 1987.

Kozloff, Sarah. *Invisible Storytellers: Voice-Over in American Fiction Film*. Berkeley, Los Angeles, London: University of Chicago Press, 1983.

———. *Overhearing Film Dialogue*. Berkeley, Los Angeles and London: University of California Press, 2000.

Lawrence, Amy. *Echo and Narcissus: Women's Voices in Classical Hollywood Cinema*. Berkeley, Los Angeles and Oxford: University of California Press, 1991.

Neale, Steve. "Melodrama and Tears." *Screen* 27, no. 6 (November/December 1986): 6–22.

Turim, Maureen. *Flashbacks in Film: Memory and History*. New York and London: Routledge, 1989.

Walker, Janet. *Couching Resistance: Women, Film and Psychoanalytical Psychiatry*. Minneapolis: University of Minnesota Press, 1993.

Wilson, George. *Narration in Light: Studies in Cinematic Point of View*. Baltimore: Johns Hopkins University Press, 1986.

# Film Sound and Music

Adorno, Theodor, and Hanns Eisler. *Composing for the Films*. New York: Oxford University Press, 1947; London and Atlantic Highlands, N.J.: The Athlone Press, 1994.

Altman, R., ed. *Sound Theory Sound Practice*. New York and London: Routledge, 1992.

Atkins, Irene Kahn. *Source Music in Motion Pictures*. Rutherford, Madison, Teaneck: Fairleigh Dickinson University Press; London and Toronto: Associated University Press, 1983.

Brown, Royal S. *Overtones and Undertones: Reading Film Music*. California and London: California University Press, 1994.

Chion, Michel, edited and translated by Claudia Gorbman. *Audio-Vision: Sound on Screen*. Paris: Editions Nathan, 1990; New York and Chichester, West Sussex: Columbia University Press, 1994.

Flinn, Caryl. *Strains of Utopia: Gender, Nostalgia, and Hollywood Film Music*. Oxford and Princeton: Princeton University Press, 1992.

Gorbman, Claudia. *Unheard Melodies: Narrative Film Music*. Bloomington: Indiana University Press, 1987.

Kalinak, Kathryn. *Settling the Score: Music and the Classical Hollywood Film*. Madison: University of Wisconsin Press, 1992.

Laing, Heather. *Wandering Minds and Anchored Bodies: Music, Gender and Emotion in Melodrama and the Woman's Film*. Unpublished PhD thesis, University of Warwick, 2000.

Prendergast, Roy M. *Film Music: A Neglected Art*. New York and London: Norton, 1977, 1992.

Russell, Mark, and James Young. *Film Music: Screencraft*. Switzerland: Rotovision, 2000.

Weis, Elisabeth, and John Belton, eds. *Film Sound: Theory and Practice*. New York: Columbia University Press, 1985.

# The English Patient

"Aims without Frontiers." *Screen International* no. 1103 (11 April 1997): 12.

Alexander, Jeff. *"The English Patient." Premiere* 10, no. 3 (November 1996): 27.

Amidon, Stephen. "Romancing the Prose." *Sunday Times: Section II* (26 January 1997).

Andrews, Nigel. "Class Act for a Sandblown Haiku." *Financial Times* (13 March 1997): 19.

Bakewell, Joan. "The Patient in Need of a Get Well Card." *Sunday Times: Section 5* (9 March 1997): 5.

Benedict, David. "Cutting to the Quick." *Independent: Tabloid* (6 March 1997): 4–5.

Billson, Anne. "Cinema." *Sunday Telegraph Review* (16 March 1997): 9.

Boshoff, Alison. "Oscar Knives Are Out for the Un-English Patient." *Daily Telegraph* (24 March 1997): 5.

Braund, Simon. "'We Lost Fox Because We Wouldn't Go for a Big Name for Kristin's Part . . .'" *Empire*, no. 100 (October 1997): 206.

Brooks, Richard. "Real-Life English Patient Adored Africa, Cigarettes, Guns—and Men." *Observer* (17 August 1997): 3.

Brown, Geoff. "Minghella Serves Up Oscar's Just Desserts." *Times* (13 March 1997): 31.

Curtis, Quentin. "Passion Where Worlds Collide." *Daily Telegraph* (14 March 1997): 26.

de Lisle, Tim. "A British Film to Swoon For." *Independent on Sunday* (9 March 1997): 14.

Dempster, Nigel. "Casting His Lot." *Daily Mail* (24 January 1996): 33.

"DNH Bends Own Rules to Claim Patient As British." *Screen Finance* (23 March 1997).

Dobson, Patricia. *"The English Patient." Screen International* no. 1046 (23 February 1996): 22.

Dorminey, Bruce. "War's First Casualty Is Love." *Evening Standard* (11 January 1996): 29.

"Dubai Cuts *The English Patient.*" *Guardian* (1 May 1997).

Dunn, Kate. "Sandstorm over Desert Hero's Nazi Deal." *Independent on Sunday* (12 January 1997): 4.

Emery, Sharyn. "'Call Me By My Name': Personal Identity and Possession in *The English Patient*." *Literature/Film Quarterly* 28, no. 3 (2000): 210–13.

"*English Patient* 'in the Red.'" *Evening Standard* (21 March 2000): 4.

"Film Role Suits Jaeger's Image." *Sunday Times: Section 3* (23 February 1997): 12.

Forshey, Gerald E. "*The English Patient*: From Novel to Screenplay." *Creative Screenwriting* 4, no. 2 (Summer 1997): 91–98.

French, Philip. "Rich, Exhilarating, First-Class." *Observer: Review* (16 March 1997): 12.

Glaister, Dan. "Film Revives a Classic." *Guardian* (20 March 1997): 6.

Glass, Charles. "Casualties of Amour." *Premiere* 10, no. 4 (December 1996): 96–102.

Goodridge, Mike. "Executive Suite: Anthony Minghella." *Screen International* no. 1094 (7 February 1997): 44.

Gristwood, Sarah. "Medical Miracle." *Guardian: Section 2* (29 November 1996): 4–5.

Gritten, David. "The Brits Are Back in Hollywood." *Daily Telegraph* (25 November 1996): 21.

Harris, Ed. "300,000 Back *The Patient* As Our Prospects Get Better and Better." *Evening Standard* (18 March 1997): 3.

"It's All Wight on the Night for Minghella." *Daily Telegraph* (26 March 1997): 10.

Jackson, Kevin. "Never Mind the Hype, Prepare to Be Seduced." *Independent* (16 March 1997): 11.

Jaggi, Maya. "Journey to Hollywood." *Guardian: Section 2* (6 March 1997): 9.

James, Nick. "*The English Patient*." *Sight and Sound* 7, no. 3 (March 1997): 45–46.

Katz, Ian. "British Film-maker Walks on Water after Oscar Glory." *Guardian* (26 March 1997): 2.

——— "Film Awards Turn Spotlight on Britain." *Guardian* (20 December 1996): 11.

Keenan, Steve. "Tunisia Aims to Cash in on Oscar Film." *Times* (13 March 1997): 31.

Lane, Harriet. "Mr. Motivator." *Observer Life Magazine* (© Harriet Lane, *Guardian Newspapers Limited*) (9 March 1997): 22, 24.

Linklater, Magnus. "For an Oscar, Play It Safe." *Times* (29 March 1997): 20.

Lyttle, John. "*The English Patient* Has 12 Oscar and 13 BAFTA Nominations. But, Asks John Lyttle, Why All This Fuss over a Dressed-Up Costume Drama with Nowhere to Go?" *Independent: Tabloid* (27 February 1997): 10.

Mahjoub, Jamal. "*The English Patient*." *Wasafiri* no. 26 (Autumn 1997): 75–76.

"Making History." *Time Out* (7–17 May 1997): 6.

Malcolm, Derek. "A Fiennes Romance." *Guardian: Section 2* (14 March 1997): 6–7.

———. "Hollywood's Secrets and Lies." *Guardian: Section 2* (26 March 1997): 13.

Mars-Jones, Adam. "A Deceptive Beauty: *The English Patient*." *Independent* (13 March 1997): 6.

Margolis, Jonathan. "'Biggles Meets Barbara Cartland': Is There a Backlash against *The English Patient*?" *Sunday Times: Section II* (27 April 1997): 4–5.

McCarthy, Todd. "*Patient* Charts Difficult Terrain." *Variety* (11 November 1996): 57, 62.

Minghella, Anthony. *The English Patient: A Screenplay by Anthony Minghella*. London: Methuen Drama, 1997.

———. "I Don't Have a Speech. I Look Terrible in a Tuxedo. What Could Possibly Go Right?" *Observer: Review* (30 March 1997): 3–4.

———. "Anthony Minghella on . . . the Evocative Marta Sebestyen [sic]." *Evening Standard* (24 April 1997): 27.

Nathan, Ian. "*The English Patient*." *Empire* no. 94 (April 1997): 34.

———. "*The English Patient*." *Empire* no. 125 (November 1999): 146.

O'Kelly, Sebastian. "The Real Laszlo de Almasy [sic]." *Daily Telegraph: Weekend* (1 March 1997): 19.

Ondaatje, Michael. *The English Patient*. London and Basingstoke: Picador, 1993.

"Patient's Triumph." *Evening Standard* (25 March 1997): 9.

Parkinson, David. "What Makes an Oscar-Winner?" *Radio Times* 292, no. 3814 (8 March 1997): 52–53.

Reynolds, Nigel. "'Rejected' Film in Line for 13 Bafta Awards." *Daily Telegraph* (26 February 1997): 5.

———. "Nigel Reynolds Looks at How a Starring Role in a Movie Has Put the Classical Author Herodotus Back in the Spotlight." *Daily Telegraph* (19 March 1997): 3.

————. "*English Patient* on Cloud Nine after Oscars Triumph." *Daily Telegraph* (26 March 1997): 10.

————. "Rush to Cash in on Herodotus." *Daily Telegraph* (28 March 1997): 1.

Roddick, Nick. "British Disease Strikes." *Moving Pictures International* no. 25 (March 1997): 40.

Rundle, Lisa. "From Novel to Film—*The English Patient* Distorted." *Borderlines* no. 43 (April 1997): 9–13.

Sadashige, Jacqui. "Sweeping the Sands: Geographies of Desire in *The English Patient*." *Literature/Film Quarterly* 26, no. 4 (1998): 242–54.

"A Sensuous Journey through Uncharted Depths of Mind." *Asian Age* (19 November 1996): 14.

Shone, Tom. "Just Dessert." *Sunday Times Magazine* (9 March 1997): 34, 37–38.

————. "An Affair to Remember." *Sunday Times Section II* (16 March 1997): 11–12.

Stenberg, Douglas. "A Firmament in the Midst of the Waters: Dimensions of Love in *The English Patient*." *Literature/Film Quarterly* 26, no. 4 (1998): 255–62.

Stringer, Robin, and Jerry Watson. "A Very English Oscar Triumph." *Evening Standard* (25 March 1997): 1, 3.

Stuart, Jan. "From a Passionate Read to a Passionate Journey." *Newsday* (23 March 1997): C08.

Summers, Sue. "The Patient English Director." *Daily Telegraph: Weekend Magazine* (22 February 1997): 34, 36, 38.

Thomas, Bob. "*English Patient* Is Best Film." *Asian Age* (26 March 1997): 14.

Thomson, David. "How They Saved the Patient." *Independent on Sunday* (22 February 1996): 15, 17.

Walker, Alexander. "Love on a Grand Scale." *Evening Standard* (13 March 1997): 26–27.

Whittell, Giles. "*English Patient* Tops Golden Globe List." *Times* (20 December 1996): 9.

Wolf, Matt. "Sit Back and Relax While *The Patient* Rocks You." *Asian Age* (21 November 1996): 14.

————. "Monarch of All He Purveys." *Times* (3 March 1997): 19.

Younis, Raymond Aaron. "Nationhood and Decolonization in *The English Patient*." *Literature/Film Quarterly* 26, no. 1 (1998): 2–9.

# INDEX

# About the Author

HEATHER LAING holds degrees in both music and film studies, including a Ph.D. in Film and Television Studies from the University of Warwick. She has taught at the University of Warwick and Southampton Institute of Higher Education and is currently a freelance researcher and writer on film music and film studies. She is the author of "Emotion by Numbers: Music and Song in the Musical" in R. Stilwell and B. Marshall (eds.) *Musicals: Hollywood and Beyond* (Exeter, England, and Portland, Ore.: Intellect, 2000).

**DAT**